CW01271660

Walk in the Light Series

The Redeemed

An Examination of Israel, the Church and the Chosen People

Todd D. Bennett

Shema Yisrael Publications

The Redeemed
An Examination of Israel, the Church and the
Chosen People

First printing 2008

Unless otherwise noted, Scripture passages are
translated by the author.

Copyright © 2008 by Shema Yisrael Publications.

For information write:
Shema Yisrael Publications
123 Court Street
Herkimer, New York 13350

ISBN: 0-9768659-5-5
Library of Congress Number: 2008910968

Printed in the United States of America

Please visit our website for other titles:

www.shemayisrael.net

For information regarding publicity for author
interviews call (866) 866-2211

The Redeemed

An Examination of Israel,
the Church
and
the Chosen People

"And they shall be called,
'The Set Apart People, the Redeemed of YHWH.'"
Isaiah (Yeshayahu) 62:12

Table of Contents

Acknowledgments

I must first and foremost acknowledge my Creator, Redeemer and Savior who opened my eyes and showed me the Light. He never gave up on me even when, at times, it seemed that I gave up on Him. He is ever patient and truly awesome. His blessings, mercies and love endure forever and my gratitude and thanksgiving cannot be fully expressed in words.

Were it not for the patience, prayers, love and support of my beautiful wife Janet, and my extraordinary children Morgan and Shemuel, I would never have been able to accomplish this work. They gave me the freedom to pursue the vision and dreams that my Heavenly Father placed within me and for that I am so very grateful. I love them all more than they will ever know.

Loving thanks to my father for his faithfulness along with his helpful comments and editing. He tirelessly watched and held things together at the office while I was away traveling, researching, speaking and writing.

Introduction

"²⁰ Everyone who does evil hates the light, and will not come into the light for fear that his deeds will be exposed. ²¹ But whoever lives by the truth comes into the light, so that it may be seen plainly that what he has done has been done through God."
John 3:20-21 NIV

This book is part of a larger body of educational work called the "Walk in the Light" series. The book and the entire series were written as a result of my search for the truth. Having grown up in a major Protestant Christian denomination since I was a small child I had been steeped in doctrine which often times seemed to contradict the very words contained within the Scriptures.

I always considered myself to be a Christian although I never took the time to research the origins of Christianity or to understand exactly what the term Christian meant. I simply grew up believing that Christianity was right and every other religion in the world was wrong or deficient. I also assumed that despite the seeming contradictions between Christian doctrine and the clear words of the Scriptures, there must be some reasonable explanation – even if I did not know what it was.

My beliefs were founded on more than simply blind faith. I had experienced a "living God," my life had been transformed by a loving Redeemer and I had been filled with a powerful Spirit. I knew that I was on the right track, regrettably I always felt something was lacking. I was certain that there was something more to this religion called Christianity; not in terms of a different God, but what composed this belief system which I subscribed to, and this label which I wore like a badge.

Throughout my Christian walk I experienced many highs and some lows, but along the way I never felt like I fully understood what my faith was all about. Sure, I knew that "Jesus died on the cross for my sins" and that I needed to believe in my heart and confess with my mouth in order to "be saved." I "asked Jesus into my heart" when I was a child and sincerely believed in what I had done, but something always felt like it was missing. As I grew older, I found myself progressing through different denominations, each time learning and growing, always adding some pieces to the puzzle, but never seeing the entire picture.

College ministry brought me into contact with the baptism of the Holy Spirit and more charismatic assemblies yet, while these people seemed to practice a more complete faith than those in my previous denominations, many of my original questions remained unanswered and even more questions arose. It seemed that at each new step in my faith I added a new adjective to the already ambiguous label "Christian." I went from being a mere Christian to a Full Gospel, New Testament, Charismatic, Spirit Filled, Born Again Christian; although I could never get away from the lingering uneasiness that something was still

missing.

For instance, when I read Matthew 7:21-23 I always felt uncomfortable. In that Scripture, the Messiah says: *"Not everyone who says to Me, Lord, Lord, will enter the kingdom of heaven, but he who does the will of My Father Who is in heaven. Many will say to Me on that day, Lord, Lord, have we not prophesied in Your name and driven out demons in Your name and done many mighty works in Your name? And then I will say to them openly (publicly), I never knew you; depart from Me, you who act wickedly [disregarding My commands]."* The Amplified Bible.

This passage of Scripture always bothered me because it sounded an awful lot like the modern day Christian Church, in particular, the charismatic churches which I had been attending where the gifts of the Spirit were "operating." According to the Scripture passage it was not the people who *believed* in the spiritual manifestations that were being rejected, it was those who were *actually doing* them. I would think that this would give every Christian pause for concern.

First of all "in that day" there are *many* people who will be calling the Messiah "Lord." They will also be performing incredible spiritual acts allegedly in His Name. Ultimately though, the Messiah will openly and publicly tell them to depart from Him. He will tell them that He never knew them and specifically He defines them by their actions, which is the reason for their rejection - they acted wickedly or lawlessly. In short, they disobeyed His commandments.

Also, it seems very possible that while they thought they were doing these things in His Name, they were not, because they may have never known His Name.

In essence, they did not know Him and He did not know them.

I think that many Christians are haunted by this Scripture because they do not understand who it applies to or what it means and if they were truly honest they must admit that there is no other group on the face of the planet that it can refer to except for the "Christian Church." This series provides the answer to that quandary and should provide resolution for any who have suffered anxiety over this verse.

Ultimately, my search for answers brought me right back to the starting point of my faith. I was left with the question: "What is the origin and substance of this religion called Christianity?" I was forced to explore the very foundations of my faith and to examine many of the beliefs which I subscribed to and test them against the truth of the Scriptures.

What I found out was nothing short of earth shattering. I experienced a parapettio which is a moment in Greek tragedies where the hero realizes that everything he knew was wrong. I discovered that many of the foundations of my faith were not rocks of truth, but rather the sands of lies, deception, corruption and paganism. I saw the Scripture in Jeremiah come true right before my eyes. In many translations, this passage reads: *"O LORD, my strength and my fortress, My refuge in the day of affliction, The Gentiles shall come to You from the ends of the earth and say, Surely our fathers have inherited lies, worthlessness and unprofitable things. Will a man make gods for himself, which are not gods?"* Jeremiah 16:19-20 NKJV

I discovered that I had inherited lies and false doctrines from the fathers of my faith. I discovered that

the faith which I had been steeped in had made gods which were not gods and I saw very clearly how many could say "Lord, Lord" and not really know the Messiah. I discovered that these lies were not just minor discrepancies but critical errors which could possibly have the effect of keeping me out of the New Jerusalem if I continued to practice them. (Revelation 21:27; 22:15).

While part of the problem stemmed from false doctrines which have crept into the Christian religion, it also had to do with anti-Semitism imbedded throughout the centuries and even translation errors in the very Scriptures that I was basing may beliefs upon. A good example is the next verse from the Prophet Jeremiah (Yirmeyahu) where most translations provide: *"Therefore behold, I will this once cause them to know, I will cause them to know My hand and My might; and they shall know that My Name is the LORD."* Yirmeyahu 16:21 NKJV.

Could our Heavenly Father really be telling us that His Name is "The LORD"? This is a title, not a name and by the way, won't many people be crying out "Lord, Lord" and be told by the Messiah that He never knew them? It is obvious that you should know someone's name in order to have a relationship with them. How could you possibly say that you know someone if you do not even know their name. So then we must ask: "What is the Name of our Heavenly Father?" The answer to this seeming mystery lies just beneath the surface of the translated text. In fact, if most people took the time to read the translators notes in the front of their "Bible" they would easily discover the problem.

You see the Name of our Creator is found in the Scriptures almost 7,000 times. Long ago a false doctrine

was perpetrated regarding speaking the Name. It was determined that the Name either could not, or should not, be pronounced and therefore it was replaced. Thus, over the centuries the Name of the Creator which was given to us so that we could know Him and be, not only His children, but also His friends, (Isaiah 41:8, James 2:23, John 15:15) was suppressed and replaced. You will now find people using descriptions, titles and variations to replace the Name such as: God, Lord, Adonai, Jehovah and Ha Shem ("The Name") in place of the actual Name which was given in Scriptures. What a tragedy and what a mistake!

One of the Ten Commandments, also known as the Ten Words, specifically instructs us not to take the Name of the Creator "in vain" and *"He will not hold him guiltless who takes His Name in vain."* (Exodus 20:7). Most Christians have been taught that this simply warns of using the Name lightly or in the context of swearing or in some other disrespectful manner. This certainly is one aspect of the commandment, but if we look further into the Hebrew word for vain - שׁוא (pronounced shav) we find that it has a deeper meaning in the sense of desolating, uselessness or naught.

Therefore, we have been warned not only to avoid using the Name lightly or disrespectfully, but also not to bring it to naught, which is exactly what has been done over the centuries. The Name of our Creator which we have the privilege of calling on and praising has been suppressed to the point where most Believers do not even know the Name, let alone use it.

This sounds like a conspiracy of cosmic proportions and it is. Anyone who believes in the Scriptures must

understand that there is a battle between good and evil. There is an adversary, hashatan, who understands very well the battle which has been raging since the creation of the physical universe. He will do anything to distract or destroy those searching for the truth and he is very good at what he does. He is a master of deception and a liar. He does not want the truth to be revealed. His goal is to steal, kill and destroy. (John 10:10). The enemy has operated openly and behind the scenes over the centuries to infect, deceive, distract and destroy Believers with false doctrine. He truly is a wolf in sheep's clothing and his desire is to rob the Believer of blessings and life.

As you read this book I hope that you will see how he has worked to deceive mankind from the very beginning. Since the temptation in the garden the adversary has continually tried to get mankind to disobey the commandments. We are given wonderful promises in the Scriptures concerning blessings for those who obey the commandments. Sadly, many Believers have been robbed of those blessings due to false doctrines which teach them to not keep the commandments thus turning them into lawless individuals and removing them from the true Assembly of Believers. Their belief is not followed by righteous works making their faith empty and, to some extent, powerless.

My hope is that every reader has an eye opening experience and is forever changed. I sincerely believe that the truths which are contained in this book and the "Walk in the Light Series" are essential to avoid the great deception which is being perpetrated upon those who profess to believe in, and follow the Holy One of Yisrael.

This book, and the entire series, is intended to be

read by anyone who is searching for the truth. Depending upon your particular religion, customs and traditions, you may find some of the information offensive, difficult to believe or contrary to the doctrines and teachings which you have read or heard throughout your life. This is to be expected and is perfectly understandable but please realize that none of the information is meant to criticize anyone or any faith, but merely to reveal truth.

In fact, the information contained in this book had better stir up some things or else there would be no reason to write it in the first place. The ultimate question is whether the contents align with the Scriptures and the will of the Creator. My goal is to strip away the layers of tradition which many of us have inherited and get to the core of the faith which is described in the Scriptures commonly called "The Bible."

This book should challenge your thinking and your beliefs and hopefully aid you in your search for truth. My prayer for you is that of the Apostle Paul (Shaul) in his letter to the Ephesian assembly: *"[17] that the Father of glory, may give to you the spirit of wisdom and revelation in the knowledge of Him, [18] the eyes of your understanding being enlightened; that you may know what is the hope of His calling, what are the riches of the glory of His inheritance in the saints, [19] and what is the exceeding greatness of His power toward us who believe, according to the working of His mighty power."* Ephesians 1:17-19 NKJV.

I

In the Beginning

The subject of this book, as the title plainly states, is about the Redeemed, often referred to as the People of God, God's Chosen, the Saints or the Elect. The identity of this group is based upon their unique relationship with the Creator of the Universe. To be redeemed – a person must be purchased for a price – this is the very essence of the meaning of the word "redeem."

In order to determine the identity of the members of this particular group, it is first essential to understand and properly recognize their Redeemer – the One that has purchased them. There is no better place to start this investigation than with the Scriptures. If you open a English version of the Bible and turn to the first page you will read the following words: "*In the beginning God created the heavens and the earth.*" Genesis 1:1.

From this one sentence we can learn much. In fact, even the first letter of the first word provides us with meaning, but it is necessary to explore the original Hebrew in order to glean the spiritual messages provided in the text.

The first Hebrew word in the Scriptures is "beresheet" - spelled בראשית in modern Hebrew. Since the

Hebrew language reads from right to left, the first letter is beit (ב) which means: "house." The ancient Hebrew script is written as a pictograph and provides a more vivid understanding. We can see that beit "ℷ" represents the layout or footprint of an ancient dwelling or a tent. So right from the beginning we recognize that creation was about the Creator building a "house" or a "tent" which is also known as a "tabernacle."

We could spend an enormous amount of time and space simply delving into the word "beresheet" but there is other information located in the Hebrew text which needs mentioning before we proceed. The word used to describe the Creator of the universe is "God" in the English text, but again, it is important to realize that these words were originally written in Hebrew. In the Hebrew text you will not read the word God, but rather Elohim (אלוהם).[1]

Elohim has a plurality associated with it, and this is the first title used to describe the Creator. While God has become an almost universal term to describe the Creator it is neither authentic nor accurate. The term "god" actually has pagan origins[2] and using a capital "G" or inserting a hyphen (G-d) as some are accustomed to doing does not change that fact.

It is fundamental that if a person or religion claims to know and worship the Creator, then they should understand and use a proper title and Name. This is an extremely important subject for every person to grasp although it is one not given much thought or study in the realm of modern theology.

In any event, during the Creation account we are told that Elohim created all that exists, including mankind. We are also told that man was made in *the image of Elohim.*

Genesis (Beresheet)[3] 1:27. The name given to this man was "Adam" which describes that he came from the "ground." Now he was made in the image of Elohim because the "breath of life" was breathed into him. (Beresheet 2:7). It was this sharing of life which made Adam like his Creator and it could be said that Adam was the first "chosen."

We read that Adam was given a "bride" who was taken from his side. She was not created from the ground as he was, nor was the breath of life breathed directly into her, as was the case with Adam. She was literally birthed from the man. We are told that during this "birthing process" Adam was placed in a "deep sleep."

The Hebrew word used is tardemah (תרדמה) - which means more than just deep sleep. In fact, it means: "trance or stunned - like death." What we see is a picture of Adam dying so that his bride could live. Adam was then brought back to life, or "resurrected," so that he and his bride could dwell together in paradise.

The word for man is aish (איש) in Hebrew and the word for woman is aishah (אשה). Aishah means "taken out of man." Notice that there is a Hebrew letter hey (ה) added to the word. The hey (ה) has changed over the centuries and in ancient Hebrew script it symbolizes a man standing with arms raised (𐤀) and means: "behold." It is meant to announce something and can also mean: "to reveal." The hey (ה) also represents breath which is life - the Spirit of Elohim. This entire birthing process is an important event that we are meant to learn from.

Clearly both the man and the woman were unique in their beings and the fashion which they were created. Now along with man, the woman was chosen to dwell in a special place and to perform a specific purpose. The

woman was created to be a "help mate" for man which begs the question: "Help him do what?"

The Scriptures record that Adam was placed in the garden of Eden and charged *"to tend it and keep it."* Beresheet 2:15. In the Hebrew text we read two very important words: abad (עבד) which means "to work, to serve, to tend" and shamar (שמר) which means "to hedge about, to keep, to guard, to protect." The underlying Hebrew text implies that Adam was to act as a gardener and a watchman.

This is important to understand because the word for garden in Hebrew is "gan" (גן) which means: "an enclosed space." The word provides a picture of a place surrounded by a hedge. Adam was charged with the cultivation and the protection of this place - a place where man could directly commune with his Creator.

This paradise represented the very House of Elohim and as with any house - it had rules. Adam was given a set of instructions which, if he obeyed, he could partake of the Tree of Life and dwell forever with his Creator. Disobedience, on the other hand, led to expulsion and death.

We all know the ending to this tragedy - a tragedy for all of mankind. The man and the woman disobeyed a direct command not to partake of the tree of knowledge of good and evil and as a result they were cursed. This is a general principle throughout the Scriptures - obedience leads to blessings and life while disobedience leads to curses and death.

The man and the woman were evicted because they did not abide by the rules. Blood was thereafter shed as an atonement or covering for their sin, and they were each clothed with the skin of the animal which was slaughtered

because of their disobedience. They were literally and figuratively clothed in death. From that point forward man was expelled with no immediate hope of returning.

This appeared to be the end, but it was really only the beginning of mankind's journey back to Eden.

2

The Patriarchs

Despite the fact that Adam was expelled from the garden, he still knew what conduct was pleasing to Elohim. As we read through the Scriptures and look at the Ancestors in the faith it is evident that they knew the straight way and how to walk in it.

The Scriptures record that Adam lived for 930 years and as the first man, made in the image of Elohim, he surely would have continued to be an influence on mankind. He was unique from all others because he was not born from a woman, rather he was created by Elohim. Since he was taken from the ground he also had an intimate connection with the planet. As a result, the earth has also been impacted by his sin.

While Adam was made in the image of Elohim all of mankind, beginning with Seth, was born in Adam's image. (Beresheet 5:1-4). He had walked and fellowshipped with Elohim and was the one who could teach mankind the ways of Elohim. He likely functioned as a High Priest for all of mankind and surely would have given instruction concerning things such as worship and sacrifice.

For instance, Abel, whose name is actually Hebel (הבל) in Hebrew, provided acceptable sacrifices which

were pleasing to Elohim while Cain, or rather Qayin (ק ין), did not. (Beresheet 4:4-5).[4]

We read in a popular English version of the Scriptures how these two sons presented offerings to Elohim. "*² Now Abel kept flocks, and Cain worked the soil. ³ In the course of time Cain brought some of the fruits of the soil as an offering to the LORD. ⁴ But Abel brought fat portions from some of the firstborn of his flock. The LORD looked with favor on Abel and his offering, ⁵ but on Cain and his offering he did not look with favor. So Cain was very angry, and his face was downcast.*" Beresheet 4:2-5 NIV.

Beside the fact that the names of Hebel and Qayin have been changed, there is something very important that we can learn from this passage. To begin, Adam's two sons did not present their offerings to "The LORD." If you look at the original Hebrew text you will discover that they actually presented their offerings to 𐤄𐤅𐤄𐤉. Now unless you can read ancient Hebrew script you will not know how to pronounce this word which is actually the Name of the Creator. In Modern Hebrew it is spelled יהוה and in the English language the consonants are transliterated as YHWH or YHVH.[5]

This is a good example of how translations do not always provide us with the accurate or complete meaning found in the original text. In an effort to regain the original understanding of the Creator it is important that we know and use His Name. As a result, throughout this book the Name of the Creator will be rendered as YHWH.

We can also see from this text that while Qayin brought <u>some</u> of the fruits of the soil, Hebel brought fat from the firstborn. In other words, Hebel brought a proper first fruits offering while Qayin did not – he did not give

the best portion to YHWH. Both were obviously taught by their father the difference between acceptable and unacceptable offerings.

As a result of this incident Qayin ended up killing his brother, continuing the sin that his father and mother brought to the Earth. Qayin was banished and the righteous line was seemingly cut off until the birth of Seth, who was given in place of Hebel. We read that the woman, whose correct Hebrew name was Hawah,[6] not Eve, stated: *"Elohim has granted me another child in place of Hebel, since Qayin killed him."* Beresheet 4:25. We then read that: *"Seth also had a son, and he named him Enosh. At that time men began to call on the Name of YHWH."* Beresheet 4:26.

This was the progression of the righteous seed that started with Adam and in 1 Chronicle 1 we are provided with a list of ten righteous generations from Adam to Noah as follows: *"1 Adam, Seth, Enosh, 2Kenan, Mahalalel, Jared, 3 Enoch, Methuselah, Lamech, Noah."* 1 Chronicles 1:1-3. While there were many other genealogical lines stemming from Adam, it was this line which was unique, you could say - chosen.

Adam amazingly lived to see the birth and know each one of these men except for Noah. Interestingly, it was after the death of Adam and during the life of Noah that we are told how horribly wrong things were on the planet. The event in Eden came full circle and most of the planet was now living in opposition to the righteous conduct required by YHWH.

We read that: *"5 YHWH saw that the wickedness of man was great in the earth, and that every intent of the thoughts of his heart was only evil continually. 6 And YHWH was sorry that He had made man on the earth, and He was grieved in*

His heart. ⁷ So YHWH said, I will destroy man whom I have created from the face of the earth, both man and beast, creeping thing and birds of the air, for I am sorry that I have made them. ⁸ But Noah found favour in the eyes of YHWH." Beresheet 6:5-8.

The account of Noah continues by stating: *"Noah was a <u>just</u> man, <u>perfect</u> in his generations. Noah <u>walked</u> with Elohim."* Beresheet 6:9. The Hebrew word translated as "just" is tzedek (צדיק) which means: *"straight or righteous."* The Hebrew word translated as "perfect" is tamiyim (תמים) which means: *"clean or unblemished."* The Hebrew word translated as "walked" is halak (הלך) which is where we get halakah - a word used to describe our walk with YHWH. Our halakah is the way we live in a manner which is pleasing to Him - according to His instructions found within the Torah.⁷

Therefore, Noah walked with the Almighty and was righteous which meant that he followed the instructions of YHWH and was obedient. Because of his walk, he found favor in the eyes of YHWH and he and his family were spared from the flood. Noah obviously knew the distinctions between right and wrong, righteousness and unrighteousness, clean and unclean - he was actually described as "clean" and "righteous."

We can see an example of this knowledge when He collected seven pairs of clean and one pair of unclean animals onto the Ark. Also, when the flood waters receded he slaughtered only clean animals (Beresheet 7:2-4). I was always taught to believe that all of the animals entered the Ark "two by two" and that only two of

every species were on the Ark.

This is a good example of an inherited tradition which has no basis in truth, although the tradition can actually become more powerful than truth. This is one of the dangers of religion which often heaps traditions upon truth that can cloud, distort and hide the truth that it purports to profess.[8]

Noah was not a religious man, he was a righteous man. He obeyed the instructions of YHWH and he and his entire family lived as a result. It was the rest of mankind, choosing not to live righteously, that fell under judgment. After the flood we read that a covenant was made with Noah that extended to his offspring – the future generations of the planet.

Notice that the entire family of Noah was covered because of his conduct - not just Noah. Also, the covenant made with him included future generations. We see this as a common pattern in the covenants made between YHWH and man. A mediator is often chosen to represent those in his "household" who would then benefit from the promises of the covenant.

Now many think of a covenant as a contract or an agreement but it has a much deeper meaning. In Hebrew the word for covenant is brit (ברית) and it literally means "cutting." This is why we see sacrifices as part of covenants. Typically, when making an ancient blood covenant the parties to the covenant would cut the sacrifice in two and then pass between the pieces – literally walking in the blood of the covenant.[9]

This was intended to symbolize the consequences to anyone who broke the covenant: "may they be as the slaughtered animal" (Jeremiah 34:18). If you break

a contract in most societies it is deemed a civil matter, and there are usually monetary damages assessed for the breach. When you break a blood covenant, someone is supposed to die - just as the sacrifice died when the covenant was formed.

Covenants are a wonderful example of the favour of YHWH - which is often mislabeled as grace. He did not have to enter into any covenants with man, but He did so as a gesture of His kindness and mercy and as part of His Plan to restore His creation. When Adam and Hawah transgressed His commandments He could have just killed them and scrapped all of creation. Likewise when the planet was corrupted during the age of Noah, He could have just destroyed everything. Instead He continued to work with certain people to bring about a restoration.

All of the covenants are specifically designed to bring about the restoration of all things – to get mankind back into Eden. Thanks to the mercy of YHWH and the obedience of Noah we are all here today to participate in this process.

Noah and his righteous seed continued to act in the priestly role for mankind, just as Adam had once done. He was now like Adam in the sense that he would populate the world with his seed and we are provided with specific accounts of three of his descendants. In the case of Adam we are given information concerning Qayin, Hebel and Seth. In the case of Noah we are given information concerning Shem, Ham and Japheth (Yapheth).

The righteous line of Noah descended through his son Shem and when Noah pronounced a blessing over Shem he called YHWH the Elohim of Shem and he prayed that Elohim would *dwell in the Tents of Shem.*"

According to extra-Scriptural records Shem confronted Nimrod and Babylonian sun god worship. These ancient writings even refer to The Academy of Shem where he taught the ways of the Almighty to mankind. The Scriptures record ten more generations from Noah through Shem to a man named Terah who also had three sons: Abram (Avram), Nahor and Haran. (Beresheet 11:26).

The man Avram, later renamed Avraham, was called out of the Land of Ur of the Chaldees – a sacred place known for moon worship.[10] This man who was raised in the midst of a pagan society was called out by YHWH Who told him to leave his father's household and travel to the Land of Canaan.

He promised the following to Avram:

"I will make you into a great nation
and I will bless you;
I will make your name great,
and you will be a blessing.
I will bless those who bless you,
and whoever curses you I will curse;
and all peoples on earth
will be blessed through you."
Beresheet 12:2-3 NIV

Leaving his father's household was no small thing. It meant leaving the life that he knew and had labored to build. It meant leaving his family and the security of the position that he held in his society. It meant traveling through unknown lands and dwelling in those lands as a stranger. Add the fact that Avram was 75 years old and it

is clear that this must have been a momentous decision.

We do not know if Avram struggled with this decision, all we know is that he obeyed by going to the Land of Canaan. Had Avram not gone as instructed then he never would have seen the Land and he would not have then entered into covenant with YHWH. His obedience was important to get him to the place where he could covenant with YHWH.

He lived a life exemplified by obedience. We know that he obeyed the Torah because the Scriptures clearly tell us that he did. In Beresheet 26:4-5 we read: "⁴ YHWH *appeared to Yitshaq and said: 'In your seed all the nations of the earth shall be blessed;* ⁵ *because Avraham obeyed My voice and* kept My charge, My commandments, My statutes, *and My* **Torah.'"** ¹¹

The word shamar (שמר) is found in this passage as he kept and guarded the Torah - just as Adam was to keep and guard the Torah. We see in the life of this man a covenant which was made between YHWH and a man, including the seed of the man.

Unlike other covenants made between men, this covenant was different in that only YHWH passed between the pieces of the slaughtered animals. We read about it in Beresheet 15:9-11 when YHWH told Avram: "'⁹ *Bring me a three year old heifer, a three year old female goat, a three year old ram, a turtledove and a young pigeon'.* ¹⁰ *Then he brought all of these to Him and cut them in two, down the middle, and placed each piece opposite the other, but he did not cut the birds in two.* ¹¹ *And when the vultures came down on the carcass, Avram drove them away."*

Notice that he cut the three animals and did not cut the two birds. This provided eight pieces through which

the parties were to walk in order to confirm the covenant - only that did not happen. Interestingly vultures, which were unclean birds, were attempting to take the clean animals that were part of the covenant process. Avram had to guard and protect the pieces until the covenant was executed.¹²

"¹² *Now when the sun was going down, a deep sleep fell upon Avram, and behold, dread and great darkness fell upon him.* ¹³ *Then He said to Avram know certainly that your descendants will be strangers in a land that is not theirs, and will serve them, and they will afflict them four hundred years.* ¹⁴ *And also the nation whom they serve I will judge, afterward they will come out with great possessions.* ¹⁵ *Now as for you, you shall go to your fathers in peace, you shall be buried at a good old age.* ¹⁶ *But* <u>*in the fourth generation they shall return here,*</u> *for the iniquity of the Amorites is not yet complete.* ¹⁷ *And it came to pass – then the sun went down and it was dark, that* <u>*behold there appeared a smoking oven and a burning torch that passed between those pieces.*</u> ¹⁸ <u>*On the same day YHWH made a covenant with Avram saying*</u>: '*To your descendants I have given this Land, from the river of Egypt to the great river, the River Euphrates -* ¹⁹ *the Kenites, the Kennizites, the Kadmonites,* ²⁰ *the Hittites, the Perrizites, the Rephaim, the Amorites, the Canaanites, the Girgashites, and the Jebusites.*" ¹³

There is one very important thing to point out: The covenant promise has never been completely fulfilled. This Land grant is enormous - far greater than Ancient Israel or the Modern State of Israel ever experienced. It extends from Egypt through the Arabian Peninsula, Syria, Lebanon, Jordan, Iraq and possibly other countries in the Middle East and Africa.

Another important point is that YHWH put

Avram into what is described as a "deep sleep." Notice also that horror and great darkness fell upon him. This is a picture of death and the Hebrew word used here is tardemah (תרדמה). This was the same word used in Beresheet 2:21 when Hawah was taken from the side of Adam.

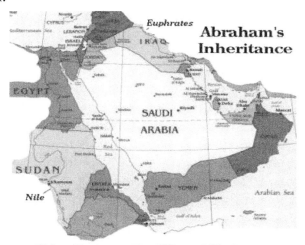

Abraham's Inheritance

All land between the Nile and Euphrates

These events parallel one another and something very important is going on in each instance. We read in Beresheet 17:5 after YHWH entered into covenant with Avram, He later confirmed the covenant when Avram was 99 years old. At that time YHWH changed his name to Avraham by adding a hey (ה) to his name. YHWH then detailed the covenant of circumcision (Beresheet 17:10 - 14). The covenant involved cutting his flesh and shedding his blood - not just the flesh and blood of the animals previously sacrificed. The fact that it was cut in the male organ is extremely significant since this covenant was made with Avraham <u>and his seed</u>.

In Beresheet 17:15 YHWH also changed the name of Avraham's wife from Sarai to Sara<u>h</u>. He added a hey (ה) to her name also. This reveals that the covenant would pass from the seed of Avraham through the cutting into the womb of Sarah. Just as Hawah was a bride for Adam - YHWH is showing us that through Avraham and Sarah - He was preparing a Bride for Himself. Interestingly, we see two heys (ה) added to this union and we find the hey (ה) two times in the Name of YHWH (יהוה).[14]

An important part of the original execution of this covenant is the fact that Avraham <u>did not</u> pass through the cuttings. At Beresheet 15:17 we are told to "behold," which is hineh (הנה) in Hebrew or (𐤄𐤍𐤄) in ancient Hebrew. The ancient language is particularly interesting in this instance because the character surrounded by each hey (𐤄) is a nun (𐤍) which means: "continue" or "perpetuate." It is specifically pointing to the "seed" continuing through this covenant which is made while one of the participants is virtually "dead."

We read that a smoking firepot and a burning torch passed through the cuttings as a demonstration that YHWH would bear the responsibility for both of the parties. All Avraham was responsible to do was to obey and carry the sign of the covenant in his flesh through circumcision. Avraham was instructed to circumcise himself and <u>every male in His household</u> - not just his physical seed.

This is a very critical point to understand - Avraham had an enormous household that traveled with him. They were not all his physical seed but they were part of his household and they dwelled within his tents. Therefore, the covenant was made with him and included

all of his household. The sign of this covenant was for all of the household of Avraham, just as the rainbow was the sign of the covenant made previously with Noah and all of his household in perpetuity.

The significance of the circumcision was that Avraham's seed would pass through the cutting of the covenant and then the promises of the covenant would pass through with the seed. The male child would then be circumcised on the eighth day and when that child grew up to become a man - his seed would in turn pass through the cutting of the covenant and so on - it was an everlasting covenant.

Notice the connection between the eight pieces of flesh that YHWH passed through and the eighth day circumcision when the flesh of the male child is cut. The number eight typically signifies a "new beginning" after the completion of the Scriptural cycle of seven that began on the first day of creation and continues to this day. The number eight is the same as the letter het (ח) in Hebrew which means: "a fence" or "separation." This can be plainly seen in the ancient Hebrew script - "ᄍ".

Therefore, from this covenant we can see that the seed of Avraham was to be set apart, surrounded by the hedge of the Torah as we saw in the Garden. This is very clear in the Scriptures. In fact, here is what YHWH said about Avraham in Beresheet 18:19: *"For I have known him, in order that he may command his children and his household after him, that they **keep** the Way of YHWH, to do righteousness and justice, that YHWH may bring to Avraham what He has spoken to him."*

We read in the Hebrew text the word *shamar* (שמר) again which has been translated as "keep." Avraham

watched and kept the hedge around his children and his entire household - all those who dwelled with him - and he instructed them all in the Way - which is the Torah.

This is a constant thread throughout the Scriptures although it is not always clearly recognized. Mankind knew the ways of YHWH <u>before</u> they were given to Israel at Mount Sinai and those who obeyed were considered righteous. They had faith **and** they demonstrated that faith by the way they walked. This does not mean that they were perfect in every way. They all came up short but they placed their faith in the promises made to them by YHWH.

If you follow YHWH, then you serve the same Elohim as did Avraham, who was our example in the faith. He obeyed YHWH and He worshipped YHWH in the midst of pagan peoples. It is a traditional belief that he was an "evangelist" for YHWH. His tent was always open to the stranger and he was hospitable to all. He used these opportunities to share his Elohim and he developed an entourage with him which was his household. If you joined with Avraham and dwelled under his tents, then you would also join into the covenant by following the ways of the Elohim of Avraham.

Noah and Avraham both provide us with a picture of what happens when you have faith combined with obedience. They demonstrated the importance of covenanting with the Creator which can only occur if we obey Him.

While Noah provides us with an example of faith coupled with obedience which delivers us from judgment, the life of Avraham provides us with an example of faith coupled with obedience that produces blessings. Both

covenants were everlasting covenants made with a man and his offspring.

The offspring of Noah constitutes the entire population of the earth, including Avraham and his offspring while the blessings of the offspring of Avraham extended through his promised son Isaac.

3

Isaac

While Avraham was promised great blessings which would be given to his seed, he found himself an old man without seeing that promise fulfilled. As a result, he started looking for ways to get things going. He thought that his servant Eliezer of Damascus might inherit his estate (Beresheet 15:2). He later had a son through Hagar when he was 86 years old and he hoped that this child, Ishmael, would be his heir. (Beresheet 17:18).

Needless to say, the Scriptures make it clear that neither of these options were the avenue that YHWH had in mind. The promised seed was specifically to pass from Avraham to the womb of Sarah and the child was to be named Isaac, more correctly Yitshaq (יצחק). (Beresheet 17:19).

It was not until Avraham was 99 years old, and Sarah was 89, that YHWH indicated He would fulfill His promise the following year at *"the Appointed Time."* Beresheet 18:14.[15] This is quite significant because these words were spoken immediately prior to the judgment that was about to befall Sodom and Gomorrah.

Since we are provided some hints that Lot was eating unleavened bread (Beresheet 19:3) this event likely

occurred at the time of Passover. Just as the righteous were delivered from Egypt hundreds of years later, Lot and his family were delivered from judgment during Passover. Thus, *"the Appointed Time next year"* in which Yitshaq was born would have likely been Passover.[16]

This is important because the life of Yitshaq as a pattern for the Son of Elohim. We know this through his fulfillment of the Appointed Times. We can also see this from direct references to Yitshaq as the "only son" of Avraham. This was specifically stated three times when Avraham was instructed to sacrifice Yitshaq at Moriah.

After Yitshaq was born and grown Elohim said to Avraham: *"Take your son, your only son, Yitshaq, whom you love, and go to the region of Moriah. Sacrifice him there as a burnt offering on one of the mountains I will tell you about."* Beresheet 22:2.

Imagine that! This promised son, a miracle child that was given to Avraham and Sarah in their old age, was now to be sacrificed. I doubt that Avraham told Sarah. Instead, early the next morning he arose and took Yitshaq and two servants. On the third day[17] they arrived in the land  of Moriah and Avraham placed the wood of the sacrifice on the shoulders of Yitshaq.

Yitshaq must have known that something was amiss. Avraham was probably not himself as he struggled to obey this difficult command. They typically would have brought their sacrifice with them, leading Yitshaq to ask the question: *"Where is the lamb?"* Avraham's response

was: "*Elohim Himself will provide the lamb for the burnt offering, my son.*" Beresheet 22:8. A direct translation from the Hebrew reads: "*Elohim will provide Himself a lamb.*"

After that Avraham bound Yitshaq and laid him on the altar to sacrifice him. It is important to note that there is nothing to indicate that Yitshaq struggled or protested. He was a grown man while Avraham was very old. According to the Book of Yasher he was 37 years old so he likely could have escaped, but it appears that he willingly laid down his life. (Yasher 22:41,53).

As Avraham was about to kill his son he was stopped by the Messenger of YHWH and told not to touch his son. The Messenger then went on to state: "*Now I know that you fear Elohim, because you have not withheld from me your son, your only son.*" Beresheet 22:12. "*¹⁵ The messenger of YHWH called to Avraham from heaven a second time ¹⁶ and said, I swear by Myself, declares YHWH, that because you have done this and have not withheld your son, your only son, ¹⁷ I will surely bless you and make your descendants as numerous as the stars in the sky and as the sand on the seashore. Your descendants will take possession of the cities of their enemies, ¹⁸ and through your offspring all nations on earth will be blessed, because you have obeyed me.*" Beresheet 22:15-18.

There is so much more going on in this passage than we can possibly imagine by just reading the English. On the surface we see a great promise that the descendents or rather "the seed" of Avraham will be incredibly numerous and powerful and all the nations of the earth would be blessed because of them.

As with many passages we can only understand the

profound depth of the Scriptures by reading and studying the original Hebrew. For instance, this entire passage is filled with the untranslated aleph-taw (את) which is a clear indication that it is a Messianic reference.[18]

There are three times that Yitshaq is refered to Avraham as *"your son, your only son."* In each of those three references there are three occurrences of the untranslated aleph-taw (את). In Beresheet 22:9, the passage where it describes Avraham as laying the wood on the altar and binding Yitshaq, there are three occurrences of the untranslated aleph-taw (את). Also in the following passage when Avraham was prepared to slay Yitshaq there are three occurrences of the untranslated aleph-taw (את). Also, remember that they arrived at Moriah on "the third day."

It could not be any clearer that this incident, often referred to as "the Akida," was a shadow picture of the fact that Elohim would provide a Lamb, His only Son - the Lamb of Elohim - Who would be slain and the promise to Avraham that *"all nations would be blessed"* would extend through this Lamb. This is powerful information and it can only be fully seen in the Hebrew text.[19]

Therefore, while Ishmael was born first, he was not the promised seed and he did not carry the promised blessings. While Ishmael was from the seed of Avram, Yitshaq was from the promised seed of Avraham. While the seed, Ishmael, passed through the uncircumcised Avram the seed, Yitshaq, passed through the circumcised cutting of Avraham - he literally passed through the covenant as did YHWH when He executed the covenant with Avraham.

Unlike Ishmael, who was circumcised when he

was 13 years old, Yitshaq was circumcised on the 8th day in accordance with the covenant. As such, his seed would thereafter pass through the cutting of his circumcision, which was the sign of the covenant.

In another Messianic reference concerning Yitshaq, we read how he married a virgin bride named Rivkah, who was the daughter of Bethuel. Interestingly the Hebrew word for virgin is Bethula (בתולא) while her mother's name is Bethuel (בתואל), almost the identical word only it means "desolate." It turns out that this apparent Hebrew word play is quite significant.

Rivka is brought to Yitshaq from a far off land by Avraham's servant Eliezer, the same Eliezer that Avraham thought might be his heir. Eliezer means: "El is my helper" or "El is my protector." He left the Promised Land to search out a bride for Yitshaq after swearing an oath to Avraham not to take Yitshaq with him back to Haran.

Many Scriptures record that he made the oath by placing his hand "under the thigh" of Avraham but it was much more explicit. Eleizer actually placed his hand on the circumcision of Avraham while swearing this oath because this act of finding a bride for Yitshaq was an integral part of the covenant which, in turn, was linked with the Promised Land. It was imperative that Yitshaq and his Bride be married <u>in the Promised Land</u> as his life was a pattern established for the Messiah

Eliezer went to the land of Mesopotamia, the land where Avraham had come from, to find a bride for Yitshaq. We know that after praying, Eliezer found Rivkah and gave her gifts: a nose ring and two bracelets of gold weighing ten sheqels. After negotiating the bride

price and giving gifts to her family Eliezer transported Rivkah along with her maids and Avraham's servants on ten camels. We shall see further on in this book the significance of the bride and the number ten.

When Yitshaq first meets Rivkah we read in the Scriptures that he takes her into his mother's tent and "marries" her. The Hebrew is more to the point as it states: "*he took Rivkah and she became his wife, and he loved her.*" Beresheet 24:67. This was no ordinary "church wedding" as Yitshaq apparently skipped the nuptuals and consummated their relationship without delay.

In this passage we have a clear Messianic reference as can plainly be seen in the Hebrew text. Between the words "took" and "Rivkah" is an untranslated אֵת which represents the Messiah consummating His marriage with His virgin Bride.

We read about Avraham's family as follows: "*[19] This is the genealogy of Yitshaq, Avraham's son. Avraham begot Yitshaq. [20] Yitshaq was forty years old when he took Rivkah as wife, the daughter of Bethuel the Armite of Padan Aram, the sister of Laban the Aramite. [21] Now Yitshaq pleaded with YHWH for his wife, because she was barren; and YHWH granted his plea, and Rivkah his wife conceived. [22] But the children struggled together within her; and she said, 'If all is well, why am I like this?' So she went to inquire of YHWH. [23] And YHWH said to her: 'two nations are in your womb, two peoples shall be separated from your body; one people shall be stronger than the other, and the older shall serve the younger.' [24] So when her days were fulfilled for her to give birth, indeed there were twins in her womb. [25] And the first came out red. He was like a hairy garment all over; so they called his name Esau. [26] Afterward his brother came out, and*

his hand took hold of Esau's heel; so his name was called Jacob. Yitshaq was sixty years old when she bore them. [27] *So the boys grew. And Esau was a skillful hunter, a man of the field; but Jacob was a mild man, dwelling in tents.* [28] *And Yitshaq loved Esau because he ate of his game, but Rivkah loved Jacob."* Beresheet 25:19-28.

Rivkah, was indeed barren as we saw through the word play between her mother's name and the word virgin. Through prayer she eventually conceived what would become two nations. Her younger son who wrestled with life, even from the womb, would be named Jacob.

4

Jacob

Many people assume that the great characters of faith whom we read about in the Scriptures led exemplary lives. Interestingly, this is not always the case. As with all humans these people made mistakes and had character flaws. Despite these obvious imperfections, YHWH used imperfect men and women in His plan and we should all take comfort from that fact. Just because they were called or chosen did not mean that they were better than anyone else.

The life of Jacob is filled with much deception and intrigue. He was a twin who wrestled with life, even prior to being born. We read from the account of his birth how he struggled to be the firstborn and came out of the womb grasping his brother Esau's heel. Thus the name Jacob, which is Yaakov (יעקב) in Hebrew, and means "supplanter".

From his birth it appears that Yaakov desired the firstborn status and he was reminded daily, through his name, just how close he came to having it. After he was grown we read how Esau sold his birthright to him for a bowl of stew. The legitimacy of this agreement is debatable since Esau was arguably under duress and the price was obviously not fair. Further, there is the question

of whether Esau had the right to sell something which did not necessarily belong to him. While the birthright status was attained at birth, it still needed to be given by the father, an act which usually occurred later on in life. There were times when the firstborn could give up or lose that right – so Esau sold something which had not yet been given to him. He may have been the first person to deal in futures.

The real story is not whether the sale was legitimate, but rather what was revealed in the hearts of these individuals. What Yaakov desperately wanted, Esau treated with disdain. This is why in Malachi 1:2-3 we read: "² *Was not Esau Yaakov's brother? YHWH says. Yet I have loved Yaakov, ³ but Esau I have hated, and I have turned his mountains into a wasteland and left his inheritance to the desert jackals." Esau despised those things which were to be treasured and he showed contempt for the ways of his father."* (see Beresheet 28:8-9). Yaakov and Esau were veritable opposites.

The desperation of Yaakov is compounded later when he actually deceived his elderly father by pretending to be his brother Esau. As a result of this deception Yitshaq, almost reluctantly, blesses Yaakov with the blessing of the firstborn - an act which apparently could not be undone. Only after he had actually lost the blessing was Esau filled with anguish and rage which required Yaakov to flee the Land that his fathers were promised and find safe haven with his Uncle Laban.

On his way to Paddan-Aram in Mesopotamia he stopped to rest and experienced a great vision at a place called Bethel. It was at that place where he set up the stone that he had used to rest his head and poured oil over it. He

then made a vow to Elohim saying: "*²⁰ If Elohim will be with me and will watch over me on this journey I am taking and will give me food to eat and clothes to wear ²¹ so that I return safely to my father's house, then YHWH will be my Elohim ²² and this stone that I have set up as a pillar will be Elohim's house, and of all that you give me I will give you a tenth.*" Beresheet 28:20-22.

He went on to prosper in the household of Laban although just as he had deceived his father, he too was deceived into marrying Laban's oldest daughter Leah when he thought it was Rachel. While outside the Land he had eleven sons by his two wives, Leah and Rachel, and two concubines, Bilhah and Zilpah. His sons were Reuben, Simeon, Levi, Judah, Dan, Naphtali, Gad, Asher, Issachar, Zebulun and Joseph.

After the birth of Joseph, and 20 years after he began working for Laban, Yaakov departed from the household of Laban and returned to the Land of his fathers. He had been mistreated by Laban, his wages had been changed 10 times and Laban was unwilling to let him go. Yaakov was a virtual slave of Laban, yet he prospered immensely and his family grew in size.

Unbeknown to Yaakov, Rachel stole her father's household idols before leaving Paddan-Aram. Yaakov thereafter crossed the Euphrates River and fled with his family and belongings westward to the hill country of Gilead. On the third day Laban was told of Yaakov's departure and gave chase.

After seven days Laban caught up with Yaakov and confronted him wherein they entered into a covenant together. Just as Yaakov had done after originally leaving his home, he again took a stone and set it up as a pillar.

He named the place "Galeed" which means "witness" in Hebrew. (Beresheet 31:45-47).

There were two witnesses at this ceremony, the standing stone which represented YHWH, the Elohim of Avraham, the Fear of Yitshaq and the Elohim of Yaakov, as opposed to the heap of rocks as a witness representing the god of Nahor, the grandfather of Avraham, and the god of Laban. Despite the fact that the Elohim of Yaakov had just spoken to Laban in a dream, he stubbornly clung to his gods, represented by the gold and silver idols that his daughter Rachel had stolen and was hiding from him. (Beresheet 31).

The standing stones set up by Yaakov stood as two giant parentheses to this portion of his life. It established a pattern which would be repeated by his progeny. After this event Yaakov then turned his attention to confronting his brother Esau, who he thought might want to kill him after the deception concerning his birthright.

When he left Laban he saw two messengers and called the place "mahanaim" which means "two camps" in Hebrew. This is significant because it explains what Yaakov does next. When he was informed that Esau was coming to meet him he divided his family – his tribes – into two camps or two households. (Beresheet 32:8). He did this to protect them in the event that Esau attacked them believing that if one were attacked the other could escape. It was also a prophetic event.

In preparation of the impending conflict Yaakov sent gifts ahead of him. He sent his family and possessions to the other side of the ford of Yabbok. It is here, when he was alone, that he wrestled with a man until the break of day. The man touched the socket of his hip which was

wrenched. Regardless of this inflicted injury, Yaakov would not let go until he received a blessing. The man told him: *"Your name will no longer be Yaakov, but Israel, because you have struggled with Elohim and with men and have overcome."* Beresheet 32:28. He then blessed Yaakov but he would not tell him his name.

Yaakov called the place Penuel, saying, *"It is because I saw Elohim face to face, and yet my life was spared."* Beresheet 32:30. This was a turning point in the life of Yaakov who became a new man, Yisrael.[20] He left his home and the Land as Yaakov and now he was returning as Yisrael. He left with nothing and returned prosperous. He left with his brother hating him and returned to find his brother Esau rejoicing and weeping to see him.

After his return, the first place that he set up camp was a place called Succot. This is highly significant because it is another pattern which has great significance in the future.[21] He later moved to Shechem and purchased a plot of land for 100 pieces of silver where he pitched his tent. He set up an altar and called it El Elohe Yisrael – which can mean El the Elohim of Yisrael or mighty is the Elohim of Yisrael. Either is appropriate for all that Yaakov had just experienced.

While at Shechem, Yaakov was horrified by an incident involving his daughter Dinah. His two sons, Simeon and Levi, after deceiving the males at Shechem, killed them three days after they had become circumcised. As a result of this incident, Yaakov commanded everyone

in his household to get rid of their foreign gods, get pure and change their garments. They then moved to Bethel and set up an altar and called it El Bethel.

At this point in the Scriptures we read a very interesting account as follows:

"*⁹ After Yaakor returned from Paddan Aram, Elohim appeared to him again and blessed him. ¹⁰ Elohim said to him, <u>Your name is Yaakov, but you will no longer be called Yaakov; your name will be Yisrael.</u> So He named him Yisrael. ¹¹ And Elohim said to him, I am El Almighty; be fruitful and increase in number. A nation and a community of nations will come from you, and kings will come from your body. ¹² The Land I gave to Avraham and Yitshaq I also give to you, and I will give this Land to your descendants after you. ¹³ Then Elohim went up from him at the place where He had talked with him. ¹⁴ Yaakov set up a stone pillar at the place where Elohim had talked with him, and he poured out a drink offering on it; he also poured oil on it. ¹⁵ Yaakov called the place where Elohim had talked with him Bethel (Beit El).*" Beresheet 35:9-15

This change of name is quite significant. Yaakov had to get cleaned up and go back to where his journey began – Beit El – the House of Elohim. He had fled the Land promised to his fathers and lived in exile – a veritable slave to his father-in-law. He returned a different man – a man with direction and purpose – a man in covenant with YHWH. This "new man" was to be named Yisrael (יׁשראל), signifying that he was not the same person as the last time he was there.

After leaving Bethel we read that Rachel gave birth to Benjamin, the last of the twelve sons, just outside of

Bethlehem. Rachel was also the mother of Joseph, who was the youngest son when they lived outside the Land. Interestingly, he was the last in the procession to enter and dwell in the Land when Yisrael divided his household. Benjamin, on the other hand, was the only child to be born in the Land and he remained the youngest of the sons of Yisrael. Sadly, Rachel died while giving birth to Benjamin.

The birth of Benjamin must have been bittersweet for Yisrael as his favored wife, Rachel, was now dead. Yisrael eventually returned to his father Yitshaq who was living in Hebron. It was there that he saw his father die when he was 180 years old. Both Esau and Yisrael buried Yitshaq there, a very siginificant place where Avraham was also buried.

As the twelve sons of Yisrael grew up in the Land we read of a conflict which arose between Joseph and the rest of his brothers. The Scriptures record that Joseph was the favored son of Yisrael who  had made him a special robe. Joseph was treated as the firstborn son due to the sins of his brothers, who were extremely jealous. Joseph even had dreams of his entire family bowing down to him which only exacerbated the situation.

As a result of their deep seeded jealousy, his brothers conspired to kill him, but ended up throwing him into a pit and determined to sell him into slavery. In the meantime, a caravan of Midianite merchants came along and his brothers pulled him out of the pit and sold him to Ishmaelites for 20 pieces of silver. He was then brought to

Egypt where he became a slave.

His brothers then killed a goat and put the blood of the goat on his garment. They told Yisrael that Joseph had been killed and for all intents and purposes, Joseph was dead. Joseph was thrown into prison but received favor from YHWH. Through his interpretations of Pharoah's dreams he was responsible for saving Egypt and the surrounding nations from famine and starvation. Through Joseph's actions, Pharoah increased in wealth and power.

As a result of these actions he rose to the level of viceroy in the Egyptian kingdom, second only to Pharoah. While in Egypt he married the daughter of a pagan priest who gave birth to two children, Manasheh and Ephraim. His brothers and father later came to Egypt during a time of famine, just as Avram had done in the past. As a result of their need for food, they were reunited and restored with Joseph who fed them. To his father Yisrael, it was as if Joseph had come back from the dead.

The symbolism found in the life of Joseph is profound and it is full of Messianic patterns from which there is much to learn. Before he died, Yisrael blessed his children and something very profound occurred relative to Joseph and his two sons.

Here is the account as it is stated in the Torah:

"*13 And Joseph took both of them, Ephraim on his right toward Yisrael's left hand and Manasheh on his left toward Yisrael's right hand, and brought them close to him. 14 But Yisrael reached out his right hand and put it on Ephraim's head, though he was the younger, and*

crossing his arms, he put his left hand on Manasheh's head, even though Manasheh was the firstborn. ¹⁵ Then he blessed Joseph and said, May the Elohim before whom my fathers Avraham and Yitshaq walked, the Elohim who has been my Shepherd all my life to this day, ¹⁶ the Messenger who has delivered me from all harm - may He bless these boys. <u>May they be called by my name and the names of my fathers Avraham and Yitshaq, and may they increase greatly upon the earth.</u> ¹⁷ When Joseph saw his father placing his right hand on Ephraim's head he was displeased; so he took hold of his father's hand to move it from Ephraim's head to Manasheh's head. ¹⁸ Joseph said to him, No, my father, this one is the firstborn; put your right hand on his head. ¹⁹ But his father refused and said, I know, my son, I know. He too will become a people, and he too will become great. <u>Nevertheless, his younger brother will be greater than he, and his descendants will become a group of nations.</u> ²⁰ He blessed them that day and said, In your name will Yisrael pronounce this blessing: May Elohim make you like Ephraim and Manasheh. <u>So he put Ephraim ahead of Manasheh.</u>" Beresheet 48:13-20.

What happened here is quite significant. Yisrael actually adopted the children of Joseph as his own. These two boys were born in Egypt to an Egyptian mother who was the daughter of a pagan priest. They had Egyptian blood and they were the only children of Yisrael that were adopted. They were not only adopted, Ephraim, the youngest, was elevated to first born status of all of the children of Yisrael. This event has great prophetic significance as we shall examine later in this text.

After speaking the blessings over Ephraim and

Manasheh, Yisrael then went on to call his remaining sons and blessed them as follows: "² *Assemble and listen, sons of Yaakov; listen to your father Yisrael. ³ Reuben, you are my firstborn, my might, the first sign of my strength, excelling in honor, excelling in power. ⁴ Turbulent as the waters, you will no longer excel, for you went up onto your father's bed, onto my couch and defiled it. ⁵ Simeon and Levi are brothers - their swords are weapons of violence. ⁶ Let me not enter their council, let me not join their assembly, for they have killed men in their anger and hamstrung oxen as they pleased. ⁷ Cursed be their anger, so fierce, and their fury, so cruel! I will scatter them in Yaakov and disperse them in Yisrael. ⁸ Judah, your brothers will praise you; your hand will be on the neck of your enemies; your father's sons will bow down to you. ⁹ You are a lion's cub, O Judah; you return from the prey, my son. Like a lion he crouches and lies down, like a lioness - who dares to rouse him? ¹⁰* <u>The scepter will not depart from Judah, nor the ruler's staff from between his feet, until Shiloh comes to whom it belongs and the obedience of the nations is His.</u> *¹¹* <u>He will tether his donkey to a vine, his colt to the choicest branch; he will wash his garments in wine, his robes in the blood of grapes.</u> *¹²* <u>His eyes will be darker than wine, his teeth whiter than milk.</u> *¹³ Zebulun will live by the seashore and become a haven for ships; his border will extend toward Sidon. ¹⁴ Issachar is a rawboned donkey lying down between two saddlebags. ¹⁵ When he sees how good is his resting place and how pleasant is his land, he will bend his shoulder to the burden and submit to forced labor. ¹⁶ Dan will provide justice for his people as one of the tribes of Yisrael. ¹⁷ Dan will be a serpent by the roadside, a viper along the path, that bites the horse's heels so that its rider tumbles backward. ¹⁸ I look for your deliverance, O YHWH. ¹⁹ Gad will be attacked by a band of raiders, but he will attack them at their heels. ²⁰ Asher's food will be rich; he*

will provide delicacies fit for a king. ²¹ *Naphtali is a doe set free that bears beautiful fawns.* ²² *Joseph is a fruitful vine, a fruitful vine near a spring, whose branches climb over a wall.* ²³ *With bitterness archers attacked him; they shot at him with hostility.* ²⁴ *But his bow remained steady, his strong arms stayed limber, because of the hand of the Mighty one of Yaakov, because of the Shepherd, the Rock of Yisrael,* ²⁵ *because of your father's Elohim, who helps you, because of the Almighty, who blesses you with blessings of the heavens above, blessings of the deep that lies below, blessings of the breast and womb.* ²⁶ *Your father's blessings are greater than the blessings of the ancient mountains, than the bounty of the age-old hills. Let all these rest on the head of Joseph, on the brow of the prince among his brothers.* ²⁷ *Benjamin is a ravenous wolf; in the morning he devours the prey, in the evening he divides the plunder.* ²⁸ *All these are the twelve tribes of Yisrael, and this is what their father said to them when he blessed them, giving each the blessing appropriate to him."* Beresheet 49:2-28.

Yisrael began as a man who inherited the promises of his fathers. This man originally named Yaakov eventually became Yisrael whose children were divided into tribes, soon to become a nation. His son Joseph inherited the birthright while Judah received the kingship. This is an important distinction with much significance which must be recognized and understood.

After blessing his children, Yisrael died and while he was brought back to Hebron and buried with his fathers, his children remained in Egypt.

5

Yisrael

What began as twelve sons of a man who wrestled with life and with his Creator soon became twelve tribes that grew into a nation within a nation. The Scriptures tell us: "*⁶ Now Joseph and all his brothers and all that generation died, ⁷ but the Yisraelites were fruitful and multiplied greatly and became exceedingly numerous, so that the land was filled with them.*" Exodus (Shemot)²² 1:6-7.

What began as a blessing under Joseph eventually became a curse. The Yisraelites came to Egypt as free men, escaping famine, but they ended up becoming slaves.

Egypt was the land inhabited by the descendants of Mitsrayim, the son of Ham, and the word Mitsrayim in Hebrew has come to be likened with "bondage."²³ The Yisraelites grew into a nation while in Egypt until the set time came for them to leave. This, of course, was all part of the pattern and the plan foretold to Avram by YHWH.

When YHWH entered into the covenant with Avram He stated: "*¹³ Know for certain that your descendants will be strangers in a country not their own, and they will be enslaved and mistreated four hundred years. ¹⁴ But I will punish the nation they serve as slaves, and afterward they will come out with great possessions.*" Beresheet 15:13-14.

Moses (Mosheh)[24] was raised through the household of Pharoah to lead the Yisraelites out of bondage. Just as Joseph had been grafted into the Egyptian power structure to bring Yisrael into Egypt, now Mosheh was grafted in to lead them out.

Mosheh was adopted into Pharoah's family and was actually a prince of Egypt. He began his life as a veritable orphan under a death sentence and then lived a life of royalty until around the age of forty. After murdering an Egyptian he fled to the land of Midian where, like Joseph, he married the daughter of a pagan priest.

While in Midian he returned to the heritage of his family and became a shepherd of flocks. This life in Midain was quite different than in Egypt. It must have been a humbling experience since shepherding was a lowly profession in Egyptian society. This was important training as he was preparing to lead the flock of Yisrael.

Around the age of eighty, YHWH appeared to Mosheh in the burning bush and charged him to return to Egypt and deliver His people – His sheep - out of bondage.[24] This once strong and bold man was now unsure of himself and his ability to speak so YHWH instructed Mosheh to use his brother Aaron as his mouthpiece.

Mosheh and Aaron attempted to obtain the permission of Pharoah to let the Yisraelites go into the desert for three days to hold a festival to YHWH. The Scriptures detail the confrontation: *"¹ Afterward Mosheh and Aaron went to Pharaoh and said, This is what YHWH, the Elohim of Yisrael, says: 'Let my people go, so that they may hold a festival to me in the desert.' ² Pharaoh said, 'Who is YHWH, that I should obey him and let Yisrael go? I do not know YHWH and I will not let Yisrael go.' ³ Then they said,*

'The Elohim of the Hebrews has met with us. Now let us take a three-day journey into the desert to offer sacrifices to YHWH our Elohim, or he may strike us with plagues or with the sword.'" Exodus 5:1-3.

It is quite interesting to note that Pharoah, the ruler of a major portion of the civilized word, did not know the Name of the Elohim of a large part of his population. That was about to change because YHWH prepared a great deliverance for His people so that the whole world would thereafter know his Name.

"*13* Then YHWH said to Mosheh, Get up early in the morning, confront Pharaoh and say to him, This is what YHWH, the Elohim of the Hebrews, says: 'Let My people go, so that they may worship Me, *14* or this time I will send the full force of my plagues against you and against your officials and your people, so you may know that there is no one like Me in all the earth. *15* For by now I could have stretched out My Hand and struck you and your people with a plague that would have wiped you off the earth. *16* But I have raised you up for this very purpose, that I might show you My power and that My Name might be proclaimed in all the earth.*" Shemot 9:13-17.

Notice that YHWH identified Himself as "The Elohim of the Hebrews." Avraham being the first Hebrew represented a people who followed YHWH. The household of Avraham consisted of many people who were not his direct offspring but if they lived under his tent – they too were Hebrews if they followed the Elohim of Avraham.

This is important because after YHWH had decimated Egypt through a series of plagues, it was time to deliver the Hebrews which consisted of the children of Yisrael along with those who desired to follow YHWH

and become part of Yisrael by obeying YHWH.

Their obedience began with the Passover, known as Pesach (פֶּסַח) in Hebrew, which occurred prior to the Exodus. YHWH instructed that every house slaughter a lamb as follows:

"²¹ Then Mosheh summoned all the elders of Yisrael and said to them, 'Go at once and select the animals for your families and slaughter the Passover lamb. ²² Take a bunch of hyssop, dip it into the blood in the basin and put some of the blood on the top and on both sides of the doorframe. Not one of you shall go out the door of his house until morning. ²³ When YHWH goes through the land to strike down the Egyptians, He will see the blood on the top and sides of the doorframe and will pass over that doorway, and He will not permit the destroyer to enter your houses and strike you down. ²⁴ Obey these instructions as a lasting ordinance for you and your descendants. ²⁵ When you enter the Land that YHWH will give you as He promised, observe this ceremony. ²⁶ And when your children ask you, 'What does this ceremony mean to you?' ²⁷ then tell them, 'It is the Passover sacrifice to YHWH, Who passed over the houses of the Yisraelites in Egypt and spared our homes when He struck down the Egyptians.' Then the people bowed down and worshiped. ²⁸ The Yisraelites did just what YHWH commanded Mosheh and Aaron. ²⁹ At midnight YHWH struck down all the firstborn in Egypt, from the firstborn of Pharaoh, who sat on the throne, to the firstborn of the prisoner, who was in the dungeon, and the firstborn of all the livestock as well. ³⁰ Pharaoh and all his officials and all the Egyptians got up during the night, and there was loud wailing in

Egypt, for there was not a house without someone dead."
Shemot 12:21-30.

Now we do not know precisely who obeyed and who did not obey. There was clearly a distinction made between Yisrael and Egypt. The Yisraelites were those who obeyed the instructions of YHWH delivered through Mosheh and the Egyptians were those who did not obey. The firstborn of the Yisraelites were delivered from death while the firstborn of the Egyptians were killed.[25]

The households of all who obeyed - all that were protected by the blood of the lamb - were delivered from death. But there was more to the promise than mere salvation from physical death of the firstborn. There was still much more to be completed at Sinai. Just as Adam was connected to YHWH and that connection was broken through disobedience, YHWH had plans to reconnect that relationship through the union of marriage with those who obeyed.

The children of Yisrael had been immersed in a pagan culture for centuries and it was time for Elohim to deliver on His promises to Avraham, Yitshaq and Yaakov. He plagued the land of Egypt, led the multitude out through divided waters and subsequently destroyed the army of Pharaoh. The Scriptures tell us that this was all done in such a dramatic fashion so that the entire world would know the Name of YHWH. (Shemot 9:16).

This is the concept that many people fail to recognize - it is the desire of YHWH that the entire world might know Him. This was the reason why He chose to deliver Yisrael and make them a nation of priests. "Priests to what?" you might ask. Priests to YHWH and to the nations!

The children of Yisrael were miraculously delivered from Egypt, not by themselves, but along with a mixed multitude of people. According to Shemot 12:37-38: *"³⁷ The children of Yisrael journeyed from Rameses to Succot, about six hundred thousand men on foot, besides children. ³⁸ **A mixed multitude went up with them also**, and flocks and herds - a great deal of livestock."*

This is a very important point that is often overlooked. Remember that as a result of Joseph and his leadership Egypt owned much land and possessions. People had come from all over the world seeking food and many sold themselves into servitude. The children of Yisrael were probably not the only slaves in Egypt.

I would imagine that if you were a slave and you just saw your slavemaster decimated by a Mighty Elohim — if you had the opportunity to leave with His people you would probably take it. This is not to say that everyone that went with Yisral was a slave. There were likely a variety of people from every level of Egyptian society. This mixed multitude consisted of a diversity of people from a range of cultures and languages.

It was the children of Yisrael, along with this mixed multitude, that was redeemed. At this point in the Scriptures we begin to clearly see the redemption plan that YHWH was implementing. In ancient days the process of redemption typically involved purchasing something that used to belong to you or a kinsman. It might be land, property or even a person.

The Exodus from Egypt was an act of redemption and those who were redeemed are repeatedly referred to as the people of YHWH - Yisrael. This concept of redemption is essential to understand because it implies

either ownership, right or title to something or someone. It was because of this relationship that Yisrael was redeemed and the price of redemption was the blood of the Lamb which was demonstrated through the Passover. This redemption was for a reason higher than merely freeing slaves. The redemption was meant to restore that which had been lost in Eden.

When the redeemed reached Mt. Sinai, Mosheh went up the mountain to meet with YHWH. While the instructions had been revealed to mankind from the beginning, something different happened at Sinai - just like something different happened with Avraham. It was another step in the process of restoration. This time the Torah was written and incorporated into a covenant with these redeemed people called Yisrael.

YHWH had told Avraham that his descendants would be afflicted for 400 years. When the time was up - the promise was fulfilled through the seed of Avraham that passed through Yitshaq to Yaakov - whose name was changed to Yisrael.

The primary difference between the covenant made with Avraham and the Sinai covenant was that YHWH was completing the marriage covenant and included within that covenant were those who dwelled with Yisrael. The Torah was still at the center of the covenant - like a Ketubah or a written marriage contract between a husband and a wife. The covenant was made between YHWH and Yisrael through Mosheh the Mediator.[26]

The first place that they camped was Succot, just as their father Yisrael had first camped at Succot when he returned to the Land.[27] These were not the same physical locations but they obviously are meant to tell

us something. Succot, as it turns out, is a very important Feast of YHWH. It is an Appointed Time when all who love and obey Him dwell in succas, which are temporary dwellings.

We are supposed to celebrate Succot every year as a rehearsal for a future event. It is an Appointed Time of YHWH, not a Jewish Holiday as some incorrectly believe. It is a time for everyone to obey and some day the entire planet will be celebrating this Feast.[28]

You see, anybody could sojourn with Yisrael as long as they agreed to obey the Holy One of Yisrael - just like anyone could live with Avraham and enter into the covenant if they were circumcised and followed the Ways of YHWH. The Assembly of Yisrael always included non-native Yisraelites and the Torah was never considered to be the exclusive domain of those who had the right genes – i.e. full blooded offspring of the man named Yisrael.

The Torah was for all mankind, as it was from the beginning. Remember, Adam was not a Hebrew, a Yisraelite, a Jew or a Christian - he was a man created in the image of YHWH. After the sin of Adam and Hawah, it was then necessary to restore individuals and mankind back into a right relationship and standing before the Creator.

YHWH was always concerned about the individual and when He established Yisrael as a nation it did not mean that He forgot about those who came prior to Yisrael nor does it mean that He was not concerned about the other nations that surrounded Yisrael. In fact, He established Yisrael to reveal Himself to those very nations.[29]

Therefore, anyone who wanted to enter into

this covenant relationship with the Creator could do so provided that they observed the terms of the covenant - which was the Torah. This is specifically stated in Leviticus (Vayiqra)[30] 19:33-34: "[33] And if a stranger dwells with you in your Land, you shall not mistreat him. [34] The stranger who dwells among you <u>shall be to you as one born among you, and you shall love him as yourself</u>; for you were strangers in the land of Egypt: I am YHWH your Elohim."

There were plenty of non-native Yisraelites who had joined with Yisrael and were redeemed from Egypt. They were also with Yisrael when they became impatient with Mosheh and under Aaron's tutelage, crafted a golden calf and worshipped it as YHWH.

The problem with growing up in a pagan society is that it is hard to stay set apart from all of the pagan elements that impact your day to day life. A casual observer might ask: Why on earth would they construct a golden calf? It seems absolutely absurd, until you realize that they were doing what was familiar to them. They were worshipping YHWH the way that the gods had been worshipped in Egypt.

You see, pagan societies such as Egypt did not worship one god - they worshipped many gods. There were a multitude of gods and goddesses that symbolized different things on the earth and in the spirit realm. One of the

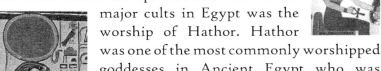

major cults in Egypt was the worship of Hathor. Hathor was one of the most commonly worshipped goddesses in Ancient Egypt who was originally considered to be the mother of Horus, the falcon god. That title eventually

went to Isis and Hathor was in later times regarded as his wife. Hathor was associated with love, fertility, sexuality, music, dance and alcohol. Who better to invite to a party - at least that is what the Yisraelites thought.

"She was sometimes represented entirely anthropomorphically, in the form of a cow, or as a woman with cow's ears. When in human form, her headdress could be one of cow's horns with a solar disc, or a falcon on a perch. She was also a sky goddess, and was regarded as a vast cow who straddled the heavens, with her four legs marking the four cardinal points."[31] She was honored as the "Lady of Byblos," the source of the word "Bible."[32]

The Yisraelites declared a Feast to YHWH which was not a feast prescribed or ordained by YHWH.[33] They built an altar and made an idol in the manner that they had learned while in Egypt. The golden calf was the child of Hathor and Apis. Thus we see an example of a pagan trinity - father, mother, child worship which is predominate in pagan systems and derives from Babylon.[34]

They took what they were used to doing in a pagan society and began doing it to YHWH. The only problem was that it was an abomination to YHWH. They were supposed to be a "holy" people which is qadosh (קדש) in Hebrew and means: "set apart." They were not supposed  to be doing pagan things and saying that they were doing them to YHWH. They were mixing abominations in their worship which is strictly prohibited. Sadly, this error was continually repeated

by Yisrael.[35]

There is no reason to think that only the non-native Yisraelites worshipped false gods. In fact, their readiness to worship false gods only days after witnessing the miraculous deliverance from Egypt only strengthens the position that many of the Yisraelites had fallen into pagan worship while enslaved in Egypt. After all, they were surrounded by these gods and goddesses which pervaded every aspect of the Egyptian culture.

These gods and goddesses had names, faces and temples where they could be worshipped. They had carved and painted images, statues and idols which could be seen and touched - they appeared real to those who worshipped them. In this pagan environment, Yisrael may have forgotten or neglected the Elohim of their father Avraham because He was invisible and without form.

This is why Elohim brought them out to the desert, to clean them up and straighten them out - to restore them. He wanted to reveal Himself to them and show them how to properly worship Him. We know that YHWH punished those who worshipped the golden calve. He also gave Yisrael a second chance to complete the marriage Covenant.

If you read the Old Testament Scriptures, better known as the Tanak,[36] you will see that time and again, Yisrael fell back into pagan worship. Their "backsliding" involved a variety of gods and goddesses from neighboring countries, some of which will be discussed further on in this book.[37]

The cleansing process which began in the wilderness has been continuing throughout the ages. In every generation He gleans those who have a heart for

Him. He is looking for a people who will follow Him wholeheartedly, a people He can redeem and dwell with.

Yisrael had to make a choice - whether they would follow the One True Elohim or whether they would chase after the false gods of the pagan nations. Yisrael consisted of anyone who wanted to follow the Elohim of Yisrael. It did not matter where you came from. If you were born outside of Yisrael you could join with Yisrael, but if you wanted to dwell with the Redeemed people, you needed to live your life according to the instructions - the Torah. The Torah told Yisrael - the Bride - exactly what YHWH - the Husband - expected of her. It established boundaries for the marriage.

The Torah was, in essence, a wedding gift to Yisrael. It was never considered to be a burden by Yisrael; it was always understood to be a blessing and a privilege to be given the Torah. In fact, it showed them how to receive blessings and it warned them of how they could be cursed.

Many people wander through life wondering how to be blessed and wondering why they are not blessed or why they feel cursed. YHWH expressly told His Bride how to prosper and how to avoid problems. He showed her the path to abundance, blessings and life.

Who would not consider that to be a great gift? As a result, at Sinai, the Assembly of Yisrael willingly agreed to obey the Torah; it was not forced upon them. In fact, YHWH delivered them from slavery and freed them without any conditions other than to follow His instructions. This is so no one could ever state that they made a decision under duress.

Once the mixed multitude was delivered from slavery, they were <u>then</u> given the option to accept the

Torah and their decision was unequivocal. After Mosheh told the people all of the words, they responded in Shemot 24:4: "*All the words that YHWH has commanded we will do.*" They freely chose to live in a manner which allowed them to dwell in the presence of a Holy Elohim - the manner prescribed by the Torah.

According to Bemidbar 15:29: "*You shall have one Torah for him who sins unintentionally, for him who is native-born among the children of Yisrael and for the stranger who dwells among them.*" Again, your skin color did not matter; neither did the genes in your body. What mattered was what you believed and consequently what you obeyed.

Yisrael later rejected the promise of the Covenant by refusing to enter the Land. This demonstrated an utter lack of faith and trust in the promises of YHWH. While they passed the first test, leaving their homes, they failed to enter into the Land of Canaan.

How remarkable that their father Avraham did so with his relatively small entourage while this mighty band of people were too afraid to enter in. This is incredible because YHWH had just recently delivered them from the most powerful nation on earth. They were about to receive the Land which was promised to them but they were afraid, despite the miracles they had just witnessed.

Their fear demonstrated that they did not trust YHWH and ultimately they did not love Him. If they loved Him, they would have done what He said, even if it meant certain death. Sadly, YHWH was intent on blessing them and they still refused to obey. We should all meditate on this point because we too can miss the blessings if we fail to obey. There may come a time in the future when we must make a similar choice. Our response

must be to obey no matter what we see with our eyes.

As a result of the choice that Yisrael made, they were made to wander in the wilderness for forty years until the next generation was raised up to enter into the Land. This was very merciful of YHWH. He could have destroyed them all because of their disobedience but instead, He let them live out the rest of their lives until only two from that generation remained.

6

The Land

Since the Land was an integral part of the Covenant made with Avraham and confirmed at Sinai, it was important for Yisrael to enter into the Land of promise. If you do not want to live in the Land then you should not expect to enter into the Covenant. The Land and the Covenant are inseparable.

Some erroneously try to differentiate or divide elements of the Covenant by stating that the Land was a part of the Covenant made with Avraham and they are part of a different Covenant that does not include the Land. This is simply not possible. All Covenants made after Avraham were in essence, the same Covenant renewed.[38]

An important point to recognize is that only two adults from the generation that left Egypt in the Exodus actually crossed over into the Promised Land: Joshua and Caleb - two of the twelve who previously explored the Land. They were the two who gave a good report to the people and encouraged them to enter into the Land - despite the presence of giants. They also took the trouble to carry out a cluster of grapes as proof of the bounty that awaited them. The reason why these two were different is specifically detailed in the Scriptures: "*not one except Caleb*

son of Yephunneh the Kenizzite and Joshua son of Nun, for they followed YHWH wholeheartedly." Numbers (Bemidbar)[39] 32:12.

Notice that Caleb was not a native Yisraelite. The Scriptures record that his father was a Kenizzite yet they became part of Yisrael. Despite the fact that his father was from a foreign land, the Scriptures list Caleb as being part of the Tribe of Judah. This means that at 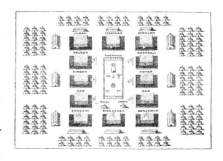 some point his family was "grafted in" to the tribe of Judah, properly known as Yahudah.[40]

This is how it worked when Yisrael camped after the Exodus. They divided into tribes and they camped around the Tabernacle. There was no "Tribe of the Mixed Multitude" - no "Tribe of the Nations." The mixed multitude was not separated from the other tribes, they became part of Yisrael as Caleb's family joined Yisrael through the Tribe of Yahudah. Anyone that wanted to join with Yisrael was ultimately "grafted in" through a tribe.

Now look at Joshua son of Nun, whose true Hebrew name was Yahushua.[41] His name was changed from Hoshea which means: "salvation" to Yahushua which means: "Yah is salvation." Yah is the short form of YHWH so the name is a declaration that it is YHWH Who saves.

Yahushua was from the Tribe of Ephraim. The Tribe of Ephraim is extremely interesting because the

name itself means: "doubly fruitful." Remember that Ephraim was a son of Joseph (Yoseph)[42] and he was born in Egypt along with his brother Manashah - unlike the other children of Yisrael. His mother Asenath was an Egyptian - the daughter of a pagan priest - just as Mosheh's wife was the daughter of a pagan priest.[43] Yisrael has always been mixed with the other nations.

Ephraim was the youngest son of Yoseph yet he received the blessing and birthright of a firstborn son. He was adopted by his grandfather Yisrael and elevated as a son. So we have this powerful picture of a child born into a pagan culture and Yisrael then adopting him, making him a tribe and blessing him - as a firstborn son! (Beresheet 48).

We also see the two men - Caleb and Yahushua - representing the tribes of Yahudah and Ephraim, both of whom were adopted into Yisrael in different ways - these being the only two to enter into the Land from their generation. How profound and encouraging for anyone born into paganism, finding themselves outside of the Covenant - not to fret, there is room for everyone.

If you still are not convinced, then read on. Before this new generation entered into the Promised Land, the Covenant was renewed at Moab. We read in Deuteronomy 29:1 *"These are the terms of the Covenant YHWH commanded Mosheh to make with the Yisraelites in Moab, in addition to the Covenant he had made with them at Horeb."* All of Yisrael was assembled, including sojourners in the midst of the assembly, to hear the words of the renewed Covenant.

"[10] All of you are standing today in the presence of YHWH your Elohim - your leaders and chief men, your elders and officials, and all the other men of Yisrael, [11] together with your

children and your wives, and the aliens living in your camps who chop your wood and carry your water. [12] You are standing here in order to enter into a Covenant with YHWH your Elohim, a Covenant YHWH is making with you this day and sealing with an oath, [13] to confirm you this day as His people, that He may be your Elohim as He promised you and as He swore to your fathers, Avraham, Yitshaq and Yaakov. [14] I am making this Covenant, with its oath, not only with you [15] who are standing here with us today in the presence of YHWH our Elohim but also with those who are not here today." Deuteronomy 29:10-15.

The Covenant was renewed with that new generation as well as with those who were not there. This points to a future people who would enter into the same Covenant - which would again be renewed.

We have an example of this happening with Ruth who was, by no coincidence, a Moabite from the very land where this Covenant was renewed. The story of Ruth provides a beautiful picture of a foreigner being grafted into Yisrael and becoming an important part of the Messianic bloodline. Her famous words are the formula for becoming grafted in to Yisrael: "*For wherever you go, I will go; and wherever you lodge, I will lodge; Your people shall be my people, and your Elohim, my Elohim.*" Ruth 1:16. Through this story we see a vivid example of redemption.[44]

Before entering in to the promised Land, the Assembly of Yisrael was specifically commanded not to worship false gods. "*You shall not bow down to their gods or serve them or do after their works; but you shall utterly overthrow them and break down their pillars and images.*" Shemot 23:24. They were also instructed not to set up poles and pillars in order to worship false gods. "*[21] You*

shall not plant for yourself any tree, as a wooden image, near the altar which you build for yourself to YHWH your Elohim. [22] *You shall not set up a sacred pillar, which YHWH your Elohim hates."* Deuteronomy 16:21-22.

The Yisraelites were supposed to live holy, set apart lives according to the Torah – their wedding contract. They were supposed to stay true to their Husband YHWH and not commit spiritual idolatry with other gods – which would constitute adultery.

In other words, as the Bride of YHWH, if they wanted to live in His house – the Land – then they needed to remain faithful to Him and His ways. Under the leadership of Yahushua, Yisrael was finally permitted to enter into the Land, which was divided between the Tribes.

7

The Kingdom

While Mosheh led Yisrael in the wilderness, it was Yahushua who would lead them into their inheritance. Yahushua had been at the side of Mosheh when he went up the mountain. Yahushua, along with Caleb, spied out the Land and brought back a good report. He was only one of two who entered into the Land from the generation that was delivered from Egypt.

As previously indicated, his original name was Hoshea son of Nun. We are told of his name change immediately before he entered into the Land with the eleven other spies. The change involved adding the Name of YHWH – which has great significance.

We know that Avram left a pagan land and crossed over to join into Covenant with YHWH and became Avraham. Yaakov left the Land as one man and returned a different person with his tribes and a new name. So too, Hoshea left Egypt as one man and entered into the Land as a different being. Hoshea left Egypt a slave and entered the Land as a leader – Yahushua.

We also learn from the Scriptures that the generation that entered into the Land with Yahushua and Caleb renewed the Covenant at Moab. Under the

command of Yahushua they crossed the Jordan (Yarden) River, which was a corporate baptism, more accurately known as a mikvah.[45] They were circumcised and then celebrated the first Passover in the Land. They then went on a campaign to conquer the Land and drive out the inhabitants, including giants, which the previous generation had been afraid to confront.

The Scriptures record that Yisrael settled into the Land and then renewed the Covenant again at Mount Gilboa near Shechem. These renewals did not involve new Covenants, they were the same Covenant. This is something that Christianity fails to recognize, erroneously believing that the Messiah came and entered into a "New" Covenant - which He did not do. He simply "renewed" the Covenant with Yisrael which had been done many times in the past. He followed a pattern which had been established by Mosheh and Yahushua.

Despite renewing the Covenant, the tribes were constantly struggling within themselves, between each other, with their leaders, with their neighbors and with YHWH. While Yisrael remained tribal in structure, they were bound by a common system of worship with the High Priest as their spiritual leader. This failed to unify all of the tribes and they often found leadership from individuals who would function in a role known as a "Judge."[46]

From the time that they conquered the Land under the leadership of Yahushua, there was a period of approximately 393 years that elapsed until YHWH would raise up a leader who would unite the tribes as a cohesive nation.

The people eventually cried out for a king. This was

inevitable and even foretold by Mosheh. (Deuteronomy (Devarim)[47] 17:14). At that time Samuel (Shemuel)[48] was the undisputed authority figure in Yisrael. Shemuel was a unique individual who was a nazarite from the tribe of Ephraim. He was dedicated to YHWH by his mother Hannah and, in essence, adopted by Eli the High Priest. This was likely the case because he served as a priest and only a Levite could serve in the Mishkan.[49]

It was Shemuel who attended to the Mishkan after the death of Eli, since his two sons Hophni and Phinehas died in a battle against the Philistines, and it was Shemuel who had the authority from YHWH to annoint the first King of the Kingdom of Yisrael. How fascinating that this very unique man from the tribe of Ephraim would stand as a Judge of Yisrael at the time when Yisrael transitioned into a kingdom.

Shemuel anointed Shaul, who was from the tribe of Benyamin. Benyamin was the only one of the 12 sons of Yisrael that was born in the Land and the tribe of Benyamin was the smallest amongst the tribes. This tribe was nearly decimated after the sin of Gibeah. (see Judges 19-20). This tribe was located geographically between Yoseph, the largest tribe and Yahudah. Yoseph and Benyamin were the two youngest sons of Yisrael and they shared the same mother – Rachel.

The reign of Shaul did not last long because he did not diligently obey the commandments. Here is what Shemuel told Shaul: "[13] *You have done foolishly. You have not kept the commandment of YHWH your Elohim, which He commanded you. For now YHWH would have established your kingdom over Yisrael forever.* [14] *But now your kingdom shall not continue. YHWH has sought for Himself a man after His own*

heart, and YHWH has commanded him to be commander over His people, because you have not kept what YHWH commanded you." 1 Shemuel 13:13-14.

Shaul failed just as Adam had failed. He did not keep, guard, watch over and protect (shamar) the commandments.[50] Therefore, YHWH found a man like Yahushua and Caleb - a man who would follow Him with his WHOLE heart. David was a giant slayer as were Yahushua and Caleb. He trusted in his Elohim and we know from the Psalms (Tehillim)[51] that he loved the Torah. These are the character traits of a man that YHWH will allow to lead His people – Yisrael.

David was the youngest child of Jesse (Yeshai) and was born and raised in Bethlehem. The reign of King David is looked upon as the Golden years of Yisrael. He made mistakes but his heart for YHWH never wavered. As a result, YHWH covenanted with David that the throne would never depart from his offspring. David was responsible for moving the capital of the Kingdom to Jerusalem. It is no coincidence that this was the location from which the Melechzedek reigned that Avraham tithed to – this was a fulfillment of the Avrahamic covenant.

David established his throne in Jerusalem and endeavored to build a House for YHWH. Up until then the Tabernacle made in the wilderness was still being used and moved to various locations. David set his heart to build a permanent house.[52]

At the direction of the prophet Gad, David purchased the threshing floor of Araunah, along with oxen to slaughter.[53] There he built an altar to YHWH and it was chosen as the location of the House of YHWH. A threshing floor is a specially flattened surface made either

of rock or beaten earth where the farmer would thresh the grain harvest. The threshing floor was either owned by the entire village or by a single family. It was usually located outside the village in a place exposed to the wind.[54]

Once the grain was threshed, a process of separating it from the stalks, usually through beating, it needed to be separated from the chaff through a process known as winnowing. The fact that the location of the House of YHWH was a threshing floor has profound implications when you consider that the Appointed Times, known as the moadim, were centered around the harvests.[55]

It is even more profound that it was at this very location that the Messenger of YHWH stopped during a plague on Yisrael due to the sin of David. This event took place while wheat was being threshed so it would have been around Shavuot. Seventy thousand Yisraelites had died and the plague stopped at the threshing floor around the Feast of Weeks (Sevens).

While David purchased the land, he was not permitted to build the House because he had blood on his hands. He was responsible for making the plans and preparations for building the House, as well as developing the songs, the instruments and other aspects of the worship service.[56]

After the reign of King David, things deteriorated very rapidly. His son, Solomon (Shlomo),[57] built and dedicated the House of YHWH. He also built other great structures and he accrued incredible wealth. He was known for his great wisdom, but sadly he fell into serious idolatry at the end of his life.

Read how his heart turned away from YHWH: "*¹ But King Shlomo loved many foreign women, as well as the*

daughter of Pharaoh: women of the Moabites, Ammonites, Edomites, Sidonians, and Hittites - ² from the nations of whom YHWH had said to the children of Yisrael, 'You shall not intermarry with them, nor they with you. Surely they will turn away your hearts after their gods.' Shlomo clung to these in love. ³ And he had seven hundred wives, princesses, and three hundred concubines; and his wives turned away his heart. ⁴ For it was so, when Shlomo was old, that his wives turned his heart after other gods; and his heart was not loyal to YHWH his Elohim, as was the heart of his father David. ⁵ For Shlomo went after Ashtoreth the goddess of the Sidonians, and after Milcom the abomination of the Ammonites. ⁶ Shlomo did evil in the sight of YHWH, and did not fully follow YHWH, as did his father David. ⁷ Then Shlomo built a high place for Chemosh the abomination of Moab, on the hill that is east of Jerusalem, and for Molech the abomination of the people of Ammon. ⁸ And he did likewise for all his foreign wives, who burned incense and sacrificed to their gods. ⁹ So YHWH became angry with Shlomo, because his heart had turned from YHWH Elohim of Yisrael, who had appeared to him twice, ¹⁰ and had commanded him concerning this thing, that he should not go after other gods; but he did not keep what YHWH had commanded. ¹¹ Therefore YHWH said to Shlomo, because you have done this, and have not kept My Covenant and My statutes, which I have commanded you, I will surely tear the kingdom away from you and give it to your servant. ¹² Nevertheless I will not do it in your days, for the sake of your father David; I will tear it out of the hand of your son. ¹³ However I will not tear away the whole kingdom; I will give one tribe to your son for the sake of My servant David, and for the sake of Jerusalem which I have chosen." 1 Kings 11:1-13.

So a man who began his reign renowned for his wisdom ended up an idolater. He failed to keep (shamar)

the commandments which separated him from the One Who had blessed him so greatly. The Scriptures are very clear that it was his disobedience which led to his demise. The Torah specifically forbids kings from obtaining great wealth or taking many wives. (Devarim 17:16-17) They were supposed to prepare their own Torah Scroll to remind them to live and rule according to the instructions of YHWH. (Devarim 17:18).

Shlomo was provided with everything he needed to be a great king but he failed miserably and ended up being involved in abominable conduct, some of the worst pagan rituals that existed, including the sacrifice of children. He blatantly disobeyed the commandments and the Kingdom would suffer as a result. Before his death, it was prophesied by Ahiyah of Shiloh that the Kingdom would be torn apart.

The prophet confronted the servant of Shlomo, Jereboam, as he was leaving Jerusalem. Ahiyah took a new cloak and tore it into 12 pieces. He told Jereboam to take 10 pieces and spoke the following to him:

"³¹ See, I am going to tear the kingdom out of Solomon's hand and give you ten tribes. ³² But for the sake of my servant David and the city of Jerusalem, which I have chosen out of all the tribes of Yisrael, he will have one tribe. ³³ I will do this because they have forsaken me and worshiped Ashtoreth the goddess of the Sidonians, Chemosh the god of the Moabites, and Molech the god of the Ammonites, and have not walked in my ways, nor done what is right in my eyes, nor kept my statutes and laws as David, Solomon's father, did. ³⁴ But I will not take the whole kingdom out of Solomon's hand; I have made him ruler all the days of his life for

*the sake of David my servant, whom I chose and who
observed my commands and statutes. ³⁵ I will take the
kingdom from his son's hands and give you ten tribes. ³⁶
I will give one tribe to his son so that David my servant
may always have a lamp before me in Jerusalem, the
city where I chose to put my Name. ³⁷ However, as for
you, I will take you, and you will rule over all that
your heart desires; you will be king over Yisrael. ³⁸ If
you do whatever I command you and walk in my ways
and do what is right in my eyes by keeping my statutes
and commands, as David my servant did, I will be with
you. I will build you a dynasty as enduring as the one
I built for David and will give Yisrael to you. ³⁹ I will
humble David's descendants because of this, but not
forever."* 1 Kings (Melakim) 11:31-39.

This was an incredible prophecy given to Jereboam
– an Ephraimite. The Scriptures record that Jereboam was
a mighty man of valour - he was a powerful man. Shlomo
recognized this and placed him in charge of the whole
labor force of the House of Yoseph, but Jereboam rebelled
against Shlomo. His people were being oppressed and
YHWH chose Jereboam to punish Shlomo. He also gave
Jereboam great promises if he would only do what Shlomo
failed to do – be like David – obey and guard (shamar) the
commands, walk in His ways and do what was right.[58]

8

Division

After the death of King Shlomo, the prophecy given by Ahiyah came to pass. The House of Yisrael, also known as the Northern Kingdom, petitioned Solomon's son, King Rehoboam, essentially asking for tax relief. In the past, King Shlomo, had put a heavy burden on the people while amassing great wealth and building mighty structures.

Instead of taking the advice of the elders, Rehoboam heeded the counsel of his young friends and responded to the apparent reasonable request by stating: "*My father laid on you a heavy yoke; I will make it even heavier. My father scourged you with whips; I will scourge you with scorpions.*" 1 Kings (Melakim) 12:11 NIV.

His "unwise" response resulted in a split in the Kingdom of Yisrael. The House of Yisrael, which consisted of the Ten Northern Tribes, aligned with Jeroboam son of Nebat. The House of Yahudah, which consisted of the Southern Tribes, aligned with Rehoboam. While the House of Yahudah maintained the worship of YHWH in Jerusalem the Northern Tribes set up their own false worship system. This is where things started to go bad for the House of Yisrael.

Apparently, Jeroboam feared that if the House of Yisrael continued to go to Jerusalem they would eventually join up with the House of Yahudah and reunite the Kingdom of Yisrael. This notion was unfounded, self serving and contrary to the promise given to him by YHWH. Therefore, after seeking and following some bad advice of his own, he set up pagan worship in the north.

"²⁶ _Jeroboam thought to himself, The kingdom will now likely revert to the house of David._ ²⁷ _If these people go up to offer sacrifices at the House of YHWH in Jerusalem, they will again give their allegiance to their master, Rehoboam king of Yahudah. They will kill me and return to King Rehoboam._ ²⁸ _After seeking advice, the king made two golden calves._ He said to the people, 'It is too much for you to go up to Jerusalem. Here are your gods, O Yisrael, who brought you up out of Egypt._ ²⁹ _one he set up in Bethel, and the other in Dan.'_ ³⁰ _And this thing became a sin; the people went even as far as Dan to worship the one there._ ³¹ _Jeroboam built shrines on high places and appointed priests from all sorts of people, even though they were not Levites._ ³² _He instituted a festival on the fifteenth day of the eighth month, like the festival held in Yahudah, and offered sacrifices on the altar._ This he did in Bethel, sacrificing to the calves he had made. And at Bethel he also installed priests at the high places he had made._ ³³ _On the fifteenth day of the eighth month, a month of his own choosing, he offered sacrifices on the altar he had built at Bethel._ So he instituted the festival for

the Yisraelites and went up to the altar to make offerings." 1 Kings (Melakim) 12:26-33.

This is really quite incredible because Jereboam was already promised a perpetual throne like David's if he would simply obey. Instead of trusting the word of YHWH, he tried to hold onto power using his own intellect and setting up his own system of worship – in direct contravention to the ways of YHWH!

Jeroboam not only established new places of worship, he also established different appointed times and set up a false priesthood.[59] The sin of Jeroboam was even worse than the sin of his predecessors at Sinai. Despite warnings, Jeroboam refused to repent and therefore, as a result of this great sin, Yisreal was scheduled for punishment. It was not a mystery that they would be punished, Mosheh had told them long ago but they apparently did not remember or they just did not care.

As you can probably imagine, not everyone in this new breakaway kingdom was pleased with the idolatry that was introduced by Jeroboam. While most people would have surely appreciated the tax relief, they needed to decide whether the trade was worth it or not – they had a choice to make.

The Scriptures record the following: *"[13] And from all their territories the priests and the Levites who were in all Yisrael took their stand with him. [14] For the Levites left their common-lands and their possessions and came to Yahudah and Jerusalem, for Jeroboam and his sons had rejected them from serving as priests to YHWH. [15] Then he appointed for himself priests for the high places, for the goat and the calf idols which he had made. [16] And after them, those from all the tribes of Yisrael, such as set their heart to seek YHWH Elohim of Yisrael, came*

to Jerusalem to sacrifice to YHWH Elohim of their fathers. ¹⁷ So they strengthened the kingdom of Yahudah, and made Rehoboam the son of Solomon strong for three years, because they walked in the way of David and Solomon for three years." 2 Chronicles 11:13-17

So we see that at least the Levites from the Northern Kingdom left and went to dwell with Yahudah. Also, others from the Northern Kingdom "*came to Jerusalem to sacrifice.*" We can safely assume from the statement: "*they strengthened the kingdom of Yahudah*" that they were added to the kingdom by moving to Judea. This will be important to remember later in the discussion because it is highly likely that the Southern Kingdom was a mixture of all of the tribes, although primarily Yahudah, Benyamin and Levi.

Sadly, the entire ordeal stemmed from a continuing sibling rivalry between Ephraim and Yahudah. Jeroboam, after all, was from the tribe of Ephraim (1 Melakim 7:46) and Rehoboam was from the tribe of Yahudah. We will see this as a common theme throughout the Scriptures and it is a very important concept to understand – the struggle between the first born status and the rulership.

The matter was aptly summarized in 1 Melakim 12:19: "*So Yisrael has been in rebellion against the house of David to this day.*" The split in the kingdom was no accident as proclaimed by Shemayah, the man of Elohim, as Rehoboam was about to suppress the rebellion of the House of Yisrael. "*This is what YHWH says: 'Do not go up to fight against your brothers, the Yisraelites. Go home, every one of you, for this is My doing. So they obeyed the word of YHWH and went home again, as YHWH had ordered.'*" 1 Melakim 12:24. YHWH had a plan for this division which

was much greater than people could imagine.

As we read from Scriptures, neither Rehoboam or Jeroboam followed good advice. Both Kingdoms ended up getting into trouble, although the sin of the House of Yisrael was much worse than that of the House of Yahudah. As a result of their sins, both Kingdoms received the promised curses of YHWH which are found within the Torah.

Since they were divided and acting independently of one another, YHWH treated them differently. They committed different sins and were given different punishments. The House of Yahudah staved off judgment as they went in and out of idolatry throughout the succession of many kings. Eventually, both ended up suffering the punishment foretold by Mosheh - expulsion from the Land.

9

Exile

Before the tribes of Yisrael entered the Land they were given detailed and repeated guidance concerning the blessings of obedience and the curses of disobedience. Just as with Adam and Hawah, they were given commandments and they were warned of the punishment that awaited them if they disobeyed. Likewise, as with Adam and Hawah, if they wanted to dwell in the Household of YHWH they needed to obey the rules of the House. Yisrael could live in the Land as long as they obeyed the Torah.

There are many who proclaim that the Torah, which they call "the Law," was too difficult for Yisrael to obey. This is simply untrue. After detailing the blessings and the curses to Yisrael, Mosheh specifically stated: "[11] _Now what I am commanding you today is not too difficult for you or beyond your reach._ [12] _It is not up in heaven, so that you have to ask, 'Who will ascend into heaven to get it and proclaim it to us so we may obey it?'_ [13] _Nor is it beyond the sea, so that you have to ask, 'Who will cross the sea to get it and proclaim it to us so we may obey it?'_ [14] _No, the word is very near you; it is in your mouth and in your heart so you may obey it._" Devarim 30:11-14 NIV.

One of the penalties of disobedience was exile. It was specifically provided that if Yisrael did not obey the Torah: "*³⁶ YHWH will drive you and the king you set over you to a nation unknown to you or your fathers. There you will worship other gods, gods of wood and stone. ³⁷ You will become a thing of horror and an object of scorn and ridicule to all the nations where YHWH will drive you.*" Devarim 28:36-37.

Again they were told: "*⁶⁴ Then YHWH will scatter you among all nations, from one end of the earth to the other. There you will worship other gods - gods of wood and stone, which neither you nor your fathers have known. ⁶⁵ Among those nations you will find no repose, no resting place for the sole of your foot. There YHWH will give you an anxious mind, eyes weary with longing, and a despairing heart. ⁶⁶ You will live in constant suspense, filled with dread both night and day, never sure of your life. ⁶⁷ In the morning you will say, 'If only it were evening!' and in the evening, 'If only it were morning!' - because of the terror that will fill your hearts and the sights that your eyes will see. ⁶⁸ YHWH will send you back in ships to Egypt on a journey I said you should never make again. There you will offer yourselves for sale to your enemies as male and female slaves, but no one will buy you.*" Devarim 28:64-68.

There was also provision for multiplying their punishment. In Vayiqra 26 the Yisraelites were told on three separate occasions that their punishment would be multiplied seven times if they continued to disobey. This is extremely important to understand when examining the duration of the exiles for the different kingdoms.

Mosheh told the children of Yisrael that they would, in fact, be exiled. He also provided them with the hope of an eventual restoration described as follows:

"*¹ When all these blessings and curses I have set*

before you come upon you and you take them to heart wherever YHWH your Elohim disperses you among the nations, ² *and when you and your children return to YHWH your Elohim and obey Him with all your heart and with all your soul according to everything I command you today,* ³ *then* <u>*YHWH your Elohim will restore your fortunes and have compassion on you and gather you again from all the nations where He scattered you.*</u> ⁴ **Even if you have been banished to the most distant land under the heavens, from there YHWH your Elohim will gather you and bring you back.** ⁵ *He will bring you to the Land that belonged to your fathers, and you will take possession of it. He will make you more prosperous and numerous than your fathers.* ⁶ <u>*YHWH your Elohim will circumcise your hearts and the hearts of your descendants, so that you may love Him with all your heart and with all your soul, and live.*</u> ⁷ *YHWH your Elohim will put all these curses on your enemies who hate and persecute you.* ⁸ *You will again obey YHWH and follow all his commands I am giving you today.* ⁹ <u>*Then YHWH your Elohim will make you most prosperous in all the work of your hands and in the fruit of your womb, the young of your livestock and the crops of your Land. YHWH will again delight in you and make you prosperous, just as He delighted in your fathers,* ¹⁰ *if you obey YHWH your Elohim and keep His commands and decrees that are written in this Scroll of the Torah and turn to YHWH your Elohim with all your heart and with all your soul.*</u>" Devarim 30:1-10.

So we see a pattern being repeated - just as Adam and Hawah were cut off and expelled from the "household" because of their disobedience – so were the two Houses

of Yisrael. This is an interesting parallel because, as we shall see, all of the tribes of Yisrael were not exiled together. Rather the Kingdom was divided in two and the House of Yisrael was exiled separately from the House of Yahudah.[60]

Let us first read what happened to the House of Yisrael:

"[1] In the twelfth year of Ahaz king of Yahudah, Hoshea son of Elah became king of Yisrael in Samaria, and he reigned nine years. [2] He did evil in the eyes of YHWH, but not like the kings of Yisrael who preceded him. [3] Shalmaneser king of Assyria came up to attack Hoshea, who had been Shalmaneser's vassal and had paid him tribute. [4] But the king of Assyria discovered that Hoshea was a traitor, for he had sent envoys to So king of Egypt, and he no longer paid tribute to the king of Assyria, as he had done year by year. Therefore Shalmaneser seized him and put him in prison. [5] The king of Assyria invaded the entire land, marched against Samaria and laid siege to it for three years. [6] In the ninth year of Hoshea, the king of Assyria captured Samaria and deported the Yisraelites to Assyria. He settled them in Halah, in Gozan on the Habor River and in the towns of the Medes. [7] All this took place because the Yisraelites had sinned against YHWH their Elohim, who had brought them up out of Egypt from under the power of Pharaoh king of Egypt. They worshiped other gods [8] and followed the practices of the nations YHWH had driven out before them, as well as the practices that the kings of Yisrael had introduced. [9] The Yisraelites secretly did things against YHWH their Elohim that were not right. From watchtower to fortified city they built themselves high places in all their towns. [10] They set up sacred stones and Asherah poles on every high

hill and under every spreading tree. ¹¹ At every high place they burned incense, as the nations whom YHWH had driven out before them had done. They did wicked things that provoked YHWH to anger. ¹² They worshiped idols, though YHWH had said, 'You shall not do this. ¹³ YHWH warned Yisrael and Yahudah through all His prophets and seers: Turn from your evil ways. Observe My commands and decrees, in accordance with the entire Torah that I commanded your fathers to obey and that I delivered to you through My servants the prophets.' ¹⁴ But they would not listen and were as stiff-necked as their fathers, who did not trust in YHWH their Elohim. They rejected His decrees and the covenant He had made with their fathers and the warnings He had given them. They followed worthless idols and themselves became worthless. They imitated the nations around them although YHWH had ordered them, 'Do not do as they do,' and they did the things YHWH had forbidden them to do. ¹⁶ <u>They forsook **all** the commands of YHWH their Elohim and made for themselves two idols cast in the shape of calves, and an Asherah pole. They bowed down to all the starry hosts, and they worshiped Baal.</u> ¹⁷ <u>They sacrificed their sons and daughters in the fire. They practiced divination and sorcery and sold themselves to do evil in the eyes of YHWH, provoking Him to anger.</u> ¹⁸ <u>So YHWH was very angry with Yisrael and removed them from His presence. **Only the tribe of Yahudah was left,**</u> ¹⁹ <u>and even Yahudah did not keep the commands of YHWH their Elohim. They followed the practices Yisrael had introduced. ²⁰ Therefore **YHWH rejected all the people of Yisrael; He**</u>

afflicted them and gave them into the hands of plunderers, until He thrust them from His presence. [21] *When He tore Yisrael away from the house of David, they made Jeroboam son of Nebat their king. Jeroboam enticed Yisrael away from following YHWH and caused them to commit a great sin.* [22] *The Yisraelites persisted in all the sins of Jeroboam and did not turn away from them* [23] *until YHWH removed them from his presence, as he had warned through all his servants the prophets. So the people of Yisrael were taken from their homeland into exile in Assyria, and they are still there.*" 2 Melakim 17:1-24.

The Assyrians actually removed all of the House of Yisrael from the Land. This is a fact debated by some but the Scriptures clearly state that "*YHWH rejected ALL the people of Yisrael*" and "*ONLY the Tribe of Yahudah was left.*" Remember that a remnant of the Northern Tribes, along with the Levites, likely "moved in" with the House of Yahudah after Jeroboam set up his idolatrous system of worship. Therefore, while Assyria removed the Northern Tribes from their Land, there was probably a remnant of these Tribes who lived in Judea and joined the House of Yahudah.

As was their custom, Assyrian Kings did not just defeat their enemies – they transplanted them in order to better gain control of the territories that they conquered. In the case of the House of Yisrael, this appears to have been a process which took place through the reigns of three Assyrian Kings, Tiglath-pileser III, Shalmaneser V and Sargon II – possibly others.

One can read in the Khorsebad Annals how

Sargon II took Samaria and carried away 27,290 of the population of Yisrael. This is often used by those who desire to contradict the Scriptures by claiming that not all of the House of Yisrael was sent into exile. That is a weak argument because this particular incident recorded by Sargon II was only one event of many which occurred in the 700's BCE.

"In the late 1800's some clay Assyrian cuneiform tablets were discovered and they were finally translated in the 1930's. These tablets were Assyrian records of this 700's [Y]israelite deportation. There were records of four deportations, which proved the ten tribes of the northern Nation of [Y]israel were assembled into Assyrian culture and became identifiable as the C[i]merians, the Sythians, and the Goths. Our records of ancient history show that over several hundred years, and through different paths, the Sycthian, C[i]merian and the Goths migrated essentially to northwest Europe and became known as the Anglo-Saxon Celtic people. Linguistic analysis of the word 'Anglo-Saxon' shows the word 'Saxon' means 'sons of Isaac.'"[61]

The exile of the northern tribes was a result of their grievous sins – YHWH had to remove them from His presence. They were participating in the worst forms of idolatry, even offering their children as sacrifices – likely to the god Chemosh. Not only were the Yisraelites removed from

their Land, they were replaced by foreigners.

"²⁴ _The king of Assyria brought people from Babylon,_
Cuthah, Avva, Hamath and Sepharvaim and settled
them in the towns of Samaria to replace the Yisraelites.
They took over Samaria and lived in its towns. ²⁵ When
they first lived there, they did not worship YHWH; so
YHWH sent lions among them and they killed some
of the people. ²⁶ It was reported to the king of Assyria:
The people you deported and resettled in the towns of
Samaria do not know what the Elohi of that country
requires. He has sent lions among them, which are
killing them off, because the people do not know what
He requires. ²⁷ Then the king of Assyria gave this order:
'Have one of the priests you took captive from Samaria
go back to live there and teach the people what the god
of the land requires.' ²⁸ So one of the priests who had
been exiled from Samaria came to live in Bethel and
taught them how to worship YHWH. ²⁹ Nevertheless,
each national group made its own gods in the several
towns where they settled, and set them up in the shrines
the people of Samaria had made at the high places. ³⁰
The men from Babylon made Succoth Benoth, the men
from Cuthah made Nergal, and the men from Hamath
made Ashima; ³¹ the Avvites made Nibhaz and Tartak,
and the Sepharvites burned their children in the fire as
sacrifices to Adrammelech and Anammelech, the gods
of Sepharvaim. ³² _They worshiped YHWH, but they_
also appointed all sorts of their own people to officiate
for them as priests in the shrines at the high places. ³³
They worshiped YHWH, but they also served their
own gods in accordance with the customs of the nations
from which they had been brought. ³⁴ To this day they

persist in their former practices. They neither worship YHWH nor adhere to the decrees and ordinances, the laws and commands that YHWH gave the descendants of Yaakov, whom He named Yisrael. [35] When YHWH made a Covenant with the Yisraelites, He commanded them: 'Do not worship any other gods or bow down to them, serve them or sacrifice to them. [36] But YHWH, who brought you up out of Egypt with mighty power and outstretched arm, is the one you must worship. To Him you shall bow down and to him offer sacrifices. [37] You must always be careful to keep the decrees and ordinances, the laws and commands he wrote for you. Do not worship other gods. [38] Do not forget the Covenant I have made with you, and do not worship other gods. [39] Rather, worship YHWH your Elohim; it is He who will deliver you from the hand of all your enemies.' [40] They would not listen, however, but persisted in their former practices. [41] Even while these people were worshiping YHWH, they were serving their idols. To this day their children and grandchildren continue to do as their fathers did." 2 Melakim 17:24-41.

Notice that YHWH sent lions to destroy these new settlers because they too were not worshipping Him. As a result, the King of Assyria sent back a priest to instruct the foreigners how to serve YHWH, which they did <u>along</u> with their pagan worship. We can still see the descendents of those foreigners living in Samaria. The Samaritans have continued their hybrid religion centered at Mount Gerizim to this day.

How interesting that the Kingdom of Yisrael was chosen to be a kingdom of priests who, through their obedience were to shine as a light to the nations. They

were delivered from Egypt and brought to their own Land so that they could be set apart and obey YHWH. Through their obedience they would be blessed and all the world would see it. Instead, they disobeyed, but even through their disobedience they would give testimony to the nations, only now they would be scattered throughout the nations and the nations were brought into the Land.

The Scriptures indicate that the House of Yahudah also followed the ways of the House of Yisrael, although their punishment was withheld due to their repentance and restoration which occurred under the reigns of various kings. While the tribes of the House of Yisrael were removed from their Land and scattered by around 721 – 722 BCE, the House of Yahudah was not exiled until around 586 BCE.

Ezekiel (Yehezqel)[62] was one of the major prophets who prophesied to the House of Yahudah concerning their sin during their exile. He began his prophetic ministry in the *"fifth year of King Jehochin's captivity."* Yehezqel 1:2. Jehochin was the king of Yahudah who was taken captive by Babylon about 610 BCE. Accordingly, this would place the beginning of Yehezqel's prophecies at about 606 BCE.

The last dates which Yehezqel mentions in his prophecy are the "twenty-seventh year" and "the twenty fifth year of our captivity" Yehezqel 29:17, 40:1. Therefore, Yehezqel prophesied for at least 20 years among the captives, until 584 BCE. The Babylonians exiled captives from Jerusalem in three different stages. In an early campaign around 618 BCE, the prophet Daniel was among the Yahudim taken to Babylon. A second attack against the city occurred in 610 BCE, when many more captives were taken. Yehezqel was likely taken captive at this time.

Then in the extensive campaign of 601 BCE - 599 BCE, Nebuchadnezzar destroyed Jerusalem and took most of the remaining inhabitants into exile.[63]

Thus we have the House of Yisrael, often referred to as Ephraim, separated from the House of Yahudah and completely removed from the Land by the Assyrians. We later see the House of Yahudah removed by the Babylonians. Both Kingdoms strayed from YHWH. As we previously saw Ephraim (represented by Yahushua) and Yahudah (represented by Caleb) enter in to the Land because they followed YHWH wholeheartedly (Devarim 1:36) – now both Houses were expelled because of their disobedience.

There were different prophets sent to the different Kingdoms to warn them and they would often stand in the gap and encourage Yisrael (Ephraim) and Yahudah to get cleaned up and get right with their Creator. These prophets acted like marriage counselors but both Kingdoms failed to heed their warnings. They refused to give up their whoring and thus they remained separated from their Husband - YHWH.

Read what YHWH spoke through the Prophet Hoshea: "⁴ *What can I do with you, Ephraim? What can I do with you, Yahudah? Your love is like the morning mist, like the early dew that disappears. ⁵ Therefore I cut you in pieces with my prophets, I killed you with the words of my mouth; my judgments flashed like lightning upon you. ⁶ For I desire mercy, not sacrifice, and acknowledgment of Elohim rather than burnt offerings. ⁷ Like Adam, they have broken the covenant - they were unfaithful to me there.*" Hoshea 6:4-7.

Notice how he speaks to Ephraim and Yahudah separately and notice the connection with Adam. Adam

was supposed to commune with YHWH. Adam was literally and metaphorically split in two when Hawah was taken from his side - and both Adam and Hawah broke the Covenant. This was similar to what happened with Yisrael. The Kingdom was divided into Ephraim and Yahudah and both of them broke the Covenant.

It might have seemed like all was lost as YHWH sent His prophets to proclaim the punishment which would beset both Houses. Thankfully, these prophets did not only proclaim judgment, they also gave hope to both the House of Yisrael and the House of Yahudah that someday they would be restored.

10

The Prophets

The exile of each House was inevitable and we can see the pattern was actually established at the Garden of Eden. Mosheh told the Children of Yisrael that they would be exiled but he also told them that they would be regathered. YHWH also sent prophets to the different Houses - because they both were unique in their circumstances YHWH gave them each specific words.

These prophecies are too numerous to detail in this text but it is important for the reader to understand the context of each individual prophecy to gain a proper understanding. Some prophets were sent exclusively to the House of Yisrael while others were sent exclusively to the House of Yahudah – some were sent to both. Since the House of Yisrael was the first to go into exile we will look at a powerful prophecy given by Hoshea concerning them. Now remember that Hoshea was the name of the assistant of Mosheh which was later changed to Yahushua – the same name as the Messiah.[64]

We are first introduced to Hoshea by being told when he was a prophet. *"The word of YHWH that came to Hoshea son of Beeri during the reigns of Uzziah, Jotham, Ahaz and Hezekiah, kings of Yahudah, and during the reign of*

Jeroboam son of Yahoash king of Yisrael." Hoshea 1:1. Hoshea was a prophet while both kingdoms were still in the Land – prior the exile of the House of Yisrael.

YHWH used the life of Hoshea to demonstrate what He was going to do to the House of Yisrael. He instructed Hoshea: "'*2 Go, take to yourself an adulterous wife and children of unfaithfulness, because the Land is guilty of the vilest adultery in departing from YHWH.' 3 So he married Gomer daughter of Diblaim, and she conceived and bore him a son. 4 Then YHWH said to Hoshea, 'Call him Yezreel, because I will soon punish the house of Yahu for the massacre at Yezreel, and I will put an end to the kingdom of Yisrael. 5 In that day I will break Yisrael's bow in the Valley of Yezreel.'*" Hoshea 1:2-5.

Yezreel means both "Elohim scatters" and "Elohim sows." As He "scattered" them under Yahu, and finally by the Assyrian deportation, so He will "sow" them again.[65] As a result, we know that the Kingdom of Yisrael would come to an end and would be scattered.

"*6 Gomer conceived again and gave birth to a daughter. Then YHWH said to Hoshea, 'Call her Lo-Ruhamah, for I will no longer show love to the House of Yisrael, that I should at all forgive them. 7 Yet I will show love to the House of Yahudah; and I will save them - not by bow, sword or battle, or by horses and horsemen, but by YHWH their Elohim.*" Hoshea 1:6-7.

The definition for the name Lo-Ruhamah is given in the passage. In essence it means "no pity, no mercy, no compassion." In other words, YHWH was going to show restraint while the House of Yisrael was scattered and suffering – He would stop showing love to them. At the same time, He would continue to show love to the House of Yahudah and would save them in a way which

they could not take credit.

After Gomer had weaned Lo-Ruhamah, she gave birth to another son. *"Then YHWH said, 'Call him Lo-Ammi, for you are not my people, and I am not your Elohim.'"* Hoshea 1:9. It could not get much worse than this. Not only would the Kingdom of Yisrael come to an end and be scattered, they would no longer be loved by YHWH and they would no longer be considered to be His people. In other words, they would be divorced from YHWH because they were adulterous.

Despite this devastating prophecy Hoshea continues with a message of hope. *"¹⁰ Yet the Yisraelites will be like the sand on the seashore, which cannot be measured or counted. In the place where it was said to them, 'You are not my people,' they will be called 'sons of the living Elohim.' ¹¹ The people of Yahudah and the people of Yisrael will be reunited, and they will appoint one leader and will come up out of the Land, for great will be the day of Yezreel."* Hosea 1:10-11.

Not only will the House of Yisrael be restored once again to the status of "sons of Elohim" they will also be reunited with Yahudah and will be too numerous to count. They will appoint one leader, which is a clear reference to the reign of the Messiah.

Before this great promise would occur, the House of Yisrael would literally lose their identity. YHWH describes this progression from rejection to restoration through the family of Hoshea. Gomer represented the present day House of Yisrael and her children represented the future House of Yisrael.

"¹ Say of your brothers, 'My people,' and of your sisters, 'My loved one.' ² Rebuke your mother, rebuke her, for she is not my wife, and I am not her husband.

Let her remove the adulterous look from her face and the unfaithfulness from between her breasts. ³ Otherwise I will strip her naked and make her as bare as on the day she was born; I will make her like a desert, turn her into a parched land, and slay her with thirst. ⁴ I will not show my love to her children, because they are the children of adultery. ⁵ Their mother has been unfaithful and has conceived them in disgrace. She said, 'I will go after my lovers, who give me my food and my water, my wool and my linen, my oil and my drink.' ⁶ Therefore I will block her path with thorn bushes; I will wall her in so that she cannot find her way. ⁷ She will chase after her lovers but not catch them; she will look for them but not find them. Then she will say, 'I will go back to my husband as at first, for then I was better off than now.' ⁸ She has not acknowledged that I was the one who gave her the grain, the new wine and oil, who lavished on her the silver and gold-which they used for Baal. ⁹ Therefore I will take away my grain when it ripens, and my new wine when it is ready. I will take back my wool and my linen, intended to cover her nakedness. ¹⁰ So now I will expose her lewdness before the eyes of her lovers; no one will take her out of my hands. ¹¹ I will stop all her celebrations: her yearly festivals, her New Moons, her Sabbath days - all her appointed feasts. ¹² I will ruin her vines and her fig trees, which she said were her pay from her lovers; I will make them a thicket, and wild animals will devour them. ¹³ I will punish her for the days she burned incense to the Baals; she decked herself with rings and jewelry, and went after her lovers, but me she forgot, declares YHWH." Hoshea 2:1-13.

YHWH vividly illustrates the adulterous conduct

of the House of Yisrael through her idolatry – chasing after other gods. When things started to go bad, Yisrael thought that she could simply return to YHWH but it was too late. All of the curses began to come upon her and she even lost the Appointed Times when the people of YHWH are supposed to meet with their Elohim. This is a vivid demonstration of the separation that she would experience.

Again, the bad news is typically followed by the good news and YHWH continues to detail how He will restore this relationship. "*14 Therefore I am now going to allure her; I will lead her into the desert and speak tenderly to her. *15 There I will give her back her vineyards, and will make the Valley of Achor a door of hope. There she will sing as in the days of her youth, as in the day she came up out of Egypt. *16 In that day, declares YHWH, you will call Me 'my husband' - you will no longer call Me 'my master.' *17 I will remove the names of the Baals from her lips; no longer will their names be invoked. *18 In that day I will make a Covenant for them with the beasts of the field and the birds of the air and the creatures that move along the ground. Bow and sword and battle I will abolish from the Land, so that all may lie down in safety. *19 I will betroth you to me forever; I will betroth you in righteousness and justice, in love and compassion. *20 I will betroth you in faithfulness, and you will acknowledge YHWH. *21 In that day I will respond, declares YHWH - I will respond to the skies, and they will respond to the earth; *22 and the earth will respond to the grain, the new wine and oil, and they will respond to Yezreel. *23 I will plant her for Myself in the Land; I will show My love to the one I called 'Not my loved one.' I will say to those called 'Not my people,' 'You are my people' and they will say, 'You are my Elohim.'" Hoshea 2:14-23.*

This passage is full of very interesting clues as to how and when the House of Yisrael will be restored. One thing is certain, the restoration of the House of Yisrael has not yet occurred. YHWH states that He will take the House of Yisrael in the desert as when she was redeemed from Egypt. So then, there will be another redemption as in the days of the Exodus and just as the song of Mosheh was sung at the first Exodus, the House of Yisrael will sing a song at their redemption.

Also, just as Yisrael was married to YHWH at Sinai after the first Exodus, the House of Yisrael will be remarried to YHWH after they are redeemed. The names of the Baals that they once worshipped will be removed from their lips[66] and YHWH will make a Covenant - The Covenant of Peace. This all clearly occurs during the Messianic era described by Isaiah (Yeshayahu).[67]

"*¹ A Shoot will come up from the stump of Jesse (Yeshai); from his roots a Branch will bear fruit. ² The Spirit of YHWH will rest on Him - the Spirit of wisdom and of understanding, the Spirit of counsel and of power, the Spirit of knowledge and of the fear of YHWH ³ and He will delight in the fear of YHWH. He will not judge by what He sees with His eyes, or decide by what He hears with His ears; ⁴ but with righteousness He will judge the needy, with justice He will give decisions for the poor of the earth. He will strike the earth with the rod of His mouth; with the breath of His lips He will slay the wicked. ⁵ Righteousness will be His belt and faithfulness the sash around His waist. ⁶ The wolf will live with the lamb, the leopard will lie down with the goat, the calf and the lion and the yearling together; and a little child will lead them. ⁷ The cow will feed*

*with the bear, their young will lie down together, and
the lion will eat straw like the ox. ⁸ The infant will play
near the hole of the cobra, and the young child put his
hand into the viper's nest. ⁹ They will neither harm nor
destroy on all My holy mountain, for the earth will be
full of the knowledge of YHWH as the waters cover
the sea. ¹⁰ In that day the Root of Yeshai will stand
as a banner for the peoples; the nations will rally to
Him, and His place of rest will be glorious. ¹¹ In that
day the Master will reach out His Hand a second time
to reclaim the remnant that is left of His people from
Assyria, from Lower Egypt, from Upper Egypt, from
Cush, from Elam, from Babylonia, from Hamath and
from the islands of the sea. ¹² He will raise a banner
for the nations and gather the exiles of Yisrael; he will
assemble the scattered people of Yahudah from the four
quarters of the earth. ¹³ Ephraim's jealousy will vanish,
and Yahudah's enemies will be cut off; Ephraim will
not be jealous of Yahudah, nor Yahudah hostile toward
Ephraim.*" Yeshayahu 11:1-13.⁶⁸

How wonderful that the House of Yisrael who are
called "*not my people*" will one day again be "*the people of
Elohim.*" What began as a dire prophecy of devastation
and rejection became a message of hope and restoration.
This event has not occurred and will only occur when
the prophesied Messiah, the Root of Yeshai, reigns on the
earth as can clearly be seen from the passage.

Jeremiah (Yirmeyahu)⁶⁹ was called a prophet to the
nations although he primarily prophesied to the House of
Yahudah concerning their impending exile. There was a
time when he prophesied to both the Northern Kingdom
and the Southern Kingdom. Just as Mosheh had told all of

the tribes of Yisrael that they would be scattered because they did not obey the Torah so too did Yirmeyahu.

"*⁶ During the reign of King Yosiah, YHWH said to me, Have you seen what faithless Yisrael has done? She has gone up on every high hill and under every spreading tree and has committed adultery there. ⁷ I thought that after she had done all this she would return to me but she did not, and her unfaithful sister Yahudah saw it. ⁸ I gave faithless Yisrael her certificate of divorce and sent her away because of all her adulteries. Yet I saw that her unfaithful sister Yahudah had no fear; she also went out and committed adultery. ⁹ Because Yisrael's immorality mattered so little to her, she defiled the Land and committed adultery with stone and wood. ¹⁰ In spite of all this, her unfaithful sister Yahudah did not return to me with all her heart, but only in pretense, declares YHWH. ¹¹ YHWH said to me, Faithless Yisrael is more righteous than unfaithful Yahudah. ¹² Go, proclaim this message toward the north: Return, faithless Yisrael, declares YHWH, I will frown on you no longer, for I am merciful, declares YHWH, I will not be angry forever. ¹³ Only acknowledge your guilt - you have rebelled against YHWH your Elohim, you have scattered your favors to foreign gods under every spreading tree, and have not obeyed me, declares YHWH. ¹⁴ Return, faithless people, declares YHWH, for I am your Husband. I will choose you - one from a town and two from a clan - and bring you to Zion. ¹⁵ Then I will give you shepherds after my own heart, who will lead you with knowledge and understanding. ¹⁶ In those days, when your numbers have increased greatly in the Land, declares YHWH, men will no longer say,*

The ark of the covenant of YHWH. It will never enter their minds or be remembered; it will not be missed, nor will another one be made. ¹⁷ *At that time they will call Jerusalem - The Throne of YHWH, and all nations will gather in Jerusalem to honor the Name of YHWH. No longer will they follow the stubbornness of their evil hearts.* ¹⁸ <u>*In those days the House of Yahudah will join the House of Yisrael, and together they will come from a northern land to the Land I gave your forefathers as an inheritance.*</u>" Yirmeyahu 3:6-18

Yirmeyahu also prophesied specifically to the House of Yahudah of their impending exile. "¹⁰ *When you tell these people all this and they ask you, Why has YHWH decreed such a great disaster against us? What wrong have we done? What sin have we committed against YHWH our Elohim?* ¹¹ *then say to them, 'It is because your fathers forsook me,' declares YHWH, 'and followed other gods and served and worshiped them. They forsook me and did not keep my Torah.* ¹² *But you have behaved more wickedly than your fathers. See how each of you is following the stubbornness of his evil heart instead of obeying me.* ¹³ *So I will throw you out of this Land into a land neither you nor your fathers have known, and there you will serve other gods day and night, for I will show you no favor.'*" Yirmeyahu 16:10-13.

He went on to proclaim: "¹ *Yahudah's sin is engraved with an iron tool, inscribed with a flint point, on the tablets of their hearts and on the horns of their altars.* ² *Even their children remember their altars and Asherah poles beside the spreading trees and on the high hills.* ³ *My mountain in the Land and your wealth and all your treasures I will give away as plunder, together with your high places, because of sin throughout your country.* ⁴ *Through your own fault you will lose the inheritance I*

gave you. I will enslave you to your enemies in a land you do not know, for you have kindled my anger, and it will burn forever." Yirmeyahu 17:1-4.

Yahudah's hearts had become like stone. Instead of the Torah being inscribed upon their hearts, as it was inscribed upon the tablets of stone, their sins were inscribed upon their hearts. Just as Mosheh smashed the tablets, and later renewed the Covenant at Sinai, Yahudah needed to have the Covenant renewed because they had broken the Covenant. This time, the Torah would be written on their hearts instead of on tablets of stone.

Like Mosheh and the other prophets, Yirmeyahu prophesied of a time when all of the tribes of Yisrael would be restored.

"¹ At that time, declares YHWH, 'I will be the Elohim of all the tribes of Yisrael, and they will be my people.' ² This is what YHWH says: 'The people who survive the sword will find favor in the desert; I will come to give rest to Yisrael.' ³ YHWH appeared to us in the past, saying: I have loved you with an everlasting love; I have drawn you with loving-kindness. ⁴ I will build you up again and you will be rebuilt, O Virgin Yisrael. Again you will take up your tambourines and go out to dance with the joyful. ⁵ Again you will plant vineyards on the hills of Samaria; the farmers will plant them and enjoy their fruit. ⁶ There will be a day when watchmen cry out on the hills of Ephraim, Come, let us go up to Zion, to YHWH our Elohim. ⁷ This is what YHWH says: Sing with joy for Yaakov; shout for the foremost of the nations. Make your praises heard, and say, O YHWH, save your people, the remnant of Yisrael. ⁸ See, I will bring them from the land of

the north and gather them from the ends of the earth. Among them will be the blind and the lame, expectant mothers and women in labor; a great throng will return. ⁹ They will come with weeping; they will pray as I bring them back. I will lead them beside streams of water on a level path where they will not stumble, because I am Yisrael's father, and Ephraim is my firstborn son. ¹⁰ *Hear the word of YHWH, O nations; proclaim it in distant coastlands:* <u>He who scattered Yisrael will gather them and will watch over his flock like a shepherd.</u> ¹¹ <u>For YHWH will ransom Yaakov and redeem them from the hand of those stronger than they.</u> ¹² *They will come and shout for joy on the heights of Zion; they will rejoice in the bounty of YHWH - the grain, the new wine and the oil, the young of the flocks and herds. They will be like a well-watered garden, and they will sorrow no more.* ¹³ *Then maidens will dance and be glad, young men and old as well. I will turn their mourning into gladness; I will give them comfort and joy instead of sorrow.* ¹⁴ *I will satisfy the priests with abundance, and My people will be filled with my bounty, declares YHWH.* ¹⁵ *This is what YHWH says: A voice is heard in Ramah, mourning and great weeping, Rachel weeping for her children and refusing to be comforted, because her children are no more.* ¹⁶ *This is what YHWH says: Restrain your voice from weeping and your eyes from tears, for your work will be rewarded, declares YHWH. They will return from the land of the enemy.* ¹⁷ *So there is hope for your future, declares YHWH.* <u>Your children will return to their own Land.</u> ¹⁸ *I have surely heard Ephraim's moaning: You disciplined me like an unruly calf, and I have been disciplined. Restore me, and*

I will return, because you are YHWH my Elohim. ¹⁹
*After I strayed, I repented; after I came to understand, I
beat my breast. I was ashamed and humiliated because I
bore the disgrace of my youth.* ²⁰ Is not Ephraim my dear
son, the child in whom I delight? Though I often speak
against him, I still remember him. Therefore My heart
yearns for him; I have great compassion for him, declares
YHWH. ²¹ *Set up road signs; put up guideposts. Take
note of the highway, the road that you take. Return,
O Virgin Yisrael, return to your towns.* ²² How long
will you wander, O unfaithful daughter? YHWH will
create a new thing on earth - a woman will surround a
man. ²³ This is what YHWH Almighty, the Elohim of
Yisrael, says: *When I bring them back from captivity,
the people in the Land of Yahudah and in its towns
will once again use these words: YHWH bless you, O
righteous dwelling, O sacred mountain.* ²⁴ People will
live together in Yahudah and all its towns - farmers and
those who move about with their flocks. ²⁵ I will refresh
the weary and satisfy the faint. ²⁶ At this I awoke and
looked around. My sleep had been pleasant to me. ²⁷ '*The
days are coming,' declares YHWH, 'when I will plant
the House of Yisrael and the House of Yahudah with
the offspring of men and of animals.* ²⁸ *Just as I watched
over them to uproot and tear down, and to overthrow,
destroy and bring disaster, so I will watch over them
to build and to plant, declares YHWH.'*" Yirmeyahu
31:1-28.

I hope that by now this sounds familiar. The plan of
YHWH was no secret, it was proclaimed by His prophets
who consistently prophesied concerning the punishment
and restoration of the House of Yisrael, sometimes

referred to as Ephraim, and the House of Yahudah. This restoration can only happen through a renewal of the Covenant according to the pattern set forth by Mosheh at Sinai. Since the House of Yisrael had been divorced from YHWH, she needs to become a virgin in order to be remarried.[70]

Remember that after YHWH had redeemed Yisrael from Egypt, He brought them to Sinai to complete the redemption ritual by marrying Yisrael – His Bride. Mosheh went up to receive the Tablets which were like a Ketubah – a marriage contract.[71]

While he was up on the mountain YHWH cut out two tablets of stone and wrote the Covenant on those tablets. Sadly, while Mosheh was on the mountain the people grew impatient and went whoring after other gods. She was unfaithful – even during the betrothal process!

As a result of her idolatry the Covenant was broken but through the mediation of Mosheh, YHWH did not destroy Yisrael. Instead, He allowed the Covenant to be renewed only this time, it was Mosheh the mediator, who had to cut out the tablets of stone and carry them up the mountain and present them before YHWH. YHWH then, once again, wrote the same Covenant - the same Torah - on those new stone tablets presented by man.

This renewal at Sinai provided a pattern for future renewal. This is what both Yirmeyahu and Yehezqel described would happen to Yisrael and Yahudah. First we will look at what Yirmeyahu prophesied concerning a renewal of the Covenant that was, once again, broken.

"'[31] The time is coming,' declares YHWH, 'when I will make a <u>renewed Covenant with the House of Yisrael and with the House of Yahudah</u>.' [32] 'It will not be like

the Covenant I made with their forefathers when I took them by the hand to lead them out of Egypt, because they broke My Covenant, though I was a Husband to them,' declares YHWH. ³³ 'This is the Covenant I will make with the House of Yisrael after that time,' declares YHWH. 'I will put my Torah in their minds and write it on their hearts. I will be their Elohim, and they will be My people. ³⁴ No longer will a man teach his neighbor, or a man his brother, saying, Know YHWH, because they will all know Me, from the least of them to the greatest, declares YHWH. For I will forgive their wickedness and will remember their sins no more.' ³⁵ This is what YHWH says, He Who appoints the sun to shine by day, Who decrees the moon and stars to shine by night, Who stirs up the sea so that its waves roar - YHWH Almighty is His Name: ³⁶ Only if these decrees vanish from My sight, declares YHWH, will the descendants of Yisrael ever cease to be a nation before Me. ³⁷ This is what YHWH says: Only if the heavens above can be measured and the foundations of the earth below be searched out will I reject all the descendants of Yisrael because of all they have done, declares YHWH. ³⁸ The days are coming, declares YHWH, when this city will be rebuilt for Me from the Tower of Hananel to the Corner Gate. ³⁹ The measuring line will stretch from there straight to the hill of Gareb and then turn to Goah. ⁴⁰ The whole valley where dead bodies and ashes are thrown, and all the terraces out to the Kidron Valley on the east as far as the corner of the Horse Gate, will be holy to YHWH. The city will never again be uprooted or demolished." Yirmeyahu 31:31-40.

Notice how Yirmeyahu indicates that there will be

a time when the Covenant would be renewed with both Houses but then goes on to describe the Covenant with the House of Yisrael. The reason is the same as what occurred at Sinai – adultery. Yehezqel further elaborates on this renewed Covenant with the House of Yisrael.

"*14 The word of YHWH came to me: 15 Son of man, your brothers-your brothers who are your blood relatives and the whole House of Yisrael - are those of whom the people of Jerusalem have said, 'They are far away from YHWH; this Land was given to us as our possession.' 16 Therefore say: This is what the Sovereign YHWH says: 'Although I sent them far away among the nations and scattered them among the countries, yet for a little while I have been a sanctuary for them in the countries where they have gone.' 17 Therefore say: This is what the Sovereign YHWH says: 'I will gather you from the nations and bring you back from the countries where you have been scattered, and I will give you back the Land of Yisrael again. 18 They will return to it and remove all its vile images and detestable idols. 19 I will give them an undivided heart and put a new spirit in them; I will remove from them their heart of stone and give them a heart of flesh. 20 Then they will follow my decrees and be careful to keep My laws. They will be my people, and I will be their Elohim. 21 But as for those whose hearts are devoted to their vile images and detestable idols, I will bring down on their own heads what they have done,' declares the Sovereign YHWH." Yehezqel 11:14-21.*

This restoration and renewal is reiterated later by the prophet as follows:

"*16 Again the word of YHWH came to me: 17 'Son of man, when the people of Yisrael were living in their own*

Land, they defiled it by their conduct and their actions. <u>Their conduct was like a woman's monthly uncleanness in My sight.</u> ¹⁸ So I poured out My wrath on them because they had shed blood in the Land and because they had defiled it with their idols. ¹⁹ <u>I dispersed them among the nations, and they were scattered through the countries;</u> I judged them according to their conduct and their actions. ²⁰ And wherever they went among the nations they profaned My holy Name, for it was said of them, These are YHWH's people, and yet they had to leave His Land. ²¹ I had concern for My holy Name, which the House of Yisrael profaned among the nations where they had gone.' ²² Therefore say to the House of Yisrael, This is what the Sovereign YHWH says: 'It is not for your sake, O House of Yisrael, that I am going to do these things, but for the sake of My holy Name, which you have profaned among the nations where you have gone. ²³ I will show the holiness of My great Name, which has been profaned among the nations, the Name you have profaned among them. Then the nations will know that I am YHWH,' declares the Sovereign YHWH, 'when I show Myself holy through you before their eyes. ²⁴ <u>For I will take you out of the nations; I will gather you from all the countries and bring you back into your own Land.</u> ²⁵ I will sprinkle clean water on you, and you will be clean; I will cleanse you from all your impurities and from all your idols. ²⁶ <u>I will give you a new heart and put a new spirit in you; I will remove from you your heart of stone and give you a heart of flesh.</u> ²⁷ <u>And I will put my Spirit in you and move you to follow my decrees and be careful to keep my laws.</u> ²⁸ <u>You will live in the Land I gave your forefathers; you will be My people,</u>

and I will be your Elohim. [29] *I will save you from all your uncleanness. I will call for the grain and make it plentiful and will not bring famine upon you.* [30] *I will increase the fruit of the trees and the crops of the field, so that you will no longer suffer disgrace among the nations because of famine.* [31] *Then you will remember your evil ways and wicked deeds, and you will loathe yourselves for your sins and detestable practices.* [32] *I want you to know that I am not doing this for your sake, declares the Sovereign YHWH. Be ashamed and disgraced for your conduct, O House of Yisrael!"* Yehezqel 36:16-32.

This chapter has included lengthy Scripture citations but it is important to realize that these are merely a small sample of the prophecies concerning the division, punishment and restoration of the House of Yisrael and the House of Yahudah. It is because of the great importance of this issue that I wanted the reader to see the actual prophecies, not just my thoughts regarding the prophecies on this subject.

This is not a topic that is taught in most mainline religions that base their faith upon the Scriptures. Sadly, if you fail to recognize this information you will not correctly comprehend the plan of YHWH and the ministry of the Messiah. Both the House of Yisrael and the House of Yahudah were given durations for their exiles. As we shall examine in the next chapter, the House of Yahudah returned to the Land precisely according to schedule while the House of Yisrael remained in exile.

II

The Return of Judah

The exile of the House of Yahudah was much different than that of the House of Yisrael. Not only was the duration different, but they also adapted to their exiles in different ways. The House of Yisrael was completely displaced from their Land by the Assyrians and relocated throughout that empire which was later conquered by the Babylonians and the Medes. They were scattered to the "four corners" of the earth and assimilated into various cultures – eventually they completely lost their identity and became, in essence, Gentiles.

The House of Yahudah, on the other hand, was conquered and exiled by the Babylonians who were later conquered by the Medes. In their exile they largely maintained their identity, and it is important to understand that not all of the Yahudim were exiled from the Land. Some remained, although it does not appear that they maintained any cohesive governmental structure and they were greatly encroached upon by their surrounding neighbors.

Historical and archaeological evidence shows that the Yahudim who were exiled to Babylonia assimilated into that culture, but maintained a distinctively Hebrew

identity. Many retained Hebrew names, they signed and witnessed contracts, they gave and received inheritances and some even operated in governmental positions. It appears that they lived and functioned as Hebrews and even had their own city called "Al Yahudah" – this was a far different exile than that of the House of Yisrael.

So while the House of Yisrael was completely removed from the Land and seemingly "lost" in history, the House of Yahudah was exiled until the time of their prophesied return. When it was time for their return, they knew who they were and they knew where they were.

The Scriptures record the following: *"²⁰ He carried into exile to Babylon the remnant, who escaped from the sword, and they became servants to him and his sons until the kingdom of Persia came to power. ²¹ <u>The Land enjoyed its sabbath rests; all the time of its desolation it rested, until the seventy years were completed in fulfillment of the Word of YHWH spoken by Yirmeyahu.</u> ²² In the first year of Cyrus king of Persia, in order to fulfill the word of YHWH spoken by Yirmeyahu, YHWH moved the heart of Cyrus king of Persia to make a proclamation throughout his realm and to put it in writing: ²³ This is what Cyrus king of Persia says: YHWH, the Elohim of heaven, has given me all the kingdoms of the earth and He has appointed me to build a House for Him at Jerusalem in Yahudah. Anyone of His people among you - may YHWH his Elohim be with him, and let him go up."* 2 Chronicles 36:20 – 23.

This portion of 2 Chronicles is referring specifically to the prophecy of Yirmeyahu wherein he stated to the House of Yahudah: *"This whole country will become a desolate wasteland, and these nations will serve the king of Babylon seventy years."* Yirmeyahu 25:11.

Again in Yirmeyahu 29 we read the warning of

judgment along with the promise of a return for the House of Yahudah: "*¹⁰ This is what YHWH says: 'When seventy years are completed for Babylon, I will come to you and fulfill my gracious promise to bring you back to this place. ¹¹ For I know the plans I have for you,' declares YHWH, 'plans to prosper you and not to harm you, plans to give you hope and a future. ¹² Then you will call upon Me and come and pray to Me, and I will listen to you. ¹³ You will seek Me and find Me when you seek Me with all your heart. ¹⁴ I will be found by you, declares YHWH, and will bring you back from captivity. I will gather you from all the nations and places where I have banished you,' declares YHWH, 'and will bring you back to the place from which I carried you into exile.'"* Yirmeyah 29:10-14.

"*And YHWH will take possession of Yahudah as His inheritance in the Holy Land, and will again choose Jerusalem.*" Zechariah 2:12. The promise of return from the Babylonian exile was fulfilled, as prophesied, and some of the descendants of those who were exiled returned to the Land. We read about this return primarily in the accounts of Haggai, Zechariah, Nehemiah and Ezra.

It is important to recognize that only the House of Yahudah was given the promise of return within seventy years and only a remnant of the House of Yahudah was returned from exile. Many attempt to imply that the House of Yisrael somehow snuck back in along the way and resettled into their tribal territories but that is simply not the case.⁷²

The House of Yisrael and the House of Yahudah both engaged in idolatry against YHWH, and both were dealt punishments. Yirmeyahu records that the House of Yisrael had been faithless and the House of Yahudah had been treacherous toward YHWH.

"¹ If a husband divorces his wife and she goes from him and belongs to another man, Will he still return to her? Will not that land be completely polluted? But you are a harlot with many lovers; Yet you turn to Me, declares YHWH. ² Lift up your eyes to the desolate heights and see: Where have you not lain with men? By the road you have sat for them like an Arabian in the wilderness; and you have polluted the Land with your harlotries and your wickedness. ³ Therefore the showers have been withheld, and there has been no latter rain. You have had a harlot's forehead; you refuse to be ashamed. ⁴ Will you not from this time cry to Me, My Father, You are the guide of my youth? ⁵ Will He remain angry forever? Will He keep it to the end? Behold, you have spoken and done evil things, As you were able. ⁶ YHWH said also to me in the days of Josiah (Yoshiyahu) the king: Have you seen what backsliding Yisrael has done? She has gone up on every high mountain and under every green tree, and there played the harlot. ⁷ And I said, after she had done all these things, Return to Me. But she did not return. And her treacherous sister Yahudah saw it. ⁸ Then I saw that for all the causes for which backsliding Yisrael had committed adultery, I had put her away and given her a certificate of divorce; yet her treacherous sister Yahudah did not fear, but went and played the harlot also. ⁹ So it came to pass, through her casual harlotry, that she defiled the Land and committed adultery with stones and trees. ¹⁰ And yet for all this her treacherous sister Yahudah has not turned to Me with her whole heart, but in pretense, says YHWH. ¹¹ Then YHWH said to me, Backsliding Yisrael has shown herself more righteous than treacherous Yahudah. ¹² Go and proclaim these words toward the north, and say: Return, backsliding Yisrael, says YHWH; I will not cause My anger to fall on you. For I am merciful, says YHWH; I will not remain angry forever. ¹³ Only acknowledge your iniquity, that you have

transgressed against YHWH your Elohim, and have scattered your charms to alien deities under every green tree, and you have not obeyed My voice, says YHWH. ¹⁴ Return, O backsliding children, says YHWH; for I am a master (husband) to you. I will take you, one from a city and two from a family, and I will bring you to Zion." Yirmeyahu 3:1-14.

When the House of Yisrael was removed from the Land, it was likened as a divorce. When the House of Yahudah was removed from the Land it showed that Yahudah was no better than Yisrael. Yahudah was cast out of the Land twice, but the second return of Yahudah in modern times signals that the return of the House of Yisrael cannot be that far away.

Because the House of Yisrael committed different sins than the House of Yahudah they were both punished separately and their exiles had different durations. Yehezqel aptly demonstrated the different periods as he was commanded to lie on his left side for three hundred and ninety days and his right side for forty days. The time that he laid on his left side represented a day for every year of sin committed by the House of Yisrael and the time that he laid on his right side represented a day for every year of sin committed by the House of Yahudah. (see Yehezqel 4).

As a result, the House of Yisrael would be in exile for 390 years times 7 or 2,730 years. If you add that number to the approximate Assyrian exile date of 721-722 BCE, you can see that the exile of the House of Yisrael or "The Time of the Gentiles" is drawing to an end.

The restoration of the divided Kingdom of Yisrael could not occur until the sins of both Houses were dealt with according to the Torah. His bride must be clean –

"without spot or blemish." (see Ephesians 5:27). This is the reason that YHWH sent His Son to die. This death provided for the atonement of the entire Commonwealth of Yisrael, and it is the prerequisite for Elohim to be married to His people. This marriage was foretold by the prophet Yeshayahu who links Messianic prophecies with the marriage of the Bride to the Land and to Elohim.

"*¹ For Zion's sake I will not keep silent, for Jerusalem's sake I will not remain quiet, till her righteousness shines out like the dawn, her salvation like a blazing torch. ² The nations will see your righteousness, and all kings your glory; you will be called by a new name that the mouth of YHWH will bestow. ³ You will be a crown of splendor in YHWH's hand, a royal diadem in the hand of your Elohim. ⁴ No longer will they call you Forsaken, or call your Land Desolate. But you will be called Hephzibah (My delight is in her), and your land Beulah (Married); for YHWH will take delight in you, and your Land married. ⁵ As a young man marries a maiden, so will your sons marry you; as a bridegroom rejoices over his bride, so will your Elohim rejoice over you.*" Yeshayahu 62:1-5.

While some of the exiles of the House of Yahudah were restored to the Land under the successive returns of Zerubbabel, Ezra and Nehemiah, among others - the House of Yisrael has yet to be restored to the Land. They fell under a different punishment and their return was prophesied to be at a different time and in a different fashion than their brethren, the House of Yahudah.

Therefore, since the exile of the House of Yisrael, the tribes that constitute the House of Yahudah have generally been the only identifiable and recognizable remnant of the Commonwealth of Yisrael within and without the Land. While it is highly probable that there was

a mixing of the Tribes after the division of the Kingdoms, those that came from the north joined with Yahudah and became part of Yahudah. Therefore, after the return from Babylon, the vast majority, if not all, of the recognizable Tribes that constituted the Commonwealth of Yisrael were from the Tribes of Yahudah, Benyamin and Levi – those that had been taken captive by the Babylonians.

It is also important to understand the apparent friction that existed between those who were exiled from Judea and those who remained in Judea during the exile. Remember that not everyone from Judea was taken captive by the Babylonians. The royalty, nobility and priests of the House of Yahudah had been taken into captivity, but others remained. As a result, there were many of the descendents of the former ruling class who were returning with a mandate to reestablish the Kingdom of Yahudah.

Those who were punished by being taken into exile believed that through their exile they had been "cleansed" or "purified" from the former sins of Yahudah and therefore in a position to reestablish the Kingdom. In contrast, the ones that stayed apparently felt that they were the righteous ones because they were not punished by being taken into exile. As a result, they put up some opposition to these returning exiles.

Because of their differences and varying attitudes, the two groups of Yahudim often clashed and experienced conflict within their ranks. Nevertheless, the Scriptures record that under the authority of Cyrus, King of Persia, Zerubabbel, a prince of Yahudah, returned to the Land and he was encouraged by YHWH to complete the work of rebuilding the Altar and the Temple. (Zechariah 4:9).

Zerubbabel was joined by Yahushua, the High

Priest, along with prophets and many Levites. They completed the House of YHWH and reestablished the altar service. They were later joined by Ezra and Nehemiah and we read about their efforts in books named after these two individuals, which are one book in the Hebrew Scriptures.

While Ezra and Nehemiah detail the ones who returned from captivity (Ezra 2; Nehemiah 7), it is important to note that many of the Yahudim remained in Babylonia. They had built homes, married wives, had children, jobs and generally life was going on for them. They apparently were content with their lives and saw no need to return – not unlike what we see today with the Modern State of Israel. While many Yahudim have returned to the Land to restore the Kingdom of Yahudah, many more continue to reside outside the Land.

Therefore, we know that some of the exiled Yahudim returned to the Land while many continued to be dispersed throught the Babylonian and Mede territories. The Yahudim also migrated south into Egypt, Ethiopia, Libya and throughout Africa and the Mediteranean region.

As a result, the return from exile was not a complete return and the House of Yahudah was never restored as a fully autonomous Kingdom, except arguably for brief periods of rebellion from the ruling empires to which they had been subjected. These Yahudim continued to be ruled and influenced by the Greeks, Selucids and Romans while the Parthians eventually ruled over the former Mede empire to the east. This was the political climate which existed in the Land when the Messiah entered the scene and there is no recorded return of the House of Yisrael up to that point in time.

Christianity, which claims to believe in the Messiah of Yisrael, rarely spends any time on this vital subject because they generally feel that Yisrael had its opportunity and failed. According to popular Christian doctrine the reigns have now been passed to "The Church," which they believe is "Spiritual Yisrael." As a result, not many are looking for the House of Yisrael or expecting their return from exile, which now appears to be imminent. This is a pity because the ministry of the Messiah largely involved restoring the House of Yisrael.[73]

The Christian religion has failed to understand that the House of Yisrael was divorced from YHWH because she committed adultery, she whored after different pagan gods. (Jeremiah 3:8). This sin was very grievous in the eyes of YHWH and as a result, the Northern Tribes were scattered throughout the nations. YHWH also declared that He would be a Husband to the House of Yisrael if she would return to Him. (Jeremiah 3:14).

In order to unite and restore the Kingdom to YHWH, the House of Yahudah and the House of Yisrael need to be cleansed from their defilements. They need to be restored to Elohim and restored to the Land.

So then, for there to be a restoration there was needed a Shepherd who could gather the sheep, a Prophet who could direct His people, a High Priest who could atone for their transgressions, a King who could rule and a Groom who could marry the Bride – what was needed was the Messiah.

12

The Messiah

It should not be any surprise that the Messiah of Yisrael would come as a Shepherd looking for His sheep, the Prophet foretold by Mosheh, a High Priest atoning for sin, a King establishing His Kingdom and a Bridegroom preparing for His Bride. These are all positions and patterns provided in the Scriptures for a reason – to point us to the Messiah.

This book is not intended to be a proof text for the identity of Messiah, that is the subject of the Walk in the Light series book entitled "The Messiah." For the purpose of this discussion it is assumed that the reader is fully cognizant of the fact that there is no other figure in history that meets the prophetic and legal prerequisites of the Messiah other than the One known as Yahushua.

Christianity has changed His Name to "Jesus" and altered many of His fundamental teachings by claiming that He came changing the Torah and forming a new religion - but this is simply not the case. Sadly, the Christian religion has adopted numerous pagan customs and traditions which have seriously clouded the true identity and teaching of the Messiah.

The Messiah of Yisrael as described in the "New

Testament"[74] was named Yahushua, not Jesus.[75] This is evident from the Good News according to Matthew when the Messenger of YHWH proclaimed to Yoseph the following: *"She will give birth to a son, and you are to give him the name Yahushua, because He will save His people from their sins."* Matthew 1:21.

Most English translations insert the name "Jesus" for "Yahushua" which is an error. They do this because most Greek manuscripts were Hellenized by substituting familiar names for unfamiliar Hebrew names.[76]

For instance, the name of the prophet Elijah (Eliyahu)[77] was substituted with the name of the pagan

sun god Helios. The name of Yahushua was substituted with the offspring of the sun god Helios named Iesas or Iesus, which was later translated to Jesus. There has never been a Hebrew named Jesus, especially 2,000 years ago when that particular English name did not even exist.[78]

There is no "J" in the Hebrew or Greek languages and it would have been linguistically impossible for the Hebrew Messiah to have such a name – this is an undisputed fact. The letter "J" is not even 500 years old, and there is no "J" in the original King James version of the Bible.

Yahushua is the same name as the Patriarch that many call Joshua. The patterns are remarkable and the Name means "YHWH saves." In other words, "YHWH will save His people from their sins" – just as the Messenger told Yoseph. His name, after all, is the purpose of His ministry.

Besides changing His Name, the Christian religion, in large part, also misrepresents the teachings of Yahushua. Most of Christianity teaches that Jesus came to do away with the Torah and establish the church. They have developed a doctrine of grace which allegedly does away with all of the Torah except for some of the Ten Commandments.

These concepts completely contradict the teachings of the Tanak and simply make no sense when subjected to any real scrutiny. Contrary to what Christianity professes, Yahushua came to restore the Kingdom of Yisrael and He did nothing to contradict or change the teaching of Mosheh, which was the very foundation - the constitution of that Kingdom.

Before we look at His ministry it is first important to look at the circumstances surrounding His birth. He was born during a period commonly referred to as the "Fall Feasts" which includes the Appointed Times known as Yom Teruah, Yom Kippur and Succot.[79] Contrary to popular belief, He was not born on December 25, which was the traditional birth date for most sun gods throughout history.[80]

He was born in Bethlehem, which means: "House of Bread." How profound that "The Bread of Life" (John 6:35, 6:48) would be born in a town named the "House of Bread." We know that Bethlehem was the home of King David, and the Prophet Micah (Michayahu)[81] prophesied: "*But you, Bethlehem Ephrathah, though you are small among the clans of Yahudah, out of you will come for me One Who will be ruler over Yisrael, whose origins are from of old, from ancient times.*" Michayahu 5:2.

Michayahu prophesied concerning Samaria and

Jerusalem during the reigns of the Kings of Yahudah. (Michayahu 1:1). So we know that a future King would come out of Bethlehem Who was not just a mere man, but this One has origins from ancient days and He would reign over all of Yisrael.

The Book of Matthew (Mattityahu)[82] meticulously provides the lineage of Yahushua from Avraham through David to Yoseph, the adoptive father of Yahushua.[83] One of the reasons for providing the lineage was to show that Yahushua was a descendant of King David and thus an heir to the throne. This explains the account of the "Wise men" that we read about in Mattityahu as follows: "*1 Now*

after Yahushua was born in Bethlehem of Yudea in the days of Herod the king, behold, wise men from the East came to Jerusalem, 2 saying, 'Where is He who has been born King of the Yahudim? For we have seen His star in the East and have come to worship Him.'" Mattityahu 2:1-2.

Contrary to popular belief these wise men, called Magi, from the East did not come to the baby while He was in the manger - they came much later. Most manger scenes are inaccurate when they show the baby Jesus in a manger with the "Three Wise Men" looking over Him.

The Scriptures do not mention three wise men, but rather three gifts: gold, frankincense, and myrrh. There were most likely many more than three of them, and they probably would have had a large entourage to carry and protect the gifts and supplies necessary for such a long journey which would have taken time to assemble. The only witnesses to the birth and the infant, according to the

Scriptures, were the shepherds who would not have been living outside in the middle of winter (Luke 2:12).

There is considerable evidence to support the fact that the "wise men" found Yahushua in the Galilee - not in Bethlehem. One significant reason is because after the Messiah was circumcised on the eighth day in accordance with the Torah and after the days of purification were completed, Yoseph and Miryam took Him to Jerusalem to present Him before YHWH and *"to offer a sacrifice according to what is said in the Torah of YHWH, a pair of turtledoves or two young pigeons."* Luke 2:34.

What this passage of Scripture is telling us is that they presented a sacrifice which a *poor person* would bring to the House of YHWH. According to the Torah: *"6 When the days of her purification are fulfilled, whether for a son or a daughter, she shall bring to the priest a lamb of the first year as a burnt offering, and a young pigeon or a turtledove as a sin offering, to the door of the tabernacle of meeting.7 Then he shall offer it before YHWH, and make atonement for her. And she shall be clean from the flow of her blood. This is the Torah for her who has born a male or a female. 8 And if she is not able to bring a lamb, then she may bring two turtledoves or two young pigeons - one as a burnt offering and the other as a sin offering. So the priest shall make atonement for her, and she will be clean."* Vayiqra 12:6-8.

Since they did not bring a lamb, they were likely quite poor. This is inconsistent with the myth that the Messiah and His family were loaded up with gold and other gifts on the night He was born. The wise men were nowhere near the manger in Bethlehem because the Scriptures later record: **"And coming into the house,** *they saw the Child with Miryam His mother, and fell down and did*

reverence Him . . ." Mattityahu 2:11.

The wise men appeared at the "house" - not at the manger when Yahushua was a "child" - not a baby. They actually found Yahushua around a year or so after His birth. It was only then that they worshipped Him and gave Him gifts. It was after that point that they were warned in a dream not to return to Herod. (Mattityahu 2:12).

Herod had already learned from the wise men exactly what time the star appeared. That is why, when he learned that he had been duped by them he ordered all children two years old and younger to be killed. Yoseph was also warned in a dream to flee to Egypt and he now could afford the trip because he had just been given the resources necessary for the journey. (Mattityahu 2:13).

Just who were these "wise men" seems to be the mystery of the ages although it is possible to piece together their identity through a historical analysis. At the time of the birth of Yahushua, the Roman Empire and the Parthian Empire were experiencing somewhat of a détente. While the Roman Empire ruled the west, the Parthian Empire ruled the east.

The wise men described in the Scriptures were likely Parthians from Persia, members of the Megistanes, who were very high officials in the Parthian Empire.[84] The historian Josephus strongly implies that these Parthians may have been Yisraelites formerly deported by the Assyrian Empire, which was later replaced by the Parthian Empire.[85]

We know from history that the Prophet Daniel was a gifted and brilliant Yisraelite who was brought captive to Babylon by Nebuchadnezzar during the exile of the House of Yahudah. He belonged to the Tribe of

Yahudah and was from nobility in the Kingdom of Yahudah. He experienced great favor, esteem and power in the Babylonian Empire and was given the governorship of the province of Babylon, and the head-inspectorship of the sacerdotal caste, which consisted of the scholars, educators and scientists, including the astrologers, astronomers, magicians, sorcerers, priests and the like, also known as Magi or wise men.

Later, when the Medo-Persians conquered the Babylonians, Daniel continued his administratorship in that Empire as well. He was given the unique responsibility of being the principal administrator of two world empires - not something too many people can put on their resume.

One of the titles given to Daniel was Rab HarTumaya (רב חרטמיא) - the Chief of the Magicians. When he continued in this role - a Hebrew from nobility, functioning in a traditional hereditary Median priesthood, it resulted in the plot which got him thrown in the lion's den from which he was miraculously delivered.

As a result of his prominence in both the Babylonian and Medo-Persian empires, Daniel likely had great riches, but he was a eunuch with no descendants. This was a barbarous custom for those who served in the oriental courts but it begs the question: What happened to the wealth of this man who had no progeny?

Being a Prophet of the Most High he was given wisdom, knowledge and revelation beyond any man of his time which he was told to "*close up and seal the words of the scroll until the time of the end.*" (Daniel 12:4). Daniel likely knew when the Messiah would come, or at least the signs to look for, since he was one prophet that was given very specific time frames for prophetic events.

As such, it is believed by some that he passed on his riches through his eventual successors, the Parthian Magi, with instructions to bring his wealth to the Messiah when the sign of His birth was seen in the Heavens. Since the Magi were a priestly line these may have actually been priests of Yisrael. When the Magi saw the sign, they knew that it signaled the birth of the Hebrew Messiah.[86] Since the prophecies indicated where the Messiah would be born (Michayahu 5:2-5) and where He would dwell (Yeshayahu 9:1), they knew where to look for Him.

Their entourage would have been enormous, likely in the thousands. They would have brought a small army with them since they were Parthian dignitaries traveling within the Roman Empire carrying great riches. This is why Herod and all of the inhabitants of Jerusalem were "*disturbed*" and "*troubled*" by their arrival. (Mattityahu 2:3). This is a scene which most people will not be presented with in Sunday School but it is supported by history and the Scriptures.

When they finally located "*the Child*" Yahushua in the Galilee they anointed Him King of Yahudah and gave Him the riches of His Kingdom. It is important to understand that Yahushua was not some theoretical or self proclaimed king. He was actually the King of Yahudah and that was the context within which you must view His appearance on Earth.

To properly understand His teachings it is also imperative that we recognize the condition of the Kingdom and the Land. When Yahushua walked the earth some 2,000 years ago, the House of Yisrael was still in exile and while a remnant of the House of Yahudah had returned, the Kingdom was not only divided, it was

occupied by foreigners and subject to the Roman Empire When the Assyrians removed the Northern Tribes, they had transplanted them with foreigners who created a quasi-Yisraelite religion and used Mt. Gerizim as their headquarters.

Since they lived in Samaria, they were called Samaritans and they were despised by the Yahudim. Not only were they foreigners who had replaced their brethren, they were also practicing a false religion which mimicked their own. Their religion was considered to be an abomination.

Further north, things were just as bad. The area

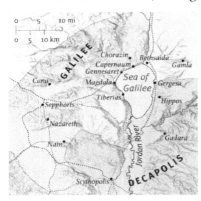

surrounding Lake Kinneret, often referred to as the Sea of Galilee was a veritable mixing pot of religions and cultures. By far, the largest population on the water was located in Tiberias, a city built by Herod and dedicated to Tiberias, the Roman Emperor. The city was located on the western shore of the Kinneret and consisted of mostly Herodians, a largely secular group of Yahudim.

Along the northern shore of the Lake was a cluster of what could be called "orthodox" Yisraelite communities. These included smaller

towns and fishing villages such as Capernum, Bethsaida and Korazim, among others. These towns were likely close knit "religiously" oriented communities as can be seen through excavations. Most of them contained a Synagogue which would have been the center of most religious and social interaction in the community.

Toward the east were the Zealots, these were the religious "extremists" who were militant in their desire to rid themselves of Roman occupation. These Zealots would use all sorts of "guerrilla" tactics to attack and kill Romans and they were centered in the strategically located area of Gamla. Gamla was located in the Northeast region of the Kinneret – in what is now known as the Golan Heights.

To the North was the city of Banias (Panias), also known as Caesarea Philippi. It was a hub of pagan worship involving some of the worst, vile and depraved forms of cult worship. This city was a center of Pan worship and included many sordid activities too disgusting to detail – suffice it to say that their worship was an abomination according to the Torah.

The region around the Kinneret to the east and to the south was referred to as the Decapolis, which was actually a collection of Hellenistic cities generally located along the eastern side of the Yarden (Jordan) River. One of these cities was located on the eastern shore of the Kinneret and was called Hippos/Sussita.

Another Decapolis city known as Bet Shean (Scythopolis) was located south of the Kinneret on the western side of the Yarden River. These cities were all pagan and included numerous temples and the worship of

various gods and goddesses such as the apparent patron goddess of Scythopolis known as Tyche to the Greeks and Fortuna to the Romans.

It was in this region of diversity, referred to as the Galilee of the Nations, or rather the Galilee of the Gentiles, that the promised Messiah lived and taught.

"*1 In the past He humbled the Land of Zebulun and the Land of Naphtali, but in the future He will honor Galilee of the Gentiles, by the way of the sea, along the Yarden - 2 The people walking in darkness have seen a great light; on those living in the Land of the shadow of death a light has dawned. 3 You have enlarged the nation and increased their joy; they rejoice before You as people rejoice at the harvest, as men rejoice when dividing the plunder. 4 For as in the day of Midian's defeat, You have shattered the yoke that burdens them, the bar across their shoulders, the rod of their oppressor. 5 Every warrior's boot used in battle and every garment rolled in blood will be destined for burning, will be fuel for the fire. 6 For to us a Child is born, to us a Son is given, and the government will be on His shoulders. And He will be called Wonderful Counselor, Mighty Elohim, Everlasting Father, Prince of Peace. 7 Of the increase of His government and peace there will be no end. He will reign on David's throne and over His kingdom, establishing and upholding it with justice and righteousness from that time on and forever. The zeal of YHWH Almighty will accomplish this. 8 The Master has sent a message against Yaakov; it will fall on Yisrael. 9 All the people will know it - Ephraim and the inhabitants of Samaria . . ."* Yeshayahu 9:1-9.

According to this, and other prophecies, many anticipated a Messiah who would restore the divided Kingdom and rule over a united Kingdom. They yearned for this Son of David to come and free them from their

oppressors.

In Jerusalem the Temple had just gone through extensive rebuilding and renovations by the tyrant Herod the Great, named King of Judea. Interestingly, Herod was the son of Antipater the Idumaean. He was an Edomite which means he descended from Esau, the brother of Yisrael. In other words, Herod did not descend from David so he was not a  legitimate King of Yahudah. Further, the priesthood which served in the Temple that he built was not a properly functioning priesthood. For many years, the High Priesthood had been a politically appointed position not dependant upon progeny.

Therefore when we look at the Land two thousand years ago we see the Kingdom of Yisrael in ruins. The Land was being desecrated, the House of YHWH was not properly constructed or administered and the leadership was illegitimate.[87]

The Priesthood was controlled by the Sadducean Sect of Yahudim. The Sadducees represented the aristocratic group of the Hasmonean High Priests, who replaced the previous High Priestly lineage that had allowed the Syrian Emperor Antiochus IV Epiphanes to desecrate the Temple of Jerusalem with idolatrous sacrifices and to martyr monotheistic Jews. The Jewish holiday of Hanukkah celebrates the ousting of the Syrian forces, the rededication of the Temple, and the installment of the new Hasmonean priestly line. The Hasmoneans ruled as 'priest-kings,' claiming both titles high priest and king simultaneously, and like other aristocracies across

the Hellenistic world became increasingly influenced by Hellenistic syncretism and Greek philosophies: presumably Stoicism, and apparently Epicureanism in the Talmudic tradition criticizing the anti-Torah philosophy of the 'Apikorsus' . . . Like Epicureans, Sadducees rejected the existence of an afterlife, thus denied the Pharisaic doctrine of the Resurrection of the Dead." [88]

The Pharisees, on the other hand, were the predominant sect that appealed to the masses. The word **Pharisees** comes from the Hebrew *perushim* from *parush*, meaning 'separated.' The Pharisees were, depending on the time, a political party, a social movement, and a school of thought among Jews that flourished during the Second Temple Era . . . After the destruction of the Second Temple, the Pharisaic sect was re-established as Rabbinic Judaism.[89] The Pharisees were famous for their development of the Oral Law which often times added to and took away from the Torah of Mosheh.[90]

Therefore, the leadership and the faith of the Yahudim living in the Land was in utter turmoil with competing sects all subject to Roman authority. Because of these conditions, some groups entirely rejected the Temple System in Jerusalem. Some like John the Baptist, whose Hebrew Name is Yahanan,[91] sought refuge and separation in the wilderness. People seeking truth would search him out and his ministry involved making the way straight for Messiah.

His message was clear in Mattityahu 3:3: *"Repent, for the Kingdom of Heaven is at hand!"* Interestingly, in Mattityahu 4:13 we read that Yahushua preached the same exact message: *"Repent for the Kingdom of Heaven is at hand!"*

This message of the Kingdom often gets overlooked

but both Yahanan and Yahushua were proclaiming the Kingdom preceded by repentance. Repentance is the act of acknowledging that one has sinned, which simply means that a person has transgressed the commandments - the Torah. After acknowledging that you have disobeyed the Torah you then need to correct your behavior by obeying the Torah.

Traditionally this act of repentance would include immersion in a mikvah which symbolically washed away the sins. In the Hebrew language, the words for "repentance" and "restoration" are one and the same. They both involve returning to the way that things used to be or were meant to be – getting rid of the filth and returning to a right relationship with YHWH.[92]

So then right from the start of His ministry – Yahushua focused on the Torah and the restoration of the Kingdom of Yisrael. While He was rightly anointed the King of the House of Yahudah, He did not reunite the Kingdom because the House of Yisrael was still scattered throughout the world. With this knowledge it helps to better understand His statements.

Yahushua said that He came *"to seek and to save what was lost."* Luke 19:10 NIV. For something to be lost, it must have first been in the possession of the owner. This begs the question: What was lost? The answer was provided by the Messiah, it was *the House of Yisrael.*

He specifically stated that He was sent *"only to the lost sheep of the House of Yisrael."* Mattityahu 15:24. Further, when He sent out the twelve disciples He instructed them: *"⁵ Do not go among the Gentiles or enter any town of the Samaritans. ⁶ Go rather to the lost sheep of the House of Yisrael. ⁷ As you go, preach this message: 'The Kingdom of Heaven is*

near.'" Mattityahu 10:5-7.

The disciples were instructed to proclaim the same message of the Kingdom that Yahanan and Yahushua preached. They were also instructed to go to the lost sheep of the House of Yisrael, showing that Yahushua came to fulfill prophecy by gathering in the lost sheep. This is why He is called the Great Shepherd (Hebrews 13:20) and the Chief Shepherd (1 Peter 5:4).

These lost sheep belonged to the House of Yisrael. His mission was to Yisrael, a fact which is not often discussed in Christianity because of its potential implications. If the House of Yisrael was still lost when Yahushua was present on earth, I do not see any other period in history when the House of Yisrael was supposedly regathered. In fact, all of the prophesies on this issue point to a future time in history.

Yahushua stated that these sheep belonged to Him. *"2 But he who enters by the door is the shepherd of the sheep.3 To him the doorkeeper opens, and the sheep hear his voice; and* **he calls his own sheep by name and leads them out.4 And when he brings out his own sheep,** *he goes before them; and the sheep follow him, for they know his voice."* Yahanan 10:2-4 NKJV.

Later in the passage Yahushua makes another reference to sheep which were not present but needed to be gathered. *"11 I am the good Shepherd. The good Shepherd lays down His life for the sheep. 12 The hired hand is not the shepherd who owns the sheep. So when he sees the wolf coming, he abandons the sheep and runs away. Then the wolf attacks the flock and scatters it. 13 The man runs away because he is a hired hand and cares nothing for the sheep. 14 I am the good Shepherd; I know My sheep and My sheep know Me - 15 just as the Father knows Me and I know the Father and I lay down My life for the*

sheep. *¹⁶ I have other sheep that are not of this sheep pen. I must bring them also. They too will listen to My voice, and there shall be one flock and one Shepherd. ¹⁷ The reason my Father loves Me is that I lay down My life - only to take it up again. ¹⁸ No one takes it from Me, but I lay it down of My own accord. I have authority to lay it down and authority to take it up again. This command I received from My Father."* Yahanan 10:11-18 NIV.

The other sheep that Yahushua is referring to are the lost sheep of the House of Yisrael. They are not of *"this sheep pen"* (House of Yahudah) because they have been scattered abroad. Those sheep also belong to Him, but they are not in the same fold or House. They are sheep who have obviously been scattered beyond the fold which Yahushua was referring to in Jerusalem – sheep that must be gathered.

The Prophet Yehezqel spoke directly to this issue. *"¹⁶ Therefore say, 'Thus says YHWH Elohim: <u>Although I have cast them far off among the Gentiles, and although I have scattered them among the countries, yet I shall be a little sanctuary for them in the countries where they have gone.'</u> ¹⁷ Therefore say, Thus says YHWH Elohim: <u>'I will gather you from the peoples, assemble you from the countries where you have been scattered, and I will give you the Land of Yisrael.</u> ¹⁸ And they will go there, and they will take away all its detestable things and all its abominations from there. ¹⁹ <u>Then I will give them one heart, and I will put a new spirit within them, and take the stony heart out of their flesh, and give them a heart of flesh,</u> ²⁰ that they may walk in My statutes and keep My judgments and do them; and they shall be My people, and I will be their Elohim. ²¹ But as for those whose hearts follow the desire for their detestable things and their abominations, I will recompense their deeds on their own heads,' says YHWH Elohim."* Yehezqel

11:16-21.

This passage is of particular interest because Yehezqel is speaking about the Northern Tribes being scattered far off among the Gentiles, but it also promises a regathering which coincides with the Renewed Covenant which Messiah came to establish.[93]

It is clear from the Scriptures that the Renewed Covenant is centered around YHWH's plan to restore the House of Yisrael and the House of Yahudah.

"*15 Again the word of YHWH came to me, saying, 16 As for you, son of man, take a stick for yourself and write on it: For Yahudah and for the children of Yisrael, his companions. Then take another stick and write on it, For Yoseph, the stick of Ephraim, and for all the House of Yisrael, his companions. 17 Then join them one to another for yourself into one stick, and they will become one in your hand. 18 And when the children of your people speak to you, saying, 'Will you not show us what you mean by these?' 19 say to them, Thus says YHWH Elohim: 'Surely I will take the stick of Yoseph, which is in the hand of Ephraim, and the tribes of Yisrael, his companions; and I will join them with it, with the stick of Yahudah, and make them one stick, and they will be one in My hand.' 20 And the sticks on which you write will be in your hand before their eyes. 21 Then say to them, Thus says YHWH Elohim: 'Surely I will take the children of Yisrael from among the Gentiles (nations), wherever they have gone, and will gather them from every side and bring them into their own Land; 22 and I will make them one nation in the Land, on the mountains of Yisrael; and one King shall be King over them all; they shall no longer be two nations, nor shall they ever be divided into two kingdoms*

again. ²³ *They shall not defile themselves anymore with their idols, nor with their detestable things, nor with any of their transgressions; but I will deliver them from all their dwelling places in which they have sinned, and will cleanse them. Then they shall be My people, and I will be their Elohim.* ²⁴ <u>*David My servant shall be King over them, and they shall all have one Shepherd; they shall also walk in My judgments and observe My statutes, and do them.*</u> ²⁵ *Then they shall dwell in the Land that I have given to Yaakov My servant, where your fathers dwelt; and they shall dwell there, they, their children, and their children's children, forever; and My servant David shall be their prince forever.* ²⁶ <u>*Moreover I will make a Covenant of peace with them, and it shall be an everlasting Covenant with them; I will establish them and multiply them, and I will set My sanctuary in their midst forevermore.*</u> ²⁷ *My tabernacle also shall be with them; indeed I will be their Elohim, and they shall be My people.* ²⁸ *The Gentiles (nations) also will know that I, YHWH, set apart Yisrael, when My sanctuary is in their midst forevermore."* Yehezqel 37:15-28.

Some say that this already occurred between 400-500 BCE, but that cannot be so. The prophecy speaks of David being their prince forever which is a Messianic reference to the Prince of Peace. It also says that the sanctuary of YHWH will be in their midst *forevermore*. For those who know their history, the House of YHWH was destroyed in 70 AD and there is currently no Sanctuary in Jerusalem.

The prophecy speaks of the Covenant of peace, which will be an everlasting covenant. There is anything but peace in the Land today. This prophecy is clearly

speaking of a time to come in the future, not of a time in the past. The prophecy speaks of a Kingdom not divided and a time when there is no more idolatry in the Land.

The Land of Yisrael is currently extremely divided into different kingdoms, in particular the mountains of Yisrael which included much of the land currently called the West Bank. The Modern State of Israel repeatedly gives up territory which was promised to the seed of Avraham. Further, that nation consists of citizens of varying race, tribe, language, religion and political party, many of whom do not follow YHWH and obey His commandments.

Therefore, as far as YHWH is concerned, the Kingdom is still divided and the prophesied restoration of Yisrael is a future event which has yet to occur. Some day soon we can expect to see the following prophecy fulfilled: *"In those days ten men from all languages and nations will take firm hold of one Yahudite by the hem of his robe (tzitzit) and say, 'Let us go with you, because we have heard that Elohim is with you.'"* Zechariah 8:23.

It is interesting that the number ten is selected

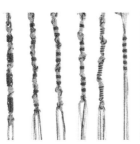 which would depict a regathering of the House of Yisrael (10 tribes) all grabbing hold of a Yahudite (House of Yahudah) which is the two sticks coming together as Yehezqel prophesied. These tzitziyot (plural) are the same tassels worn by Yahushua and every person that obeys Torah.[94]

In this same manner, Yahushua was from the House of Yahudah and he selected twelve disciples from

various tribes which represented Yisrael, although there was not one disciple from each of the twelve tribes as some were brothers, thus they belonged to the same tribe. "*² Now the names of the twelve apostles are these: first, Simon, who is called Peter, and Andrew his brother; James the son of Zebedee, and John his brother; ³ Philip and Bartholomew; Thomas and Matthew the tax collector; James the son of Alphaeus, and Lebbaeus, whose surname was Thaddaeus; ⁴ Simon the Cananite, and Judas Iscariot, who also betrayed Him. ⁵ These twelve Yahshua sent out and commanded them, saying: 'Do not go into the way of the Gentiles, and do not enter a city of the Samaritans.⁶ But go rather to the lost sheep of the House of Yisrael.'"* Mattityahu 10:2-7.

According to the Prophet Yirmeyahu: *"Yisrael is like scattered sheep; the lions have driven him away."* Yirmeyahu 50:17. Remember that lions were the method used to attack those who were transplanted into the northern kingdom and the lion is also used to depict the tribe of Yahudah. Yirmeyahu also proclaimed: *"Behold, I will send for many fishermen, says YHWH, and they shall fish them; and afterward I will send for many hunters, and they shall hunt them from every mountain and every hill, and out of the holes of the rocks."* Yirmeyahu 16:16.

This is exactly what Yahushua was training His disciples to do – become fishers of men in fulfillment of this prophecy. *"¹⁸ And Yahushua, walking by the Sea of Galilee, saw two brothers, Simon called Peter, and Andrew his brother, casting a net into the sea; for they were fishermen. ¹⁹ Then He said to them, 'Follow Me, and I will make you fishers of men.' ²⁰ They immediately left their nets and followed Him."* Mattityahu 4:18-20; Mark 1:17.

While Yahushua equipped fishers of men we

should not forget the second aspect of the regathering – the hunters. The regathering of Yisrael is to occur in two stages, a fact misunderstood by most. This is one of the main reasons why Jewish rabbis argue that Yahushua was not the Messiah, because He did not restore the Tribes of Yisrael. They do not realize that He started a process which He has yet to be complete.

The Northern tribes were clearly still scattered when Yahushua ministered in the Land, otherwise we would not read the following passage: "*33 Yahushua said, 'I am with you for only a short time, and then I go to the One who sent Me. 34 You will look for Me, but you will not find Me; and where I am, you cannot come.' 35 The Yahudim said to one another, 'Where does this man intend to go that we cannot find him? <u>Will he go where our people live scattered among the Greeks, and teach the Greeks?</u> 36 What did He mean when He said, You will look for Me, but you will not find Me, and Where I am, you cannot come?'*" Yahanan 7:33-36.

The Yahudim fully recognized that the House of Yahudah and the House of Yisrael were still scattered and they expected the Messiah to gather them back to the Land. The fact that Yahushua did not restore the Kingdom during His first appearance is why many reject Him as the Messiah, because this is one of expectations of Messiah that we read in the prophecies – Restoration of the Kingdom.

If you view the teaching, parables and miracles of Yahushua in the proper context you will see the deeper meaning. For instance, we read of two miraculous feedings in the Scriptures. One was known as the feeding of the 5,000 and the other was the feeding of the 4,000. Through these actions Yahushua spoke more powerfully to His

purpose than in words.

We can read about them from the Good News according to Mark, immediately after the disciples returned from ministering to the "lost sheep".

"*30 Then the disciples gathered to Yahushua and told Him all things, both what they had done and what they had taught. 31 And He said to them, Come aside by yourselves to a deserted place and rest a while. For there were many coming and going, and they did not even have time to eat. 32 So they departed to a deserted place in the boat by themselves. 33 But the multitudes saw them departing, and many knew Him and ran there on foot from all the cities. They arrived before them and came together to Him. 34 And Yahushua, when He came out, saw a great multitude and was moved with compassion for them, because they were like sheep not having a shepherd. So He began to teach them many things. 35 When the day was now far spent, His disciples came to Him and said, This is a deserted place, and already the hour is late. 36 Send them away, that they may go into the surrounding country and villages and buy themselves bread; for they have nothing to eat. 37 But He answered and said to them, you give them something to eat. And they said to Him, shall we go and buy two hundred denarii worth of bread and give them something to eat? 38 But He said to them, How many loaves do you have? Go and see. And when they found out they said, five, and two fish. 39 Then He commanded them to make them all sit down in groups on the green grass. 40 So they sat down in ranks, in hundreds and in fifties. 41 And when He had taken the five loaves and the two fish, He looked up to heaven, gave thanks and broke the loaves, and gave them*

to His disciples to set before them; and the two fish He divided among them all. ⁴² So they all ate and were filled. ⁴³ And they took up twelve baskets full of fragments and of the fish. ⁴⁴ Now those who had eaten the loaves were about five thousand men." Mark 6:30-44.

We know from combining the various accounts in the other Scripture passages that this event occurred near Bethsaida at a place traditionally called Tabgha. It was in that geographical area that consisted of "orthodox" Yahudim and it is generally accepted that these 5,000 men were Yahudim. As their King, Yahushua had compassion for His sheep because they were like sheep without a shepherd. As a result He fed His sheep.

After the feeding, Yahushua immediately tells His disciples to get in their boat and row to the other side of the Lake. He watches from a mountain as they struggle against the winds of a storm in the middle of the Lake. He then walks past them on the water until they cry out, at which time He talks to them and calms them down. All of this apparently happened due to the fact that: *"they had not understood about the loaves, because their heart was hardened."* Mark 6:52.

After crossing the Lake, Yahushua then continues His ministry in primarily Gentile regions. He travels up into Lebanon to the cities of Tyre and Sidon and then back down into the midst of the region of the Decapolis to the Sea of Galilee (Lake Kinneret), possibly Hippos/ Sussita. It is at this particular location that we read about the second feeding – the feeding of the 4,000.

"¹ In those days, the multitude being very great and having nothing to eat, Yahushua called His disciples to Him and said to them, ² I have compassion on the multitude, because they

have now continued with Me three days and have nothing to eat.
³ And if I send them away hungry to their own houses, they will
faint on the way; for some of them have come from afar. ⁴ Then
His disciples answered Him, How can one satisfy these people
with bread here in the wilderness? ⁵ He asked them, How many
loaves do you have? And they said, seven. ⁶ So He commanded
the multitude to sit down on the ground. And He took the seven
loaves and gave thanks, broke them and gave them to His disciples
to set before them; and they set them before the multitude. ⁷ They
also had a few small fish; and having blessed them, He said to
set them also before them. ⁸ So they ate and were filled, and they
took up seven large baskets of leftover fragments. ⁹ Now those
who had eaten were about four thousand. And He sent them
away, ¹⁰ immediately got into the boat with His disciples, and
came to the region of Dalmanutha." Mark 8:1-10.

Now it is important to recognize that there was
numerical significance in the loaves. This is emphasized
by Yahushua after both of the feedings – which were
obviously related. After the second feeding: "¹³ He left them,
and getting into the boat again, departed to the other side. ¹⁴ Now
the disciples had forgotten to take bread, and they did not have
more than one loaf with them in the boat. ¹⁵ Then He charged
them, saying, Take heed, beware of the leaven of the Pharisees
and the leaven of Herod. ¹⁶ And they reasoned among themselves,
saying, It is because we have no bread. ¹⁷ But Yahushua, being
aware of it, said to them, Why do you reason because you have
no bread? Do you not yet perceive nor understand? Is your heart
still hardened? ¹⁸ Having eyes, do you not see? And having ears,
do you not hear? And do you not remember? ¹⁹ When I broke
the five loaves for the five thousand, how many baskets full of
fragments did you take up? They said to Him, twelve. ²⁰ Also,
when I broke the seven for the four thousand, how many large

baskets full of fragments did you take up? And they said, seven. [21] *He said to them, Do you still not understand?"* Mark 8:13-20. This apparently was supposed to be quite obvious but they didn't get it.

When Yahushua fed the 5,000 He was in the region of the Yahudim acting as the King of the Yahudim without a throne, just as David did after He was anointed but before he had taken over the Kingdom from Shaul. In I Shemuel 21 we read how David was given 5 loaves of showbread to feed his men. The parallels are magnificent as Yahushua too fed His followers with five loaves. After Yahushua fed the 5,000 there were twelve baskets left over which symbolized that His reign was sufficient for the restored Kingdom of Yisrael. He had enough bread to satisfy all twelve tribes.

To demonstrate this fact He then went North as the House of Yisrael went north and eventually ended up in the midst of the Decapolis, or the midst of the Gentile region. Remember that Decapolis literally means "10 cities" and it clearly symbolized the 10 tribes of the House of Yisrael that had been scattered throughout the Gentiles. Notice that He went to feed them and there were seven loaves and there were seven baskets left over which symbolized completion. Also the combined number of loaves for both feedings was twelve, which again symbolized the feeding of the entire Kingdom including all twelve tribes.

These numbers had great symbolic significance and should have been quite apparent to the disciples. Sadly, their hearts were hardened which did not allow them to see the true significance of the miracle. This is the same condition of the hearts of many today causing them to miss the purpose of Yahushua's ministry.

After all of this He instructed His disciples to "*beware of the leaven of the Pharisees and the leaven of Herod.*" In other words, "when you go to feed Yisrael, beware of the religious entanglements in Yahudah as well as the worldly entanglements of the Gentiles" – "stay pure as David and his men were pure when they took the showbread" – "feed the people the pure bread from the table of YHWH."

His teaching and miracles had powerful messages built within them for those who had eyes to see and ears to hear. His disciples could not always get it right away because their hearts were hardened. We need to make certain that our hearts are not hardened so that we can see the real meaning of the teaching of Yahushua. He was demonstrating in a very Hebrew fashion, the purpose of His ministry.

We also see this distinction between the House of Yahudah and the House of Yisrael in His parables, which were teachings with a cloaked message. The parable of the prodigal son is often looked upon as a wonderful example of forgiveness and restoration, which it is. Sadly though, most fail to recognize the deeper significance regarding the restoration of Yisrael.

Read the account as provided in the Good News according to Luke:

"*¹¹ Then He said: A certain man had two sons. ¹² And the younger of them said to his father, Father, give me the portion of goods that falls to me. So he divided to them his livelihood. ¹³ And not many days after, the younger son gathered all together, <u>journeyed to a far country, and there wasted his possessions with prodigal living</u>. ¹⁴ <u>But when he had spent all, there arose a severe famine in that land, and he began to be in want.</u> ¹⁵ Then he went*

_and joined himself to a citizen of that country, and he
sent him into his fields to feed swine._ ¹⁶ And he would
gladly have filled his stomach with the pods that the
swine ate, and no one gave him anything. ¹⁷ But when he
came to himself, he said, How many of my father's hired
servants have bread enough and to spare, and I perish
with hunger! ¹⁸ I will arise and go to my father, and will
say to him, Father, I have sinned against heaven and
before you, ¹⁹ and I am no longer worthy to be called your
son. Make me like one of your hired servants. ²⁰ And he
arose and came to his father. But when he was still a
great way off, his father saw him and had compassion,
and ran and fell on his neck and kissed him. ²¹ And the
son said to him, Father, _I have sinned against heaven
and in your sight, and am no longer worthy to be called
your son._ ²² But the father said to his servants, Bring
out the best robe and put it on him, and put a ring on his
hand and sandals on his feet. ²³ And bring the fatted calf
here and kill it, and let us eat and be merry; ²⁴ _for this
my son was dead and is alive again; he was lost and is
found._ And they began to be merry. ²⁵ Now his older son
was in the field. And as he came and drew near to the
house, he heard music and dancing. ²⁶ So he called one of
the servants and asked what these things meant. ²⁷ And
he said to him, Your brother has come, and because he
has received him safe and sound, your father has killed
the fatted calf. ²⁸ But he was angry and would not go in.
Therefore his father came out and pleaded with him. ²⁹
So he answered and said to his father, Lo, these many
years I have been serving you; I never transgressed your
commandment at any time; and yet you never gave me a
young goat, that I might make merry with my friends. ³⁰

But as soon as this son of yours came, who has devoured your livelihood with harlots, you killed the fatted calf for him. ³¹ And he said to him, son, you are always with me, and all that I have is yours. ³² It was right that we should make merry and be glad, <u>for your brother was dead and is alive again, and was lost and is found</u>." Luke 15:11-32.

This story is about the divided Kingdom and the sons represent Yisrael and Yahudah. The prodigal son was the younger son, Ephraim - the House of Yisrael, who neglected and spent his birthright. He made a willing decision to leave his father's House just as Yisrael chose to commit adultery, being fully aprised of the consequences. He went away to a far country and was involved in unclean activities - symbolized by feeding pigs instead of sheep. He was no longer worthy to be called a son. He was Lo-Ammi, <u>not my people</u>, as prophesied by Hoshea.

He finally repented and returned to his father and his father restored him to his original status. He was lost and then found – just as was prophesied concerning the House of Yisrael. Upon his return, the robe of Joseph was placed upon him. A spectacular feast was thrown for him which makes his older brother Yahudah jealous - just as Joseph's brothers were jealous of the favor that was bestowed upon him.

All through His ministry we see Yahushua as King of Yahudah teaching and serving His sheep – getting them ready for the Kingdom. We see that He wore a fine robe of royalty which soldiers cast lots over because of its value. When asked by Pilate whether He was the King of the Yahudim, Yahushua responded: "*Yes, it is as you say.*" Mattityahu 27:11.

He was declared the King of the Yahudim by Pilate

and this statement was placed upon His execution stake. Roman soldiers even placed a crown of thorns on his head, a scarlet robe and a staff, mocking the fact that He was a King.

After His death and resurrection we read about another miracle in the Galilee region which speaks volumes if you understand the meaning. "*¹ After these things Yahushua showed Himself again to the disciples at the Sea of Tiberias, and in this way He showed Himself: ² Simon Peter, Thomas called the Twin, Nathanael of Cana in Galilee, the sons of Zebedee, and two others of His disciples were together. ³ Simon Peter said to them, 'I am going fishing.' They said to him, 'We are going with you also.' They went out and immediately got into the boat, and that night they caught nothing. ⁴ But when the morning had now come, Yahushua stood on the shore; yet the disciples did not know that it was Yahushua. ⁵ Then Yahushua said to them, 'Children, have you any food?' They answered Him, 'No.' ⁶ And He said to them, 'Cast the net on the right side of the boat, and you will find some.' So they cast, and now they were not able to draw it in because of the multitude of fish. ⁷ Therefore that disciple whom Yahushua loved said to Peter, 'It is the Master! Now when Simon Peter heard that it was the Master, he put on his outer garment (for he had removed it), and plunged into the sea. ⁸ But the other disciples came in the little boat (for they were not far from land, but about two hundred cubits), dragging the net with fish. ⁹ Then, as soon as they had come to land, they saw a fire of coals there, and fish laid on it, and bread. ¹⁰ Yahushua said to them, Bring some of the fish which you have just caught. ¹¹ Simon Peter went up and dragged the net to land, full of large fish, one hundred and fifty-three; and although there were so many, the net was not broken. ¹² Yahushua said to them, Come and eat breakfast. Yet none of*

the disciples dared ask Him, Who are You? - knowing that it was the Master. ¹³ Yahushua then came and took the bread and gave it to them, and likewise the fish. ¹⁴ This is now the third time Yahushua showed Himself to His disciples after He was raised from the dead." Yahanan 21:1-14.

The question that anyone should ask after reading this passage is: Why 153 fish? There is a wonderful mystery surrounding this passage which can only be discovered through gematria (the study of numbers) in the original Hebrew. If you only rely on English translations, you will miss an enormous amount of information in the Scriptures.

In the Hebrew language letters also have a numeric value so it is possible to place numeric values on certain words or phrases. In the Hebrew Scriptures the phrase "Sons of Elohim" calculates to 153. Sons of Elohim in Hebrew is Beni Ha-Elohim (בני האלהים). The gematria calculation for Beni Ha-Elohim goes as follows: (ב = 2) (נ = 50) (י = 10) (ה = 5) (א = 1) (ל = 30) (ה = 5) (י = 10) (ם = 40). Therefore 2+50+10+5+1+30+5+10+40 = 153.

While there are several Scripture references to the "sons of Elohim" there is only one instance in the Scriptures which refers to the "sons of the living Elohim" or literally "sons of El alive." It is found in the Book of Hosea which refers to the House of Yisrael as follows: *"¹⁰ Yet the number of the children of Yisrael shall be as the sand of the sea, which cannot be measured nor numbered; and it shall come to pass, that in the place where it was said unto them, Ye are not my people, there it shall be said unto them, Ye are the sons of the living El (sons of El alive). ¹¹ Then shall the children of Yahudah and the children of Yisrael be gathered together, and appoint themselves one head, and they shall come up out of the*

land: for great shall be the day of Yizreel." Hosea 1:10-11.

Therefore, in the context of catching the 153 fish, Yahushua was clearly showing His disciples that instead of fishing for fish they needed to be fishing for their brethren – the sons of Elohim - the lost sheep of the House of Yisrael. As if this could not be any clearer, Yahushua then instructs Peter twice to "*feed My sheep*" and once to "*tend My sheep.*" It should be plain to see that the ministry of Yahushua was very much about regathering the lost sheep of the House of Yisrael and restoring the Kingdom - a task that He passed on to His disciples.

13

Disciples

The disciples of Yahushua were a varied, interesting and misunderstood group of individuals. It is important to realize that it was not uncommon for a great rabbi to have followers, although they were not called disciples, rather they were called talmudim.

The word "talmudim" is plural and the singular form is "talmid." The word "disciple" is often used to describe a person who is a "learner" or a "student." In the Christian sense it generally refers to one of the twelve or anyone who studies, believes and follows the teachings of Jesus. In the Hebrew sense, the word "talmid" goes much deeper. A talmid not only studies and learns – but they want to be just like Yahushua. It has as much to do with living as it does with learning.

In the case of talmudim, they would eat, sleep and live with their rabbi, which was an integral part of the experience. They would walk closely behind their rabbi and rarely leave his presence. There is even a Jewish saying which captures the essence of the relationship by stating: "May you be covered in the dust of your rabbi." In other words, may you follow him so close that you get covered with the dust that he kicks up from his sandals.

Talmudim learn to live like their rabbi and it is a very intensive existence. It is much less a text book experience than it is a life experience. It is not just about acquiring knowledge and knowing what the rabbi knows - it involves becoming like the rabbi.

Generally, talmudim would ask to follow a rabbi after they had finished schooling in their mid to late teens. That would be when they made their choice to either work in a vocation or continue their studies by following a rabbi. The rabbi would watch and consider whether he would accept someone to follow him, most apparently were not accepted.

In the case of the Talmudim of Yahushua, we see most of them working, so they were either unable to follow a rabbi or maybe never even asked to follow a rabbi. They were likely quite young – unlike the portrayals that we often see in the movies.[95]

Interestingly, these Talmudim did not ask Yahushua if they could follow Him, rather He chose them without being asked. This is an important point which is emphasized in the Scriptures – "*You have not chosen Me but I have chosen you.*" Yahanan 15:16. He chose them and then taught them how to walk. He died and was resurrected – a path which they were all expected to follow as His Talmudim.

After the mandate given in the Galilee to feed His sheep, the Talmudim went to Jerusalem to keep the Feast of Shavuot, also known as the Feast of Weeks or Pentecost. On the day of the Feast, the Talmudim went to the House of YHWH where thousands would have gathered for morning prayer.[96] Let us read the account from the Book of Acts:

"*¹ When the day of Shavuot came, they were all together in one place. ² Suddenly a sound like the blowing of a violent wind came from heaven and filled the whole House where they were sitting. ³ They saw what seemed to be tongues of fire that separated and came to rest on each of them. ⁴ All of them were filled with the Set Apart Spirit and began to speak in other tongues as the Spirit enabled them. ⁵ Now there were staying in Jerusalem Yahudim, dedicated men from every nation under heaven. ⁶ When they heard this sound, a crowd came together in bewilderment, because each one heard them speaking in his own language. ⁷ Utterly amazed, they asked: 'Are not all these men who are speaking Galileans? ⁸ Then how is it that each of us hears them in his own native language? ⁹ Parthians, Medes and Elamites; residents of Mesopotamia, Yudea and Cappadocia, Pontus and Asia, ¹⁰ Phrygia and Pamphylia, Egypt and the parts of Libya near Cyrene; visitors from Rome ¹¹ both Yahudim and converts; Cretans and Arabs - we hear them declaring the wonders of Elohim in our own tongues!' ¹² Amazed and perplexed, they asked one another, 'What does this mean?' ¹³ Some, however, made fun of them and said, They have had too much wine. ¹⁴ Then Kepha stood up with the eleven, raised his voice and addressed the crowd: Men of Yudea and all of you who live in Jerusalem, let me explain this to you; listen carefully to what I say. ¹⁵ These men are not drunk, as you suppose. It's only nine in the morning! ¹⁶ No, this is what was spoken by the prophet Yoel: ¹⁷ 'In the last days, Elohim says, I will pour out my Spirit on all people. Your sons and daughters will prophesy, your young men will see visions, your old men will dream dreams. ¹⁸ Even*

on my servants, both men and women, I will pour out my Spirit in those days, and they will prophesy. ¹⁹ *I will show wonders in the heaven above and signs on the earth below, blood and fire and billows of smoke.* ²⁰ *The sun will be turned to darkness and the moon to blood before the coming of the great and glorious day of YHWH.* ²¹ *And everyone who calls on the Name of YHWH will be saved.'* ²² *Men of Yisrael, listen to this: Yahushua of Nazareth was a man accredited by Elohim to you by miracles, wonders and signs, which Elohim did among you through Him, as you yourselves know.* ²³ *This man was handed over to you by Elohim's set purpose and foreknowledge; and you, with the help of wicked men, put Him to death by nailing Him to the stake.* ²⁴ *But Elohim raised Him from the dead, freeing Him from the agony of death, because it was impossible for death to keep its hold on Him.* ²⁵ *David said about Him: 'I saw YHWH always before me. Because He is at my right hand, I will not be shaken.* ²⁶ *Therefore my heart is glad and my tongue rejoices; my body also will live in hope,* ²⁷ *because you will not abandon me to the grave, nor will you let your Holy One see decay.* ²⁸ *You have made known to me the paths of life; You will fill me with joy in your presence.'* ²⁹ *Brothers, I can tell you confidently that the patriarch David died and was buried, and his tomb is here to this day.* ³⁰ *But he was a prophet and knew that Elohim had promised him on oath that he would place one of his descendants on his throne.* ³¹ *Seeing what was ahead, he spoke of the resurrection of the Messiah, that He was not abandoned to the grave, nor did His body see decay.* ³² *Elohim has raised this Yahushua to life, and we are all witnesses of the fact.* ³³ *Exalted to the right*

hand of Elohim, He has received from the Father the promised Set Apart Spirit and has poured out what you now see and hear. ³⁴ For David did not ascend to heaven, and yet he said, YHWH said to my Master: 'Sit at My right hand ³⁵ until I make your enemies a footstool for your feet.' ³⁶ <u>Therefore let all the House of Yisrael be assured of this: Elohim has made this Yahushua, whom you crucified, both Master and Messiah.</u> ³⁷ When the people heard this, they were cut to the heart and said to Kepha and the other apostles, 'Brothers, what shall we do?' ³⁸ Kepha replied, 'Repent and be immersed, every one of you, in the name of Yahushua the Messiah for the forgiveness of your sins. And you will receive the gift of the Set Apart Spirit. ³⁹ <u>The promise is for you and your children and for all who are far off-for all whom YHWH our Elohim will call.</u>' ⁴⁰ With many other words he warned them; and he pleaded with them, Save yourselves from this corrupt generation. ⁴¹ Those who accepted his message were immersed, and about three thousand were added to their number that day." Acts 2:1-41.

The fact that 3,000 were added is profound because it parallels an occurrence that happened on the very day 1,470 years earlier after Yisrael had been brought out of Egypt. When Mosheh received the Torah on Mount Sinai, he heard the Children of Yisrael committing idolatry. He went down the mountain, broke the tablets and 3,000 Yisraelites were killed - removed from the congregation. Tradition holds that this happened on Shavuot.

The number 3,000 is further significant because Yahushua had earlier fed 5,000 and 4,000. He then told Kepha to feed His sheep. When Kepha obeyed Yahushua,

stood up in Jerusalem and preached, he was doing just that – feeding the sheep. As a result of this feeding we see that 3,000 believed, adding 3,000 to the congregation. The addition of these 3,000 sheep gave a total of 12,000 sheep being fed which is another allusion to the Kingdom being restored in Jerusalem.

Notice that those 3,000 came from all over the world, including Parthia, where the "wise men" had come from to annoint Yahushua as King. They were the dispersed of the House of Yahudah and the lands where they originated were those in which the House of Yahudah went into exile.

The event in Jerusalem beautifully parallels the event at Sinai. At Sinai, Yisrael broke the Covenant and the 3,000 were killed, the Covenant was thereafter renewed with Mosheh as the mediator of the covenant. At Jerusalem we see that Covenant with Yisrael being renewed - this time with Yahushua as the Mediator.

As people started to recognize Yahushua as the Messiah and understood His work of restoring the lost sheep to the Kingdom, they began to assemble together. It is important to realize that they did not form a new religion, but rather a new sect of Yisrael. They still obeyed the Torah - they just did not follow the leaven of the Pharisees such as the fabricated Oral Torah and commandments made up by men and enforced by their religious systems.[97]

As their community grew the original Talmudim naturally took on positions of leadership. They also continued the mandate of their Rabbi to feed His sheep through travelling, teaching and writing letters. They travelled to the regions of the world where the House

of Yisrael was known to have been exiled – this can be verified through historical documents and by the very letters written by the Talmudim.

These are the people to whom Peter (Kepha)[98] was writing. Notice how he addressed his letter: "*¹ To the pilgrims of the Dispersion in Pontus, Galatia, Cappadocia, Asia, and Bithynia, ² elect according to the foreknowledge of Elohim the Father . . .*" 1 Kepha 1:1-2. Some translations refer to the elect, the chosen, the strangers or the foreigners "who are scattered" while other translations refer to the exiles.

The Greek word for elect is eklekton which means "select or chosen." We find this same word in the following passage from Kepha: "*⁹ But you are a chosen people, a royal priesthood, a holy nation, a people belonging to Elohim, that you may declare the praises of Him who called you out of darkness into His wonderful light. ¹⁰ Once you were not a people, but now you are the people of Elohim; once you had not received mercy, but now you have received mercy.*" 1 Kepha 2:9-10.

The first thing that we must recognize is that Kepha is referring to Yisrael. The description that he uses comes straight from the Torah. "*⁵ Now therefore, if you will indeed obey My voice and keep My Covenant, then you shall be a special treasure to Me above all people; for all the earth is Mine. ⁶ And you shall be to Me a kingdom of priests and a holy nation. These are the words which you shall speak to the children of Yisrael.*" Shemot 19:5-6.

Second, by quoting the Prophet Hoshea, Kepha is making it abundantly clear that he is writing to the lost sheep of the House of Yisrael – those who once received no mercy, but now receive mercy. Those who were once not a people but now are the people of Elohim – Sons of Elohim. (Hoshea 1).

In the Letter of James, whose actual Hebrew name was Yaakov, he is even more specific as he writes: "*Yaakov, a servant of Elohim and of the Master Yahushua the Messiah, to the twelve tribes scattered among the nations.*" Yaakov 1:1.

We can clearly see that the Talmudim understood that the Kingdom had not yet been restored and their task was to follow their Rabbi, Yahushua. They continued the work of restoring the divided Kingdom by going to the nations in which the House of Yisrael had been scattered. We know that the Talmudim traveled throughout the world seeking out the lost sheep while in Jerusalem schisms occurred between the various sects of Yisraelites and the followers of Yahushua.

The Talmudim were persecuted, in large part by their own people. It appears that Yahudah did not want their Messiah, as He did not meet their expectations, nor did they desire the restoration with Yisrael which was required. We read that there was a certain Pharisee named Shaul[99] – who was a major opponent of the Talmudim of Yahushua. He was charged with rooting out these followers of Messiah and suppressing their message.

Prior to his eyes being opened to the Messiahship of Yahushua, Shaul was potentially destined to become the head of the Sanhedrin - the High Court of Yisrael. On the Road to Damascus, the Scriptures describe a powerful meeting between Yahushua and Shaul.[100] He was not converted to Christianity during this encounter as many claim - rather he was confronted by the Messiah and, while "blinded by the light" his eyes were opened concerning the fact that Yahushua was indeed the

Messiah.[101]

It is believed by some that after the encounter Shaul went to Mount Sinai in Arabia where his doctrine was corrected. The same place where Mosheh and Elijah met with YHWH is likely the place where Shaul met with YHWH.[102]

After this experience he understood that the Torah was intended to lead men to the Messiah - Who had come to restore the Kingdom. He realized that this restoration involved regathering the lost sheep of the House of Yisrael that had been scattered among the Gentiles.

Thus a man who arguably was one of the greatest Torah scholars of his day was on a mission to reveal the Messiah to the lost sheep scattered among the Gentiles who had become Gentiles - people who had little to no knowledge of the Torah because they forgot who they were or where they came from.

He attempted to explain the working of the Renewed Covenant under very difficult and complex circumstances. He was teaching about mysterious things and his teachings were often misconstrued and misunderstood by people that failed to understand history or the Torah. As a result, his writings have been used for centuries by ignorant people to alter and distort the teachings of Yahushua.

This is why Kepha specifically warned people concerning Shaul's writings: "[15] *and consider that the longsuffering of our Master is salvation - as also our beloved brother Shaul, according to the wisdom given to him, has written to you,* [16] *as also in all his epistles, speaking in them of these things, in which are some things hard to understand, which untaught and unstable people twist to their own destruction, as*

they do also the rest of the Scriptures." 2 Kepha 3:15-16.

This is exactly what has happened over the centuries. People have twisted the epistles as well as the rest of the Scriptures to meet their own end – they do so to their own destruction. Much of the time this is done because they do not understand the significance of the Torah nor do they understand the context of Shaul's writings. Sadly, they also teach their lies to the unwary and untaught who often accept them out of ignorance. Without a fundamental understanding of the Torah and the work of the Messiah this is easy enough to do.

Neither Yahushua, Shaul or any of the Talmudim ever desired to start a new religion called Christianity. On the contrary, their goal was to find the lost sheep, restore the Kingdom and teach Yisrael how to walk straight. While Shaul is often credited with starting the Christian religion which consists of converted Gentiles who allegedly replaced Yisrael, nothing could be further from the truth.

Read how Shaul addressed this issue of Yisrael: "*[1] I say then, has Elohim cast away His people? Certainly not! For I also am a Yisraelite, of the seed of Avraham, of the tribe of Benyamin.[2] Elohim has not cast away His people whom He foreknew. Or do you not know what the Scripture says of Eliyahu, how he pleads with Elohim against Yisrael, saying, [3] 'YHWH, they have killed Your prophets and torn down Your altars, and I alone am left, and they seek my life?' [4] But what does the divine response say to him? 'I have reserved for Myself seven thousand men who have not bowed the knee to*

Baal.' [5] *Even so then, at this present time there is a remnant according to the election of grace.* [6] *And if by grace, then it is no longer of works; otherwise grace is no longer grace. But if it is of works, it is no longer grace; otherwise work is no longer work.* [7] *What then? Yisrael has not obtained what it seeks; but the elect have obtained it, and the rest were blinded.* [8] *Just as it is written: 'Elohim has given them a spirit of stupor, eyes that they should not see and ears that they should not hear, to this very day.'* [9] *And David says: 'Let their table become a snare and a trap, a stumbling block and a recompense to them.* [10] *Let their eyes be darkened, so that they do not see, and bow down their back always.'* [11] *I say then, have they stumbled that they should fall? Certainly not! But through their fall, to provoke them to jealousy, salvation has come to the Gentiles.* [12] *Now if their fall is riches for the world, and their failure riches for the Gentiles, how much more their fullness!* [13] *For I speak to you Gentiles; inasmuch as I am an apostle to the Gentiles, I magnify my ministry,* [14] *if by any means I may provoke to jealousy those who are my flesh and save some of them.* [15] *For if their being cast away is the reconciling of the world, what will their acceptance be but life from the dead?* [16] *For if the firstfruit is holy, the lump is also holy; and if the root is holy, so are the branches.* [17] <u>*And if some of the branches were broken off, and you, being a wild olive tree, were grafted in among them, and with them*</u>

<u>became a partaker of the root and fatness of the olive tree,</u> ¹⁸ <u>do not boast against the branches.</u> But if you do boast, remember that you do not support the root, but the root supports you. ¹⁹ You will say then, 'Branches were broken off that I might be grafted in.' ²⁰ Well said. Because of unbelief they were broken off, and you stand by faith. Do not be haughty, but fear. ²¹ For if Elohim did not spare the natural branches, He may not spare you either. ²² Therefore consider the goodness and severity of Elohim: on those who fell, severity; but toward you, goodness, if you continue in His goodness. Otherwise you also will be cut off. ²³ And they also, if they do not continue in unbelief, will be grafted in, for Elohim is able to graft them in again. ²⁴ For if you were cut out of the olive tree which is wild by nature, and were grafted contrary to nature into a cultivated olive tree, how much more will these, who are natural branches, be grafted into their own olive tree? ²⁵ <u>For I do not desire, brethren, that you should be ignorant of this mystery, lest you should be wise in your own opinion, that blindness in part has happened to Yisrael until the fullness of the Gentiles has come in.</u> ²⁶ <u>And so all Yisrael will be saved,</u> as it is written: 'The Deliverer will come out of Zion, and He will turn away ungodliness from Yaakov; ²⁷ For this is My Covenant with them, when I take away their sins.' ²⁸ Concerning the good news they are enemies for your sake, but concerning the election they are beloved for

the sake of the fathers. ²⁹ For the gifts and the calling of Elohim are irrevocable.³⁰ For as you were once disobedient to Elohim, yet have now obtained mercy through their disobedience, ³¹ even so these also have now been disobedient, that through the mercy shown you they also may obtain mercy.³² For Elohim has committed them all to disobedience, that He might have mercy on all. ³³ Oh, the depth of the riches both of the wisdom and knowledge of Elohim! How unsearchable are His judgments and His ways past finding out! ³⁴ For who has known the mind of YHWH? Or who has become His counselor? ³⁵ Or who has first given to Him and it shall be repaid to him? ³⁶ For of Him and through Him and to Him are all things, to whom be esteem forever. Amen." Romans 11:1-36.

Many people fail to properly understand this passage which Shaul calls a "mystery." They particularly grapple with the statement that *"all Yisrael will be saved."* In the minds of most Christians, they think that there is going to be one giant "revival" and every person in the modern State of Israel is going to get "saved" or every "Jew" on earth will accept the Messiah. They think this because they fail to understand the true nature and identity of Yisrael.

When Shaul is speaking of Yisrael he is speaking about the remnant of the Set Apart Assembly of Yisrael consisting of all of those who are following YHWH *"with all the hearts, their souls and their strength."* (Devarim 6:4; Mark 12:30). He is not talking about those who are hereditarily from the Tribe of Yahudah. He is talking

about anyone, whether native born or the stranger, who obeys YHWH and His Torah and thus is a member of His family – the Kingdom.

If you understand that He is talking about the Commonwealth of Yisrael which consists of the Redeemed, The Elect, The Sheep, then you realize that he is simply reiterating the statements of the Messiah that He would not leave any sheep - they all would be gathered. Just as all of Yisrael was delivered or "saved" from Egypt, at an Appointed Time in the future, all Yisrael will be saved – none will be forgotten or left behind. (Mattityauh 18:14). YHWH will save everyone who belongs to the Set Apart Assembly – the Congregation, the Flock which is Yisrael.

The olive tree has always been understood to refer to Yisrael. The Prophet Yirmeyahu proclaimed concerning the House of Yisrael and the House of Yahudah: "*YHWH called you a thriving olive tree with fruit beautiful in form. But with the roar of a mighty storm he will set it on fire, and its branches will be broken.*" Yirmeyahu 11:16.

Shaul is referencing this prophecy and he is speaking to the House of Yisrael, which was plucked from the Land and transplanted amongst the nations, as the wild branches. Remember, they are still from an olive tree, they are just wild. Therefore, they must be grafted into the natural olive tree – Yisrael, by the Spirit of YHWH which is the binding agent – the Life that flows through and connects the tree. They must be grafted back into the root which is the source of Life.

It is important to understand that there are only two groups of people in the eyes of YHWH – those who obey and those who disobey – the righteous and the wicked – Yisrael and all other nations – the Gentiles. "Gentile"

is a term which is often misunderstood and misapplied. People often use it to refer to anyone who is not a genetic descendant of the man named Yisrael. That is not a correct definition and can lead to damaging doctrinal errors and a misunderstanding of the plan of YHWH.

It does not simply come down to genetics because there are many who come from a Hebrew bloodline that are atheists, agnostics, secular humanists etc. – these individuals are not part of Yisrael unless they repent. Further, there are many who follow YHWH that cannot prove whether or not they are a descendant of Yisrael – yet they are part of Yisrael. They can no longer be referred to as Gentiles because a Gentile is a heathen or a pagan – someone that does not follow the Torah of YHWH.

This is confirmed in another passage from Shaul: "*1 I speak the truth in Messiah - I am not lying, my conscience confirms it in the Set Apart Spirit - 2 I have great sorrow and unceasing anguish in my heart. 3 For I could wish that I myself were cursed and cut off from Messiah for the sake of my brothers, those of my own race, 4 the people of Yisrael. Theirs is the adoption as sons; theirs the divine glory, the covenants, the receiving of the Torah, the temple worship and the promises. 5 Theirs are the patriarchs, and from them is traced the human ancestry of Messiah, who is Elohim over all, forever praised! Amen. 6 It is not as though Elohim's word had failed. For not all who are descended from Yisrael are Yisrael. 7 Nor because they are his descendants are they all Avraham's children. On the contrary, it is through Yitshaq that your offspring will be reckoned. 8 In other words, it is not the natural children who are Elohim's children, but it is the children of the promise who are regarded as Avraham's offspring. 9 For this was how the promise was stated: At the appointed time I will return, and Sarah will*

have a son. *¹⁰ Not only that, but Rebekah's children had one and the same father, our father Yitshaq. ¹¹ Yet, before the twins were born or had done anything good or bad - in order that Elohim's purpose in election might stand: ¹² not by works but by him who calls - she was told, The older will serve the younger. ¹³ Just as it is written: 'Yaakov I loved, but Esau I hated.' ¹⁴ What then shall we say? Is Elohim unjust? Not at all! ¹⁵ For he says to Mosheh, 'I will have mercy on whom I have mercy, and I will have compassion on whom I have compassion.'"* Romans 9:1-15.

Shaul recognized that there is only one nation that has a Covenant with YHWH and YHWH has not given up on His people Yisrael – yet *"not all who are descended from Yisrael are Yisrael."* It is more a matter of the heart than it is with genes, that is what YHWH is revealing by mixing the House of Yisrael among the nations to the point where they became just like those gentiles that they lived amongst.

Shaul understood that there was and still is a purpose for the House of Yisrael and he specifically affirms that fact in the following passage: *"²² What if Elohim, wanting to show His wrath and to make His power known, endured with much longsuffering the vessels of wrath prepared for destruction, ²³ and that He might make known the riches of His glory on the vessels of mercy, which He had prepared beforehand for glory, ²⁴ even us whom He called, not of the Yahudim only, but also of the Gentiles? ²⁵ As He says also in Hoshea: I will call them My people, who were not My people, and her beloved, who was not beloved. ²⁶ And it shall come to pass in the place where it was said to them, 'You are not My people,' There they shall be called sons of the living Elohim."* Romans 9:22-26.

His quote from the prophecy in Hoshea is a clear reference to the regathering of the House of Yisrael. Shaul

recognizes that the House of Yisael has been mixed into the Gentile nations and it is through their regathering that YHWH will demonstrate His power and His mercy – just as He showed His power and mercy by delivering Yisrael, <u>along with the mixed multitude</u>, from Egypt.

Shaul, through His many writings, is attempting to explain a great mystery which eludes men to this day. You see, not everyone who descended from Avraham is a Hebrew and not everyone who descended from Yisrael belongs to Yisrael.

Again, whether you belong to Yisrael depends upon your heart, not your genes. This is cause for great confusion in the Assembly as there are some who attempt to divide the sheep and categorize some as "Jewish" and some as "Gentile." Now there is no harm in recognizing which tribe you belong to, although it is highly inappropriate to refer to someone in the Assembly of YHWH as a Gentile because you cannot remain in the Assembly if you are a Gentile.

The Hebrew word *goy* (גוי) is often defined as *heathen* or *gentile*. These two words generally refer collectively to all other nations other than Yisrael. They are the pagan nations who do not worship YHWH or follow His Torah. In the Tanak, there was a distinction made between a heathen nation, a heathen individual and an alien and stranger who dwelt with Yisrael. A heathen nation is a nation which refuses to follow YHWH, a heathen individual is either a person that lives in a heathen nation or an individual who refuses to follow YHWH.

If you were a heathen who wanted to serve YHWH, then your place was with Yisrael although that was not always possible. If you came to the Assembly of

Yisrael you were more than welcome to join with them, as long as you renounced your pagan ways and followed Torah. (Shemot 12:19, 12:29).

If you could not abide by these requirements then you were not welcome in the Assembly – the family of YHWH. Since YHWH dwelled with His people, there was no tolerance for disobedience in His presence – just as there was no tolerance in the Garden.

Therefore, a heathen could join with Yisrael as long as they renounced their heathen practices, at which time they no longer were a heathen. You cannot be a heathen and join with the Redeemed of YHWH because by its very definition, a "heathen" or a "gentile" means: "a pagan, or someone who lives contrary to the commands of YHWH – someone outside of the Assembly."

As a result, when someone joined with Yisrael they were referred to as an alien or a sojourner - in Hebrew the word is *towshab* (תושב). They could also be referred to as a *geyr* (גר) alien, stranger, foreigner or guest. These aliens could live and reside with Yisrael and they would be required to live according to the Torah, thus they were no longer Gentiles or Heathens because they were not living like the other nations.

With those definitions in mind we can better understand how it was the Plan of YHWH for those outside of the Assembly to join Yisrael. The prophet Yeshayahu speaks directly to this point: *"¹ Thus says YHWH: Keep justice, and do righteousness, for My salvation is about to come, and My righteousness to be revealed. ² Blessed is the man who does this, and the son of man who lays hold on it; who keeps from defiling the Sabbath, and keeps his hand from doing any evil. ³ Do not let the son of the foreigner who has*

joined himself to YHWH speak, saying, 'YHWH has utterly separated me from His people;' Nor let the eunuch say, 'Here I am, a dry tree.' ⁴ For thus says YHWH: 'To the eunuchs who keep My Sabbaths, and choose what pleases Me, and hold fast My Covenant, ⁵ Even to them I will give in My House and within My walls a place and a name better than that of sons and daughters; I will give them an everlasting name that shall not be cut off. ⁶ Also the sons of the foreigner who join themselves to YHWH, to serve Him, and to love the Name of YHWH, to be His servants - everyone who keeps from defiling the Sabbath, and holds fast My Covenant - ⁷ Even them I will bring to My holy mountain, and make them joyful in My House of prayer. Their burnt offerings and their sacrifices will be accepted on My altar; for My House shall be called a House of prayer for all nations. ⁸ YHWH Elohim, who gathers the outcasts of Yisrael, says, **Yet I will gather to Him others besides those who are gathered to Him."** Yeshayahu 56:1-8.

This is exactly what Shaul was teaching and what the Torah prescribes. Yeshayahu is showing that there is a place for those who appear to be outside of Yisrael to come and join with Yisrael. They are encouraged to "cling" and "hold fast" to the Covenant and not let go no matter what others might say. Through this process they join themselves to YHWH - they do not convert to Judaism.

This is how it likely will be when YHWH gathers the outcasts of the House of Yisrael who have been scattered amongst the Gentiles. These outcasts will be told that they cannot enter into the Covenant because they are not "Jews." Yet despite this, they are to take hold of the Covenant and when they do so, they are no longer Gentiles – they have been grafted back into the olive tree Yisrael.

Thus the Gentiles are simply all nations other than Yisrael and the term should only refer to those outside of the Assembly which were not a part of Yisrael - those not living lives according to the Torah of YHWH. Both the House of Yisrael and the House of Yahudah were expelled to live among the Gentiles because they chose not to obey YHWH. After the exile to Babylon and the return of the Yahudim to the Land, everyone else was considered a Gentile, including the Northern Tribes.

The House of Yisrael had forsaken YHWH and went whoring after pagan gods, they were banished from the Assembly. They were no longer part of Yisrael, regardless of the blood that ran through their veins. Further, because of their participation in pagan practices and assimilation into their captive's cultures, they most likely looked and acted just like the Gentiles. For all intents and purposes, they were Gentiles in the eyes of their brethren, the Yahudim.

Now this does not mean that YHWH was finished with the House of Yisrael, because He was not. As proclaimed by Yeshayahu: *"My House shall be called a House of prayer for all nations. YHWH Elohim, who gathers the outcasts of Yisrael, says, Yet I will gather to Him others besides those who are gathered to Him."* In other words, YHWH gathers those who were exiled from Yisrael and there are others – the sons of the foreigners – who will also be gathered from the nations. His House will then truly be called a House of prayer for all nations.

This is what we see happening to the Assembly of Yisrael after the death and resurrection of Yahushua. Shaul was attempting to deal with some of the issues and problems which resulted from this apparent culture clash

as Gentiles were repenting and being grafted in to the Assembly. It was not always pretty as we read in many of his Epistles. We know from history that divisions resulted between the Talmudim of Yahushua and the other sects of Yisrael.

As the Talmudim went about gathering together the outcasts of the House of Yisrael and bringing them in to the fold – tensions grew. This influx of "Gentiles" led to much dissension and division.

One important development that exacerbated the division was the Birkat ha-Minim which translates to "The Heretic Benediction." It is the Twelfth Benediction of the set daily prayer commonly referred to as the Shemoneh Esreh (the Eighteen Benedictions) or Amidah.

The Twelfth Benediction of the Genizah text reads: "For meshumaddim [apostates] let there be no hope, and the dominion of arrogance do Thou speedily root out in our days; and let the Natzrim and minim perish in a moment, let them be blotted out of the book of the living and let them not be written with the righteous." This was not a blessing as is the purpose of a benediction. Thus many have considered this to be a malediction or curse.[103]

The Shemoneh Esreh was one of the most important rabbinic prayers and was to be recited three times every day in the Synagogue. Obviously, the Natzrim, which was what they called the followers of Yahushua, would not say this prayer. It would also be difficult, if not impossible, for the Natzrim to gather and pray with people who were cursing them three times a day.

During 70 CE, Jerusalem was razed by Titus and the Roman Army. The House of YHWH was completely destroyed and many Yisraelites were slaughtered. The

Pharisees survived and established their new headquarters at Yavnah where Rabbinic Judaism developed into what we see today as a very different religion from what existed over 2,000 years ago.[104] This religion continued and expanded the Pharasaic teachings, which included the Oral Law that Yahushua opposed.

Another clear point of contention between the sects came with the Bar Kokhba revolt which occurred between 132-135 CE. The revolt started when Emperor Hadrian constructed a pagan temple in Jerusalem on the site where the House of YHWH once stood. He renamed Jerusalem, Aelia Capitolina, and forbade Torah observance. Rabbi Akiva ben Yoseph (alternatively Akiba) convinced the Sanhedrin to support the impending revolt, and regarded the chosen commander Simon Bar Kokhba to be the Messiah, according to the verse from Bemidbar 24:17: *"There shall come a star out of Jacob."* "Bar Kokhba" means "son of a star" in the Aramaic language.[105]

Sadly Akiba changed this so-called messiah's name to fit within the prophecy in Bemidbar. His original name was actually Bar Kosiba which can mean "son of a lie" which was really quite appropriate. A close examination reveals that much of what Akiba did to contrive the messiahship of Kokhba was a distortion of the truth. Despite these well known facts, Akiba is still considered to be one of the great Rabbis of Judaism.

Most historians believe that it was this messianic

claim in favor of Bar Kokhba that alienated many Natzrim, who believed that the true Messiah was Yahushua. Because the Pharasaic "Jews" rallied around the leaders of their particular religion as well as a false messiah, the Natzrim were excluded from joining the revolt because it was really not their fight. They were thus viewed with disdain by the Pharisees which created further separation and deeper division.

This was particularly a problem for the Natzrim who were native Yisraelites. The "gentile converts"[106] did not necessarily share any of the loyalties of the native Yisraelites whose failure to stand arm in arm with their brethren made them appear disloyal.

These are only a few examples of the numerous causes of division between these two sects. The conflict continued until eventually there was a complete separation between these two groups of Yisraelites which eventually "evolved" into two separate and distinct religions known as Christianity and Judaism.

14

Christianity and Judaism

After the House of YHWH was destroyed in 70 CE by Roman forces, the Pharisees became the predominant sect of Yisraelites. They survived the assault of the Romans by reaching an agreement whereby they were permitted to establish a new religious "headquarters" at Yavneh. Jerusalem was sacked and with no Temple, the Sadducees practically disappeared.

The Zealots, Ebionites, Natzrim and other sects were scattered and decimated by the Romans leaving the Pharisees as the only significant identifiable sect of Yisraelites remaining. This was the point when Pharasaic Judaism and the Rabbis assumed control over interpreting the Torah and over the people.[107]

While modern Judaism has ancient roots, contrary to popular belief, it is not what Mosheh taught in the Torah but rather it is a religion developed by rabbis. Much of Judaism is based upon Talmudic Law rather than strictly YHWH's Torah. This is an error and it is the same reason why Yahushua rebuked the Pharisees by asking: "*Why do you also transgress the commandment of Elohim because of your tradition?*" Mattityahu 15:3.

You see the Pharisees had been teaching their

traditions as if they carried the same or more weight than the commandments. At the same time, they were neglecting the commands of Elohim. This became increasingly more prevalent once they moved to Yavneh.[108]

Judaism now claims to represent the same faith as ancient Yisrael, but this is not the case. It is simply the surviving sect of many different competing sects of Yisrael. The religion of Judaism, as we see it today, does not equate to the Commonwealth of Yisrael - nor does the religion of Christianity. You do not have to convert to Judaism or Christianity to join with the Redeemed of Yisrael because currently, neither of these religions accurately represent or constitute the Assembly of Yisrael.

The religion of Christianity was created hundreds of years after the destruction of Jerusalem. While it can also be traced to the sect of Yisrael referred to as the Natzrim, it ended up incorporating many of the pagan elements from the environment in which it developed, namely the Roman Empire.

The Christian religion is not the same faith lived and taught by Yahushua and His Talmudim. In fact, there was no such religion as Christianity when Yahushua walked the earth, nor did He create a new religion after His death and resurrection. Likewise, the Christian religion did not exist during the lives of the original Talmudim nor was it created by Shaul. The early Talmudim were all Yisraelites and they never converted to any new religion - they always maintained their original faith based upon the Torah.

Most students of the Christian religion are taught that Roman Emperor Constantine "converted" to Christianity and from that point on Christianity became

the official state religion of the Roman Empire. What they do not realize is that he did not convert to Christianity – he actually helped create the religion as we know it.

Constantine was and remained a worshipper of the sun god Mithra. He had his wife and child murdered after his "so-called" conversion and it was his mother, Queen Helena, who actually used sorcery and divination to locate the holy places of this new religion.

A close analysis of history reveals that it was during the reign of Constantine when the original faith of the Natzrim was formally "repackaged" into a new religion. The "conversion" of Constantine was really a political maneuver to save his declining Empire and it actually worked for a time. Sadly, this new religion called  Christianity was littered with "leaven" from its inception.

Read what M. Turretin, wrote in describing the state of Christianity in the 4th century, saying, "that it was not so much the [Roman] Empire that was brought over to the Faith, as the Faith was brought over to the Empire; not the Pagans who were converted to Christianity, but Christianity that was converted to Paganism."[109]

Emperor Constantine was responsible for salvaging the faltering Roman Empire through reconstruction, including making Christianity the official state religion of the Roman Empire - most notably through The Council of Nicaea in 325 C.E. The official state religion created by Constantine is what we now know as the Roman Catholic Church.

Despite his claims of conversion, it is apparent

that his professed change of faith was simply an act of syncretism (ie. the blending of religions). He actually merged the faith of the Natzrim with his own pagan worship, which he continued to his death. We know this because he actually had a coin minted which depicts himself on one side and Mithra on the other side with the statement: SOLI INVICTO COMITI - Committed to the Invincible Sun.

After this not so illustrious beginning, centuries later we see that the Christian religion - having now splintered into countless denominations - has remained a repository for paganism and various cultic beliefs. At its very core is a belief in *Jesus the Christ* which has become quite different than the original faith that followed *Yahushua*  *Hamoshiach*. This is not just a difference in words, languages or names – there are critical and fundamental differences between the faith lived and taught by the original Talmudim and modern Christians.

Christianity is not the same assembly that received the outpouring of the Spirit at the Appointed Time in Jerusalem, popularly known as Pentecost, after the resurrection of the Messiah. While Christianity often claims to have picked up where Yisrael left off, this is a false doctrine called Replacement Theology. Yisrael is still the community of faith, which is often referred to as the Redeemed, and the Christian "Church" has not replaced Yisrael.

Thus we see two religions, Christianity and

Judaism, both laying claim to the same Elohim, stumbling through the centuries to this point in history where they find their destinies converging like the two sticks becoming one as prophesied in Yehezqel 37:19. Although these two religions have shared common roots, and even common Scriptures, they have also been divided by a seemingly unsurpassable chasm.

The problem is that they cannot both serve the same Elohim in two separate and distinct fashions. As Shaul aptly stated: "*4 There is one body and one Spirit, just as you were called in one hope of your calling; 5 one Master, one faith, one immersion; 6 one Elohim and Father of all, who is above all, and through all, and in you all.*" Ephesians 4:3-6.

He proclaimed: "*there is one Elohim and one Mediator between Elohim and men.*" 1 Timothy 2:5. He also stated: "*13 by one Spirit we were all immersed into one body - whether Yahudim or Hellenists, whether slaves or free - and have all been made to drink into one Spirit. 14 For in fact the body is not one member but many.*" 1 Corinthians 12:12-14. We are further exhorted by Shaul to "*stand fast in one spirit, with one mind*" and to be "*of one accord and one mind.*" Philippians 1:27; 2:2.

Yahushua Himself stated: "*20 I do not pray for these alone, but also for those who will believe in Me through their word; 21 that they all may be one, as You, Father, are in Me, and I in You; that they also may be one in Us, that the world may believe that You sent Me. 22 And the glory which You gave Me I have given them, that they may be one just as We are one: 23 I in them, and You in Me; that they may be made perfect in one, and that the world may know that You have sent Me, and have loved them as You have loved Me.*" Yahanan 17:20-23 NKJV. He also stated: "*And other sheep I have which are not of this fold;*

them also I must bring, and they will hear My voice; and there will be <u>one</u> flock and <u>one</u> shepherd." Yahanan 10:16 NKJV.

This oneness is seen throughout the Scriptures. The people of Elohim were never meant to remain divided into different nations, religions or denominations. This is evident from the command given to Yisrael that *"one Torah shall be for the native-born and for the stranger who dwells among you."* Shemot 12:49. *"¹⁴ And if a stranger dwells with you, or whoever is among you throughout your generations, and would present an offering made by fire, a sweet aroma to YHWH, just as you do, so shall he do.¹⁵ one ordinance shall be for you of the assembly and for the stranger who dwells with you, an ordinance forever throughout your generations; as you are, so shall the stranger be before YHWH.¹⁶ <u>one Torah and one custom shall be for you and for the stranger who dwells with you.</u>"* Bemidbar 15:14-16.

In other words, anyone who wanted to worship the Elohim of Yisrael and dwell in the Kingdom was subject to the same Torah as a native-born Yisraelite. There was no distinction made in the Torah concerning how people worshipped Elohim, they all were to do it in the same way - His way.

Today if a Gentile were to tell a rabbi that he or she wants to obey the Torah they will likely be met with a puzzled look. The rabbi will doubtless ask "Why?" and gently tell the person that they do not have to obey the Torah. He will then inform the Gentile that: "Only Jews need to obey the Torah, because the Torah was a gift to the Jews from Elohim."

In essence, what he is saying is that there is no need for a heathen to follow the instructions for righteous living which YHWH provides in His Torah. This is

absolutely false and completely contrary to the message provided through the Scriptures. The Torah was not given to some "elite" group of people, it is a gift to anyone who will accept it. This false teaching proffered by Rabbinic Judaism actually leads people away from YHWH. A true priest of YHWH is supposed to lead a person toward YHWH.

The plan of YHWH was not to select a privileged group and treat them special for no apparent reason and then punish the day lights out of them. Rather, it was to select a people through which He could demonstrate His love and His power for all of His Creation. This people called Yisrael, only a fraction of which were Jews (Yahudim), were called to establish a Kingdom that would shine as a light for the rest of humanity. They were supposed to show the world how to live for YHWH.

Instead, they ended up being influenced by the world and they were punished. YHWH is not finished with Yisrael, and His plan is still operating through the Covenants that He made with them. The point is that YHWH did not intend for just the genetic descendants of Yaakov to obey Him. His plan is to restore all of Creation to Him.

Remember, YHWH did not say that all native born Yisraelites must obey the Torah while all foreigners need only obey the seven Noahic Laws. This is a false teaching being propagated by some in Judaism who try to promote the idea that YHWH treats native born "Jews" different from Gentiles. It basically promotes the idea that Jews are expected to live a more set apart life than the Gentiles - while Elohim wants the Jews to obey the Torah, He only expects the Gentiles to obey the "Seven Noahic Laws."

Those who expound this teaching will tell you that Elohim does not look on Gentiles as inferior and they will be considered righteous if they just obey "The Seven Noahic Laws." Therefore, why would you want to obey the Torah which is much harder. Just be happy that you are a Gentile and obey the Seven Laws - leave the Torah to the Jews.

The so-called, Seven Noahic Laws are gleaned from Beresheet 9 as follows: 1) not to commit idolatry; 2) not to commit blasphemy; 3) not to commit murder; 4) not to commit incest and adultery; 5) not to commit theft; 6) not to eat flesh from a living animal; and 7) establish courts of justice to punish violators of the other six laws.

If you look at Beresheet Chapter 9, you will find that YHWH gave some general instructions for Noah and his offspring and He established His Covenant with all of Creation. He did not establish rules for Gentiles and later establish separate rules for just the descendents of Yaakov, who was renamed Yisrael.

Here is a typical quote from a Jewish source on this subject: "The Torah maintains that the righteous Gentiles of all nations (those observing the Seven Laws of Noah . . .) have a place in the world to come."[110]

The Torah does not make any provision for "Righteous Gentiles." This is a rabbinic teaching which is completely contrary to the Scriptures, although not unusual for Rabbinic Judaism, which often adds to, and takes away from, the Torah. This is forbidden by the Torah which proclaims: *"You shall not add to the word which I command you, nor take from it, that you may keep the commandments of YHWH your Elohim which I command you."* Devarim 4:2.

Are these proponents trying to tell me that there is some type of atonement for the sins of Gentiles provided in the "Noahic Laws?" There is none - YHWH was pointing out some fundamentals as we saw done with Adam and it is clear that He is addressing issues which ultimately led to the judgment of the planet. Teaching Gentiles that they do not need to obey the instructions of YHWH is a grave mistake and it is in direct opposition to the mission of Yisrael.

The fact that Yisrael was chosen does not mean that they were greater or better than the other nations. In fact, YHWH makes a point to let them know that is not the case. "YHWH *did not set His love on you nor choose you because you were more in number than any other people, for you were the least of all peoples . . .*" Devarim 7:7. In fact, at one point YHWH declared to Mosheh: "*⁹ I have seen this people, and indeed it is a stiff-necked people! ¹⁰ Now therefore, let Me alone, that My wrath may burn hot against them and I may consume them. And I will make of you a great nation.*" Shemot 32:9-10.

The point is that YHWH did not choose Yisrael because they were better than the other people. He chose them because He loved their fathers - their fathers who were allegedly only subject to the Seven Noahic Laws because they were not Jews. Remember, only the descendants of Yahudah are Yahudim (Jews).

To the contrary, the Scriptures make it clear that Avraham observed the Torah but according to Rabbinic tradition he should have only been subject to the Seven Noahic Laws. Would they dare say that Noah, Shem, and Avraham were Righteous Gentiles! Absolutely not - that term is an oxymoron because each word means

the opposite. A Gentile is a "heathen" and by its very definition cannot be "righteous." The Patriarchs of the true faith followed the instructions of YHWH and are part of the set apart Assembly.

Yisrael was chosen for a <u>purpose</u>. The purpose being to shine as a light to all humanity - to draw them to YHWH and teach the nations the ways of YHWH - not to try to exclude the rest of the world from the blessings that come from serving and obeying YHWH. This type of teaching is divisive and elitist.

The Scriptures do not support this divisive teaching, but rather they support the notion that YHWH is searching for a set apart people to follow and obey all of His commandments, to serve Him, to worship Him, to love Him, and to dwell with Him in His Eternal Kingdom. These are a people who will follow the One Way which He has provided – these are the Redeemed.

The Prophet Yirmeyahu speaks of the one way provided under the renewed Covenant. "*37 Behold, I will gather them out of all countries where I have driven them in My anger, in My fury, and in great wrath; I will bring them back to this place, and I will cause them to dwell safely. 38 <u>They shall be My people, and I will be their Elohim;</u> 39 <u>then I will give them one heart and one way</u>, that they may fear Me forever, for the good of them and their children after them.40 And I will make an everlasting Covenant with them, that I will not turn away from doing them good; but I will put My fear in their hearts so that they will not depart from Me.41 Yes, I will rejoice over them to do them good, and I will assuredly plant them in this Land, with all My heart and with all My soul.*" Yirmeyahu 32:37-41.

This prophecy is speaking of a future event, a time when the renewed Covenant will be established

between YHWH and His people - Yisrael. Both Judaism and Christianity are wrestling over this Covenant, but the Scriptures clearly record that the Covenant will be with Yisrael - not the modern State of Israel, a particular religious denomination or a political entity. Yisrael is simply the set apart people who obey Elohim who have taken hold of his Covenant. Yisrael are all those who are being regathered under the banner of Messiah.

While Christians and Jews (in this sense meaning adherents to Judaism) may not realize it, their destinies lie with each other through the Messiah. The Christians believe in the Hebrew Scriptures although they have added to and taken away from the Torah. They believe in the Messiah prophesied in the Scriptures and they believe that He is the one called Jesus - The Christ. Christians believe that the Messiah has already come and will come again at the end.

While Christians accept some of the teachings found in the Hebrew Scriptures, especially the prophecies concerning the Messiah, they have lost many other critical elements of their original faith - the one taught by the Messiah, not the one in Rome. As a result, Christianity has adopted pagan customs and beliefs.

The religion of Judaism has preserved the Word to some extent, but has also added numerous customs, traditions, and interpretations which have clouded the purity of the Torah. It also subscribes to the notion of an Oral Torah which stands in direct contrast to the Scriptures which state: "*³ So Mosheh came and told the people all the words of YHWH and all the judgments. And all the people answered with one voice and said, 'All the words which YHWH has said we will do.' ⁴ And Mosheh wrote all the words*

of YHWH." Shemot 24:3-4.

Adherents to Judaism have wide and diverse notions concerning the Messiah. There are some who view the Messiah as simply a concept while others do not believe in a messiah at all. Some think that there have been various messianic types and figures throughout history while others believe that Messiah has yet to come.

As with Christianity, Judaism has also inherited and incorporated pagan practices and beliefs. There are numerous archaeological sites of ancient synagogues which revealed pagan symbols and designs.[III] The Synagogue in Hamath Tiberias is an excellent example as it contains a beautiful depiction of the Temple and its implements right along side a pagan zodiac with the sun god Helios in the middle. You will find a similar mosaic, although much less  sophisticated, at the ancient Synagogue in Bet Alpha. These are examples of the mixing or acceptance of pagan concepts that occurred within Judaism.

These two groups, Christianity and Judaism, are so close yet, at the same time, they are so far apart. Judaism, in many respects, tries to exclude non-native Jews from their faith while Christians believe that they have, in essence, replaced the Jews. They are like a couple of children vying for the rights of a firstborn. In many ways, this looks like a repeat of the sibling rivalry, jealousies, and maneuvering that we read about throughout the Scriptures. Each has something that is needed by the other and they both need to get cleaned up and get into right standing before their Creator.

Only when this occurs – when Jews and Christians rid themselves of their unscriptural customs and traditions and join the Body of Messiah will they form the One Renewed Being, as Shaul described in the following passage:

> [11] *Therefore, remember that formerly you who are Gentiles by birth and called 'uncircumcised' by those who call themselves 'the circumcision' (that done in the body by the hands of men) -* [12] *remember that at that time you were separate from Messiah, excluded from citizenship in Yisrael and foreigners to the Covenants of the promise, without hope and without Elohim in the world.* [13] *But now in Messiah Yahushua you who once were far away have been brought near through the blood of Messiah.* [14] *For He Himself is our peace, Who has made the two one and has destroyed the barrier, the dividing wall of hostility,* [15] *by abolishing in His flesh the enmity - The Torah of commands in dogma - so as to create in Himself one renewed being out of the two, thus making peace,* [16] *and in this one body to completely restore to favour both of them to Elohim through the stake, having destroyed the enmity by it.* [17] *He came and preached peace to you who were far away and peace to those who were near.* [18] *For through Him we both have access to the Father by one Spirit.* [19] *Consequently, you are no longer foreigners and aliens, but fellow citizens with Elohim's people and members of Elohim's Household,* [20] *built on the foundation of the emissaries and prophets, with Messiah*

Yahushua Himself as the Chief capstone. [21] *In Him the whole building is joined together and rises to become a set apart Dwelling Place in YHWH.* [22] *And in Him you too are being built together to become a dwelling of Elohim in the Spirit.* Ephesians 2:11-22.

This passage is a good example of a text which has traditionally been poorly translated to mean something far different than the original intent of the author. The text of verse 15 was gleaned from The Scriptures, a translation published by The Institute for Scripture Research. The corrected translation helps to demonstrate that the division between the two was not the Law or The Torah as is often taught - it is the enmity of the dogma which was abolished - not the commandments.[112]

Only when this "dividing wall of hostility" is destroyed will the divided Kingdom be restored. That day will never come until both Christianity and Judaism experience true Scriptural restoration. This does not involve Jews converting to Christianity, nor does it involve Christians converting to Judaism. Rather, it requires both of these religions, shedding all of their man-made trimmings and trappings and becoming One Nation - which is the Kingdom of Elohim.

The Jews, I believe have preserved a key which Christianity has been missing for hundreds of years: The Torah. Sadly, the purity of the Torah has been obscured by a myriad of customs, traditions and interpretations which have driven Christians away from the simplicity and truth contained therein. On the other hand, I believe that Christianity has preserved a key which Judaism has been missing for almost two thousand years: The Messiah.

Regrettably, the Messiah has been obscured by layers of paganism and tradition and other clear errors which have distracted the Jews from the true identity of their Messiah.

Both groups hold a key to the restoration of the true worship of the Creator yet there exists a barrier between the two which seemingly cannot be bridged.[113] This barrier originated thousands of years ago, and was literally a wall of separation around the Temple which prohibited Gentiles from passing "under penalty of death." The Gentiles were not permitted to go as close as the Yisraelites which, in essence, kept them away from the Elohim of Yisrael. It sent a clear and resounding message to the Gentiles that they were "unclean" and not as privileged in the eyes of Elohim. They were treated as second class, which is absolutely contrary to the teaching of the Torah.

The primary reason why Yisrael was "chosen" was to shine as a light to the Gentiles and draw all men to Elohim. Sadly, those Gentiles who were drawn to Elohim and His House, were then treated as inferior to the Yisraelites and were prohibited from approaching and worshipping Elohim in the same fashion as the Yisraelites - under penalty of death.

This was one of the primary issues that the Talmudim of Yahushua had to contend with and it is a problem which continues to this day. Both Judaism and Christianity act as if they are "members only" clubs. What neither seems to realize is that there are not two different religions which YHWH established and He does not have two separate and distinct Households. YHWH does not promote Judeo-Christian values – He has His values, His commandments, His Torah – His Way.

One of the great problems as I see it, after

considering the hearts of men, is the use of semantics. Words are often used and misused in such a way as to create division. One of the greatest examples is the word "Jew." The term Jew first appears in the King James Translation of the Scriptures at 2 Melakim 16:6 which states: "*At that time Rezin king of Syria recovered Elath to Syria, and drove the Jews from Elath: and the Syrians came to Elath, and dwelt there unto this day.*"

The New American Standard uses the word "Judeans" and the NIV and NKJV use the phrase "men of Judah." Clearly, this passage was referring to people that resided in a particular geographical area known as Judea. The region known as Judea consisted of the Tribes of Benjamin and the Tribes of Yahudah and those that lived in Judea were often collectively referred to as Yahudim or "Jews," even though they consisted of more than just the Tribe of Yahudah. Remember that the Levites moved to the South after Jereboam set up pagan worship in the North. They were also accompanied by some from the Northern Tribes.

The English translation of the book of Esther was filled with the term "Jew" because the tribes that were exiled to Babylon were from the House of Yahudah or the Kingdom of Yahudah, which was located in Judea. Therefore, these exiles were referred to as Yahudim, which developed into the word Jews.

Look at the following passage from the New International Version which demonstrates this point. "*⁵ Now there was in the citadel of Susa a Jew of the tribe of Benjamin, named Mordecai son of Jair, the son of Shimei, the son of Kish, ⁶ who had been carried into exile from Jerusalem by Nebuchadnezzar king of Babylon, among those taken captive*

with Jehoiachin king of Judah." Esther 2:5-6 NIV. Mordecai was from the Tribe of Benjamin and was taken captive from his home in Judea, thus making him a Judean, or as has been translated, a Jew.

Since the House of Yisrael had effectively vanished as an identifiable people, the Yahudim began to be the ones who represented the descendants of Avraham, Yistahq and Yaakov – the people of the Covenant known as Yisraelites. Today, the word Jew is used in a very broad sense which causes much confusion concerning the identity of the Redeemed of YHWH – Yisrael.

The word "Jew" is now used to describe anyone who traces their lineage back to Yisrael. As a result, it is often being applied incorrectly to identify someone according to their genetic heritage beyond the Tribe of Yahudah. Now the word is used to describe a member of any of the twelve tribes. It is important to recognize that neither Adam, Noah, Avraham, Yitshaq, Yaakov or Mosheh were Jews. The first Jew was Yahudah, the son of Yisrael. His progeny and their companions could be considered to be of the Tribe of Yahudah making them Jews, but not the rest of Yisrael.

After the division of the Kingdoms, the label "Yahudah" was expanded to encompass all of the Tribes in the South or those who lived in the geographic region of Judea. When the Northern Tribes were exiled, the term "Jew" was eventually expanded further to describe all of Yisrael.

Beyond the genetic and geographic aspects of the term "Jew" it is also used as a religious label. In modern times it is used to describe a person according to their religious affiliation. In other words a Jew can be someone

who subscribes to the religion of Judaism.

The expansion of the definition of the word "Jew" is not authentic and often causes confusion – especially to someone that desires to enter into the Covenant with YHWH. Some who want to join with Yisrael incorrectly believe that they must join with Yahudah and subscribe to the religion of Rabbinic Judaism, which is simply an expansion of the Pharasaic sect.

This confusion is perpetuated by the fact that most Jews incorrectly refer to everyone outside of Judaism as a Gentile. Again, this is incorrect because it is basically indicating that anyone who does not subscribe to the religion of Judaism is a heathen.

I hope that it is clear how important it is that we correctly understand the Scriptural meaning of words. Just as the use of the words "Jew" and "Gentile" have been used to create division, the use of the word "Church" has added to the problem. Christianity has developed the notion of "The Church" as being a new set apart Assembly which is somehow different from the Assembly of YHWH that He calls Yisrael.

As long as people continue to use the terms "Church" and Yisrael as mutually exclusive groups, you are always going to have division and people will run into confusion when attempting to interpret the Scriptures.

The word "church" is not found anywhere in the Hebrew or Greek manuscripts of the Scriptures. It is a man made word which has been inserted into the English translations of the "New Testament" whenever they refer to the set apart Assembly of YHWH described in Greek as the "ekklesia" and in Hebrew as the "qahal." Many read about this entity "the Church" in the "New

Testament" which does not appear in the Tanak and they understandably assume that it must be something new.

Christianity uses the word "church" in a variety of contexts. Christians often refer to "the Church" as a whole; consisting of both living and non-living believers. The Church is often used in conjunction with "the Bride of Christ." It can mean an individual body of Believers in a country, state or other geographical entity. It is also often used to refer to a building where Believers assemble.

So where does this word church come from? It does not appear once in the Tanak and yet when you look in the "New Testament" it is found throughout the English text. Probably the most frequently quoted passage concerning the establishment of "the Church" is when Yahushua told Kepha: "*Upon this rock I will build my church.*" Mattityahu 16:18. He was referring, of course, to the revelation which Kepha spoke regarding His Messiahship and He actually declared that upon that truth His House of Prayer (הפלתי בית) would be built.

Yahushua never said the word "church" because it did not exist when He spoke those memorable words to Kepha. You will only read the word "church" in an English translation, not a Hebrew or Greek manuscript of Mattityahu.[114] The only other reference in the Gospels which attributes the word church to Yahushua is also found in Mattityahu as follows: "*And if he shall neglect to hear them, tell it unto the church: but if he neglect to hear the church, let him be unto thee as an heathen man and a publican.*" Mattityahu 18:17 KJV.

Again, a review of the Hebrew text reveals that Yahushua did not say the word "church" but rather qahal (קהל) which is the same word used throughout the Tanak

to describe Yisrael as a set apart Assembly or congregation. Yahushua was advising people to take their dispute to the Assembly – not the Christian Church or local church building on the corner – neither of which existed when He made that statement.

This point becomes even clearer when we look at the Septuagint,[115] which is the Greek translation of the Tanak. In the Septuagint we see that the word "ekklesia" was used in place of the Hebrew word "qahal." So the Greek work "ekklesia" was considered to mean the same thing as the Hebrew "qahal" and they almost always were used to refer to the set apart Assembly of Yisrael.

The Greek word ekklesia (εκκλεσια) derives from a compound of ek; a primary preposition denoting origin, from, out (of place, time, or cause; literal or figurative; direct or remote) and a derivative of kaleo; to "call." The word ekklesia is a "calling out" or rather "a called out assembly." Therefore what is traditionally translated as "church" should actually be translated "called out assembly" or "called out congregation."

According to Fausset's Bible Dictionary the word "church" comes from the Greek kuriakee (κυριακεε) - 'House of the lord' - a word which passed to the Gothic tongue. The Goths being the first of the northern hordes converted to Christianity, adopted the word from the Greek Christians of Constantinople, and so it came to us Anglo-Saxons. (Trench, Study of Words).

In fact, the word derives from "circus" or "kirk," which means "circle," because the oldest temples, as with the Druids, were circular in form. So then the word

"church" is actually reminiscent of pagan temples.

Further "Ekklesia in the New Testament never means the building or House of assembly, because church buildings were built long after the apostolic age. It means an organized body, whose unity does not depend on its being met together in one place; not an assemblage of atoms, but members in their several places united to the One Head, [Messiah] and forming one organic living whole (1 Corinthians 12)."[116] In other words, "ekklesia," referred to the set apart body of believers - the community of faith.

The early believers met in private houses at the House of YHWH in Jerusalem or at the synagogue. The word "synagogue" is really just a Greek word for a place of gathering. Some find this word to be crude and cold and prefer to use "shul" which is a Yiddish word that represents the house of worship as a place of prayer and study.

It is important to remember that there is only one House of YHWH and the bottom line is that there is no such thing as a Church which is separate from Yisrael. There is only one Kingdom and there is only one Assembly of Redeemed which is still called Yisrael. This is where it gets complicated because we currently have a nation called Israel that has been formed under incredible circumstances but has not been restored according to Scriptural precedent.

15

The Modern State of Israel

Today we have maps that show Israel where they formerly described Palestine over 60 years ago. A sovereign  nation was established after being non-existent for thousands of years. This appears to be an undeniable miracle - So how then do we view the modern State of Israel? The Evangelical Christian movement sees this as none other than a fulfillment of prophecies concerning Yisrael. No doubt, the formation of the current Nation of Israel is an incredible event, but it is also unique from any other historical return or restoration that we read about in the Sciptures.

In 1947 the United Nations General Assembly approved a plan to terminate the British Mandate which would facilite the creation of a "Jewish" State by 1948 in what was formerly called Palestine. The Nation of Israel thereafter declared independence on May 14, 1948, the day that the British Mandate expired and a nation was seemingly "born at once." (see Yeshayuhu 66:8).

As a result, some give the date 1948 great weight

when considering prophecy and the end times. In fact, many use this date to project future prophetic fulfillment. This typically leads to problems because 1948 is simply a date on a pagan calendar and it is not necessarily a significant date on the Scriptural calendar.[117]

I do not believe that it is within the authority of the United Nations, or any other organization for that matter, to declare whether or not the Yahudim can form a sovereign nation. YHWH promised the Land to the seed of Avraham and Sarah. He has punished the various tribes of Yisrael and only He can determine when  their punishment is complete and when restoration can occur. The United Nations has no legal significance in the eyes of YHWH and that "ungodly" organization has no authority to establish any part of YHWH's kingdom. Therefore, I do not automatically assume that the date 1948 is as significant as some believe.

Still others look to 1967 as another pivotal date because it was when the Jewish State gained control of Jerusalem. As with the date 1948 – 1967 is also just a date on a pagan calendar. Further, Israel never actually fully regained control of Jerusalem because they failed to rebuild the altar or the House of YHWH. The Mountain of YHWH, also known as the House of YHWH, is a critical part of Jerusalem and restoration. Accordingly, while many people try to use these dates as fulfillment of prophecy I am hesitant to follow suit.

Again, I do not believe that it is up to the United Nations to "rubber stamp" the existence of Israel. Interestingly, some Orthodox Jewish groups have declared that the nation is a violation of the Torah because the Messiah was not the One to establish this state.[118]

Most of Christianity has assumed that because a portion of some of the tribes have returned to the Land that this must be the Hand of YHWH and the fulfillment of prophecy, but the question must be asked: Does what began as  a Zionist movement equate to a repentant remnant? This is the question that many have struggled with for decades since the inception of the modern State of Israel.

The reason is because many of the founders of the modern State of Israel were Zionists. The Zionist movement is a political secular movement which fundamentally seeks to establish and maintain an independent "Jewish State" in the location commonly referred to as Palestine.[119] As a result, the name of the Nation of Israel might have better been named Judah or Yahudah, since the nation predominately consists of the descendants of adherents to Rabbinic Judaism.

The Modern State of Israel is, in essence, a country established by the House of Yahudah which currently makes up most of the recognizable tribes of Yisrael. Just as a remnant of the northern tribes intermingled with Yahudah in the past, so the same may hold true to this day, but that does not change the fact that we are dealing with the House of Yahudah.[120] Calling it the nation of Yahudah

might have dissipated some of the confusion surrounding the issue.

Zionism is a political movement which has fought to establish a sovereign nation primarily based upon race, but it is not pursuing YHWH wholeheartedly according to the Scriptures. YHWH is clearly not central to the Nation of Israel, which is predominantly secular, and the Torah is not the foundation of the legal system. While there are some aspects of the Torah engrained within the culture, such as the Sabbath and the dietary instructions, the Torah is not enforced as the "Law" of the Land. Further, the State of Israel is not a kingdom, but rather a parliamentary democracy.

Therefore, just because the current State of Israel calls itself "Israel" does not mean that it is the Yisrael that we read of in the Scriptures – which consists of all of the Redeemed of YHWH. While a group of genetic offspring of various tribes of Yisrael have returned to the Land, the majority have done so for reasons not entirely consistent with the type of restoration seen in the Scriptures.

Also, there are many citizens of this fledgling nation who do not descend from Yisrael at all. They derive from a variety of other tribes, cultures, races, languages and religions and they do not recognize or obey the commandments of YHWH - this is not acceptable according to the Torah. This is why the Scriptures, in a prophecy referring to our current time, call Jerusalem "Sodom and Egypt." Revelation 11:8.

Amazingly, it is now possible to have a person call themselves an Israelite that is a Muslim and worships Allah. In fact, at the time of writing this book sixteen percent of the population of this Jewish State are Muslim. In the

modern State of Israel you can also have an Israelite that believes in no god at all.

These are impossibilities, in a Scriptural sense, since a true Yisraelite is one that worships and obeys the Elohim of Yisrael – YHWH. Unless this nation is eventually restored to the Torah and its citizens live and worship in accordance with the Torah, they are not and cannot be Yisrael, despite what they call themselves.

I think that the most significant precedent in the Scriptures for what we are observing today is the restoration under Zerubbabel, Ezra and Nehemiah. The Hebrew name Zerubbabel (זרבבל) means: "sown in Babylon." As was mentioned previously, Zerubbabel was a prince of Yahudah and he was one of the first to return to Jerusalem to rebuild the altar and the Temple. He also helped restore the priestly service and reestablish the sacrificial system.

Ezra was a priest who was in exile and returned to the Land after Zerubbabel. The name Ezra (עזרה) means "help" and may be a shortened form of Azariyah (עזריה) which means "Yah has helped." Nehemiah was a Hebrew official who was part of the Babylonian exile. His name is properly pronounced Nehemyah (נחמיה) and means "comforted by Yah." He followed Zerubbabel and Ezra in a later return to the Land.

These three men, as well as many others, were used by YHWH after both the House of Yisrael and the House of Yahudah had been exiled from the Land. All of them heard the call to return and rebuild what had been destroyed by Nebuchadnezzar. They each returned at different times with a remnant of Yahudim and they each played a unique role in partially restoring the House of

Yahudah to the Land.

Upon their return they found the Land in ruins. The walls of Jerusalem had been torn down, the gates were burned and the House of YHWH destroyed. Their brethren, the House of Yisrael had been scattered and remained lost in exile. The Yahudim that were present in the Land were sometimes hostile to the returning exiles.

When Nehemyah heard about the condition of Jerusalem and his people in 444 B.C.E. he wept, fasted, and prayed. Nehemyah desired to help restore his people back to their Land and to restore the worship of their Elohim.

The Scriptures record the following prayer uttered by him: "⁵ *I pray, YHWH Elohim of heaven, O great and awesome Elohim,* <u>*You who keep Your Covenant and mercy with those who love You and observe Your commandments,*</u> ⁶ *please let Your ear be attentive and Your eyes open, that You may hear the prayer of Your servant which I pray before You now, day and night, for the children of Yisrael Your servants, and confess the sins of the children of Yisrael which we have sinned against You. Both my father's House and I have sinned.* ⁷ <u>*We have acted very corruptly against You, and have not kept the commandments, the statutes, nor the ordinances which You commanded Your servant Mosheh.*</u> ⁸ *Remember, I pray, the word that You commanded Your servant Mosheh, saying,* <u>*If you are unfaithful, I will scatter you among the nations;*</u> ⁹ <u>*but if you return to Me, and keep My commandments and do them, though some of you were cast out to the farthest part of the heavens, yet I will gather them from there, and bring them to the place which I have chosen as a dwelling for My Name.*</u> ¹⁰ *Now these are Your servants and Your people, whom You have redeemed by Your great power, and by Your strong hand.* ¹¹ *O YHWH, I pray, please let Your ear be attentive to the prayer of Your*

servant, and to the prayer of Your servants who desire to fear Your Name; and let Your servant prosper this day, I pray, and grant him mercy in the sight of this man. For I was the king's cupbearer." Nehemyah 1:5-11.

The prayer of Nehemyah is significant because it provides the outline of a prayer that gets heard by the Creator. First of all Nehemyah identifies by Name the One to Whom he is praying - YHWH. Next, he speaks of the Covenant which was made between the Creator and Yisrael and he specifically addresses YHWH as: "*You Who keep Your Covenant and mercy with **those who love You and observe Your commandments**.*" This sounds very inclusive and contrary to the predominate position in Judaism that the Torah is only for the Jews.

Nehemyah confessed not only his sins, but the sins of his fathers. He acknowledged that those sins had consequences pursuant to the Covenant, but he also remembered the promises that were contained within the Covenant. The promises were contingent upon returning to the Creator by keeping and obeying His commands.

Nehemyah asks that the prayer of "*those who desire to fear the Name*" of the Creator be heard. This prayer shows the heart of someone who confessed his sins, repented from his transgressions and desired to be restored to the Creator. This is a Hebrew praying, but it sounds an awful lot like a Christian prayer.

Repentance is heavily emphasized in Christianity for salvation, but it is not a Christian concept, and to recognize this we need only to look to the prophets. "[19] *Therefore this is what YHWH says: 'If you repent, I will restore you that you may serve Me; if you utter worthy, not worthless, words, you will be My spokesman. Let this people*

turn to you, but you must not turn to them. *²⁰ I will make you a wall to this people, a fortified wall of bronze; they will fight against you but will not overcome you, for I am with you to rescue and save you,' declares YHWH. ²¹ 'I will save you from the hands of the wicked and redeem you from the grasp of the cruel.'"* Yirmeyahu 15:19-21.

Yehezqel also speaks of repentance: *"⁶ Therefore say to the House of Yisrael, Thus says YHWH Elohim: Repent, turn away from your idols, and turn your faces away from all your abominations. ⁷ For anyone of the House of Yisrael, or of the strangers who dwell in Yisrael, who separates himself from Me and sets up his idols in his heart and puts before him what causes him to stumble into iniquity, then comes to a prophet to inquire of him concerning Me, I YHWH will answer him by Myself.⁸ I will set My face against that man and make him a sign and a proverb, and I will cut him off from the midst of My people. Then you shall know that I am YHWH.'"* Yehezqel 14:6-8.

Notice that He is speaking to the House of Yisrael <u>and</u> the strangers who dwell with them. This simply confirms the fact that Elohim's promises are available to anyone who wants to dwell with Him. Many who desire to follow YHWH get confused when they read the prophets because they are not sure how the prophecies apply to them - if at all. The answer is simple: if you are born into the Covenant or take hold of a covenant, it applies to you.

Yehezqel goes on to give some advice regarding repentance to the House of Yisrael by stating: *"³⁰ Therefore I will judge you, O House of Yisrael, every one according to his ways, says YHWH Elohim. Repent, and turn from all your transgressions, so that iniquity will not be your ruin. ³¹ Cast away from you all the transgressions which you have committed,*

and get yourselves a new heart and a new spirit. For why should you die, O House of Yisrael? ³² *For I have no pleasure in the death of one who dies, says YHWH Elohim. Therefore turn and live!"* Yehezqel 18:30-32.

Nehemyah recognized the need for change, he confessed his transgression and resolved himself to turn back to Elohim, to guard His commandments and to do them. Nehemyah's prayer was heard and he received favor from his sovereign and was permitted to return to the Land to rebuild. This restoration started with the House of Yahudah and consisted of a physical restoration of Jerusalem.

Zerubbabbel and the remnant that returned with him rebuilt the altar and the House of YHWH. Ezra and Nehemyah followed and they helped to rebuild the walls of the city. They then set up the doors and appointed gatekeepers. The walls and gates are for a defense - the remnant needed to defend themselves. Things were set in order, singers and priests were appointed and proper worship was restored.

Things were not easy, the remnant was surrounded by enemies. While they worked they were threatened, but they called upon their Elohim. They worked together and they worked hard. Some built while others defended. Even the builders were involved in the defense, they bore a load with one hand and a weapon in the other.

False prophets were sent and gave false prophecies intended to spread fear because they were hirelings sent by the enemy. (Nehemyah 6:12-13). Regardless, the people stayed focused on their goal and true to their task. They did not listen to the lies of the enemy nor did they get discouraged. They persevered and completed the work.

In some ways this sounds a lot like the Modern State of Israel which currently consists of a remnant of those who were scattered abroad. They have worked hard for decades to rebuild and defend their cities and their newly formed nation. Just as Zerubbabel, Nehemyah and Ezra received permission from Persian Kings to return and rebuild, so too, the modern State of Israel received "permission" from the United Nations to return and rebuild. The big difference with Zerubbabel, Nehemyah and Ezra was that their primary goal was to rebuild "The House of YHWH" and rebuild Jerusalem so that they could worship.

Sadly, the modern State of Israel is largely a secular state - polls have shown that the vast majority of the population is not "religious." The motivation of most of their founders was not so much to rebuild so that they could worship - if that were the case they would have rebuilt the House of YHWH decades ago.

To the contrary, the driving force was Zionism - a secular movement designed to establish a land that Jews could call their own, free from the persecution and slaughter that they had experienced for centuries. This was a noble and worthy goal, but not the same focus as Zerubbabel, Nehemyah and Ezra.

This is not to say that none of the nation's founders were motivated by their religious convictions. I am simply stating that the Torah was not necessarily at the foundation of Zionism. In fact, there was a point when one of the great founders of Zionism, Theodor Herzl, actually considered founding the State of Israel in

South America or Uganda. To some early Zionists, the actual Promised Land was not even a requisite to their founding of a Zionist Nation. This original disconnect between Zionism and the Promised Land is quite revealing.

In some instances, Zionism has actually become a religion of sorts. According to Yisrael Harel, one of the most respected of the settler movement's political commentators: "Zionism, including the religious brand, never relied on miracles. It created them . . . That is how we produced the solutions to our greatest difficulties. But that was when we still had faith in our capabilities and the justice of our cause."[121]

There is no question that the Promised Land should be settled, but it should be settled by <u>all of the tribes</u> in <u>all of the Land</u> promised to Avraham <u>and only by those who follow and obey the instructions of YHWH.</u>

This has not been the case with the modern State of Israel which is not committed to the Torah, which has and continues to give away Covenant Land and prohibits Believers from living in the Land if they do not meet their unscriptural criteria for citizenship. The cost of living is very high and many of the people are living in poverty and on credit. The country itself relies heavily on billions of dollars in foreign aid each year – this is not the prosperity which  was promised to Yisrael when they are regathered.[122]

While the recent return of the Yahudim was miraculous and no doubt aided or permitted by YHWH,

it cannot be considered a complete restoration. It appears that miracles occurred when these founders went about doing the things which they were intended to do – fight for the Land and work the Land. Sadly, those miracles seem to be disipating as they now give away the Land that their people fought and died to regain.

The Modern State of Israel is not obeying the Torah and until the nation turns to YHWH wholeheartedly, they will not see the restoration, the peace and the prosperity promised within the Scriptures. Their continuing suffering will not bring about the blessings of Elohim - only their obedience will.

One of the most significant portions of the Book of Nehemyah which relates with this generation reads as follows: "*¹ And when the seventh month came, the children of Yisrael were in their cities. <u>And all the people gathered together as one man</u> in the open square that was in front of the Water Gate; and they told Ezra the scribe to bring the Scroll of the Torah, which YHWH had commanded Yisrael.² So Ezra the priest brought the Torah before the assembly of men and women and all who could hear with understanding on the first day of the seventh month. ³ <u>Then he read from it in the open square that was in front of the Water Gate from morning until midday, before the men and women and those who could understand; and the ears of all the people were attentive to the Torah Scroll.</u> ⁴ So Ezra the scribe stood on a platform of wood which they had made for the purpose; and beside him, at his right hand, stood Mattithiah, Shema, Anaiah, Uriyah, Hilkiyah, and Maaseiyah; and at his left hand Pedaiyah, Mishael, Malchiyah, Hashum, Hashbadana, Zecharyah, and Meshullam.⁵ And Ezra opened the Scroll in the sight of all the people, for he was standing above all the people; <u>and when he opened it, all the people stood up.</u>*

6 And Ezra blessed YHWH, the great Elohim. Then all the people answered, Amen, Amen! while lifting up their hands. And they bowed their heads and worshiped YHWH with their faces to the ground. 7 Also Yahushua, Bani, Sherebiyah, Jamin, Akkub, Shabbethai, Hodiyah, Maaseiyah, Kelita, Azariyah, Yozabad, Hanan, Pelaiyah, and the Levites, helped the people to understand the Torah; and the people stood in their place. 8 So they read distinctly from the Scroll, in the Torah of Elohim; and they gave the sense, and helped them to understand the reading." Nehemyah 8:1-9.

There is much that we can glean from this passage. To begin with, the passage mentions the time that the people assembled - at the beginning of the seventh month. This was likely the Appointed Time of YHWH known as "The Day of Trumpets" or "Yom Teruah" (יום תרועה) in Hebrew.[123] This was a High Sabbath, a set apart gathering which occurred on the first day of the seventh month. The priests not only read the Word, but they taught the people and helped them to understand the Word. The Word would have been read in Hebrew and many people did not understand the language.

The Hebrew word meturgam (מתרגם) means "translator" and there were those who would translate the Torah as it was read. This was common after the exile when people spoke different languages from the countries which they had been dispersed. I believe that this is a critical point for this generation. Many people read the Word, but they do not necessarily understand what the Word is saying because of the language barrier as well as inherited customs, traditions and doctrines which conflict with the Torah and cloud their understanding. They need a correct translation and instruction to properly understand

the Word.

Now let us continue with this important lesson from Nehemyah: "*9 And Nehemyah, who was the governor, Ezra the priest and scribe, and the Levites who taught the people said to all the people, 'This day is set apart to YHWH your Elohim; do not mourn nor weep.' For **all the people wept, when they heard the words of the Torah.** 10 Then he said to them, 'Go your way, eat the fat, drink the sweet, and send portions to those for whom nothing is prepared; for this day is set apart to our Master. Do not sorrow, for the joy of YHWH is your strength.' 11 So the Levites quieted all the people, saying, 'Be still, for the day is set apart; do not be grieved.' 12 And all the people went their way to eat and drink, to send portions and rejoice greatly, because they understood the words that were declared to them.*" Nehemyah 8:9-12.

The fact that the people wept means that it had significance to them. It penetrated their hearts and impacted their lives. The Levites gave instruction on how to respond to the Word. They taught them about the Appointed Time and they instructed the people to celebrate the set apart day.[124]

I am certain that everybody was in awe at what just occurred, so the next day all the elders, priests, and Levites gathered with Ezra to study the Torah. "*14 And they found written in the Torah, which YHWH had commanded by Mosheh, that the children of Yisrael should dwell in booths during the feast of the seventh month, 15 and that they should announce and proclaim in all their cities and in Jerusalem, saying, 'Go out to the mountain, and bring olive branches, branches of olive trees, myrtle branches, palm branches, and branches of leafy trees, to make booths, as it is written.' 16 Then the people went out and brought them and made themselves booths, each one on the roof*

of his House, or in their courtyards or the courts of the House of Elohim, and in the open square of the Water Gate and in the open square of the Gate of Ephraim.[17] *So the whole assembly of those who had returned from the captivity made booths and sat under the booths; for since the days of Yahushua the son of Nun until that day the children of Yisrael had not done so. And there was very great gladness.[18] Also day by day, from the first day until the last day, he read from the Scroll of the Torah of Elohim.* And they kept the feast seven days; and on the eighth day there was a sacred assembly, according to the prescribed manner." Nehemyah 8:14-18.

This was a powerful event and all of the people learned about another Appointed Time known as Succot (סכות) or "The Feast of Booths." This is a very special time when people are instructed to go up to Jerusalem and dwell in succas, also known as booths or mangers. These are temporary structures intended to remind the children of Yisrael of when they sojourned in the wilderness. (Vayiqra 23:33).[125]

The Scriptures provide that Yahushua died at the age of 110 (Yahushua 24:29) around the year 1380 B.C.E. Therefore, over nine centuries (936 years) had elapsed since the children of Yisrael had kept the Feast in such fashion. There is no specific mention that they observed the Day of Atonement better known as Yom Kippur (יום הכפר) which falls on the tenth day of the seventh month. (Vayiqra 23:27). They likely did, since their hearts were properly prepared and they were clearly set to obey.

The Appointed Times which occur in the seventh month are extremely significant, especially in the days to come. Succot, which is also called "The Feast of Tabernacles," has prophetic significance for the end times

and just as those of the remnant started celebrating this Feast once they read about it – the same thing is occurring today. Many are beginning to learn about the Appointed Times and they are celebrating them, sometimes without knowing anything about them - they are simply acting out of obedience.

These special times do not belong to any particular religion or ethnic group, they are YHWH's (Vayiqra 23:2) and they are for all those who worship and desire to obey the Elohim of Yisrael.[126] Sadly, in the modern State of Isreal, they are celebrated by most, more as national holidays than as a religious Holy Days.

What we read about in this passage involving Nehemyah and Ezra was at the conclusion of a sabbatical year because it appears that the entire Torah was read to the Assembly during the Feast. This was commanded to be done every seven years. *"[10] At the end of every seven years, at the Appointed Time in the year of release, at the Feast of Tabernacles, [11] when all Yisrael comes to appear before YHWH your Elohim in the place which He chooses, you shall read this Torah before all Yisrael in their hearing. [12] Gather the people together, men and women and little ones, and the stranger who is within your gates, that they may hear and that they may learn to fear YHWH your Elohim and carefully observe all the words of this Torah, [13] and that their children, who have not known it, may hear and learn to fear YHWH your Elohim as long as you live in the Land which you cross the Yarden to possess."* Devarim 31:10-13.

Notice that it was not just the descendants of Yisrael that were to hear, learn, fear, and obey, but also the stranger who is within their gates, which means a person not of natural descent that chooses to dwell with Yisrael.

We see this time and time again - YHWH intended all people to know Him and obey His Torah, not just native Yisraelites.

The pattern that we see with Zerubbabel, Ezra and Nehemyah is critical. They and those who accompanied them rebuilt the altar and the House of YHWH. They studied and read the Torah and they wept because they understood that they had lost something. Through reading the Scriptures they saw that they had forgotten the Appointed Times and commandments of their Elohim. Their immediate response was to obey. They did not necessarily realize how or why they were doing certain things, they simply obeyed.

According to Ezra, when they fell into transgression by taking foreign wives their response was to acknowledge their trespass. They prayed, confessed, and again, they wept. They then made a covenant with Elohim to put away their foreign wives - which they did. (Ezra 10:1-4). They were serious in their commitment to obey YHWH and their words resonate from the past: *"Let it be done according to the Torah. Arise, for the matter is upon you . . . Be strong and act."* Ezra 10:3-4.

Be strong and act! This is the message to the remnant during this present age. This is the necessary attitude for the Redeemed to dwell in the Land. Just as Zerubbabel, Nehemyah and Ezra heard the call to return, restore, and rebuild, so too are many throughout the world hearing a call to return, restore, and rebuild.

As can plainly be seen, the major elements of this Scriptural example of restoration are lacking in the present day State of Israel. The Torah, rebuilding the House of YHWH and establishment of Torah based worship have not been the primary goal of modern Israel.

In fact, it is very likely that the Israeli Army could have regained the Temple Mount in 1967, but chose not to

 – the same holds true with the cave of Machpelah in Hebron. It appears that while the Army was prepared to fight for a homeland they either did not want these Holy sites or they did not know what to do with them.

If Israel were truly restored to the Land in 1948 then that would mean they have been back for over half of a century. The Scriptures clearly mandate that the Land is to have a Sabbath rest every seven years. To date, the Land has never completely had a Sabbath rest since the establishment of modern Yisrael.[127]

This creates quite an ironic and difficult situation because one of the reasons that the House of Yahudah was previously expelled from the Land was due to their failure to obey the command concerning the Sabbath rest for the Land. Their exile actually accomplished the requisite years of rest for the Land. (2 Chronicles 36:22).

If the State of Israel that we currently see in existence were, in fact, the fully restored Commonwealth of Yisrael, then they would have to be expelled for their disobedience. The simple fact is that this modern State is not a complete restoration and currently, most people do not even know the correct Shemittah year. So even

if they wanted to obey, which is questionable, YHWH would not punish them for disobeying something that they could not obey. He will first send His prophets which are anticipated in Jerusalem soon. (Revelation 11; see also Zekaryah 4).

Make no mistake though - YHWH is not giving the modern State of Israel a special exemption or a free pass. I sense that certain people feel that Israel's current condition is so tenuous that YHWH has suspended His commandments for the time being because He is just so happy to have His people back in the Land. A review of history reveals that this is not how He operates. While He may delay judgment for a time, He always keeps His Word.

There is currently paganism and idolatry running rampant in modern day Israel. False worship has not been purged from the Land. In fact, false religions are flourishing and mosques are being erected all around the Land. It is hard to look at the landscape of a populated area without seeing a minaret attached to a mosque and you can barely escape the wailing of the call to prayer from one of these minarets every morning, afternoon, evening and night as the name of Allah is proclaimed and exalted throughout the Land. These are abominations to YHWH which the State of Israel allows the Muslims to continue and propagate.

Instead of tearing down and destroying idols and abominations, archaeologists are actually repairing and setting up fallen sun pillars in direct contravention to the Torah. Many of the leaders have been corrupted and Tel

Aviv has become a veritable Sodom and Gomorah. Alcohol, drug abuse and sexual immorality are rampant. The youth of the Land are empty, lost and in rebellion. There was even a "Rave" party in Eilat years ago where the revelers set up a golden calf and danced around it all night long.

The government has established the "right of return," but only for people who can establish that they are "Jewish" through their mother, which is contrary to Scriptural precedent. The government actively refuses residency to those who believe that Yahushua is the Messiah, specifically targeting these people, while allowing others to become residents who believe in false messiahs, no messiah or have no faith whatsoever.

I could go on, but the point should be clear. It is not my intent to vilify modern Israelites but there is great responsibility that comes with living in the Covenant Land. The citizens of modern Israel apparently want to live in the Land, but they do not want the responsibilities associated with living in the Land. They want to live in peace without obeying the Torah. This is not possible because this is not a true and complete restoration.

While we used the restoration of Zerubbabel, Ezra and Nehemiah as an example - even that restoration was only temporary. Despite all of their efforts, the Golden years of the reign of King David were never again experienced in the Land. Centuries later, the Messiah came and they rejected Him, only to see their rebuilt Temple destroyed and the city of Jerusalem leveled.

Now that Yahudah is back in the Land they have a

choice to make and they must make it soon. We know that in the future, the House of Yahudah will be in the Land surrounded by their enemies and YHWH will *"watch over the House of Yahudah"* and *"defend the inhabitants of Jerusalem."* (Zekaryah 12:2-8).

Maybe through this process, when they are forced to place their trust and faith in YHWH, rather than their own military might, Yahudah's eyes will be opened and they will turn wholeheartedly to YHWH. It is then likely that the House of Yahudah will understand that their calling goes beyond mere Zionism. At that point, when they see the Hand of YHWH, they will accept their brethren from the House of Yisrael and welcome their return to the Land.

16

The Great Regathering

The Torah provides instruction, examples and patterns for the Redeemed so that they can learn from the mistakes of their predecessors. This is to help them avoid the curses of disobedience and prepare them to receive the blessings of obedience.

Shaul aptly states this principle in his letter to the Corinthians: *"¹ Moreover, brethren, I do not want you to be unaware that all our fathers were under the cloud, all passed through the sea, ² all were immersed into Mosheh in the cloud and in the sea, ³ all ate the same spiritual food, ⁴ and all drank the same spiritual drink. For they drank of that spiritual Rock that followed them, and that Rock was Messiah. ⁵ But with most of them Elohim was not well pleased, for their bodies were scattered in the wilderness. ⁶ Now these things became our examples, to the intent that we should not lust after evil things as they also lusted. ⁷ And do not become idolaters as were some of them. As it is written, 'The people sat down to eat and drink, and rose up to play.' ⁸ Nor let us commit sexual immorality, as some of them did, and in one day twenty-three thousand fell; ⁹ nor let us tempt Messiah, as some of them also tempted, and were destroyed by serpents; ¹⁰ nor complain, as some of them also complained, and were destroyed by the destroyer. ¹¹ Now all these things happened*

to them as examples, and they were written for our admonition, upon whom the ends of the ages have come." 1 Corinthians 10:1-11.

What we read in the Scriptures is not just a compilation of interesting and exciting tales written for our entertainment. Rather, the events that happened to the Patriarchs and Yisrael were specifically meant to provide examples and patterns for our benefit. These were given to us so that we can learn because they will be repeated, including the Exodus.

We have reviewed many Scriptures concerning the return of the outcasts of Yisrael. There are many more which confirm that the plan of YHWH is to restore the House of Yisrael when Messiah comes to rule and reign over the Earth.

"*9 For surely I will command, and will sift the House of Yisrael among all nations, as grain is sifted in a sieve; yet not the smallest grain shall fall to the ground. 10 All the sinners of My people shall die by the sword, who say, 'the calamity shall not overtake nor confront us.' 11 On that day I will raise up the tabernacle (succa) of David, which has fallen down, and repair its damages; I will raise up its ruins, and rebuild it as in the days of old; 12 That they may possess the remnant of Edom, and all the Goyim who are called by My Name, says YHWH who does this thing. 13 Behold, the days are coming, says YHWH, when the plowman shall overtake the reaper, and the treader of grapes him who sows seed; the mountains shall drip with sweet wine, and all the hills shall flow with it. 14 I will bring back the captives of My people Yisrael; they shall build the waste cities and inhabit them; they shall plant vineyards and drink wine from them; they shall also make gardens and eat fruit from them. 15 I will plant them in their Land, and no longer shall they be pulled up from the Land I have given them, says YHWH your Elohim.*" Amos 9:9-15.

So we see that the House of Yisrael was exiled among the nations. There will come a day when they will be sifted from among those nations. As was previously mentioned, sifting occurs during and after a harvest on a threshing floor. In another Messianic reference we are told that YHWH will raise up the tabernacle or rather *"succa of David."* We know that a succa is raised up during the Appointed Time of Succot. So it appears that the Messiah will be returning to pitch His succa and dwell with mankind around that time – the final harvesting of the Earth. He will likely raise up His succa on the threshing floor purchased by David.

There are currently people teaching against this future regathering. As a result, they are keeping the Redeemed, who are often referred to as the sheep, from returning to the fold. The prophet Yirmeyahu has a severe warning for these shepherds who are keeping the sheep apart. *"¹ 'Woe to the shepherds who are destroying and*  *scattering the sheep of my pasture!' declares YHWH. ² Therefore this is what YHWH, the Elohim of Yisrael, says to the shepherds who tend my people: 'Because you have scattered my flock and driven them away and have not bestowed care on them, I will bestow punishment on you for the evil you have done,' declares YHWH. ³ <u>I myself will gather the remnant of my flock out of all the countries where I have driven them and will bring them back to their pasture, where they will be fruitful and increase in number.</u> ⁴ I will place shepherds over them who will tend them, and they will no longer be afraid or terrified, nor will any be missing,' declares YHWH. ⁵ <u>'The days are coming,'</u>*

*declares YHWH, 'when I will raise up to David a righteous
Branch, a King who will reign wisely and do what is just and
right in the Land.* ⁶ *In His days Yahudah will be saved and
Yisrael will live in safety.* This is the Name by which He will
be called: YHWH Our Righteousness. ⁷ *'So then, the days are
coming,' declares YHWH, 'when people will no longer say, 'As
surely as YHWH lives, who brought the Yisraelites up out of
Egypt,'* ⁸ *but they will say, 'As surely as YHWH lives, who
brought the descendants of Yisrael up out of the land of the north
and out of all the countries where he had banished them.' Then
they will live in their own Land."* Yirmeyahu 23:1-8.

This prophecy is clearly a reference to a future
time when Messiah will reign over both Yahudah and
Yisrael. It also references an event that will bring about
the restoration for the Messianic reign. It speaks of
another Exodus besides the one when Mosheh brought the
multitude out of Egypt. It speaks of a day when Yahudah
and Yisrael will live together in safety in the Land and
the Righteous Branch, the Messiah will rule over them.
Finally, it is YHWH Himself Who will deliver His people
in a fashion, which I believe will be more spectacular than
the Exodus from Egypt.

Yirmeyahu again references such a return
and indicates that there would be an event which
overshadows the Exodus from Egypt: *"¹⁴ Therefore
behold, the days are coming, says YHWH, that it shall no
more be said, YHWH lives who brought up the children
of Yisrael from the land of Egypt, ¹⁵ but, YHWH lives who
brought up the children of Yisrael from the land of the north
and from all the lands where He had driven them. For I will
bring them back into their Land which I gave to their fathers.
¹⁶ Behold, I will send for many fishermen, says YHWH, and they*

shall fish them; and afterward I will send for many hunters, and they shall hunt them from every mountain and every hill, and out of the holes of the rocks. ¹⁷ For My eyes are on all their ways; they are not hidden from My face, nor is their iniquity hidden from My eyes. ¹⁸ And first I will repay double for their iniquity and their sin, because they have defiled My Land; they have filled My inheritance with the carcasses of their detestable and abominable idols. ¹⁹ <u>O YHWH, my strength and my fortress, my refuge in the day of affliction, the Gentiles shall come to You from the ends of the earth and say, Surely our fathers have inherited lies, worthlessness and unprofitable things.</u> ²⁰ Will a man make gods for himself, which are not gods? ²¹ Therefore behold, I will this once cause them to know, I will cause them to know My hand and My might; and they shall know that My name is YHWH." Yirmeyahu 16:14-21.

This clearly references a time when the House of Yisrael, which had been mixed amongst the Gentiles, begins to recognize that they have inherited lies and they begin to return to YHWH. Instead of calling Him "The LORD" or "God" they will know that His Name is YHWH.

They will recognize that they have worshipped false gods with pagan names. They will realize that their supposed "holy days" are actually rooted in pagan worship. They will reject the lies that they inherited and walk in truth. As a result, they will participate in a return to the Land which will make the Exodus from Egypt pale in comparison.

In another direct Messianic reference on this subject, Yeshayahu prophesies as follows: *"¹⁰ In that day the Root of Yeshai will stand as a banner for the peoples; the nations will rally to Him, and His place of rest will be glorious.*

*¹¹ In that day YHWH will reach out His Hand a second time
to reclaim the remnant that is left of his people from Assyria,
from Lower Egypt, from Upper Egypt, from Cush, from Elam,
from Babylonia, from Hamath and from the islands of the sea.
¹² He will raise a banner for the nations and gather the exiles
of Yisrael; He will assemble the scattered people of Yahudah
from the four quarters of the earth.* ¹³ Ephraim's jealousy will
vanish, and Yahudah's enemies will be cut off; Ephraim will not
be jealous of Yahudah, nor Yahudah hostile toward Ephraim.
¹⁴ They will swoop down on the slopes of Philistia to the west;
together they will plunder the people to the east. They will lay
hands on Edom and Moab, and the Ammonites will be subject to
them. ¹⁵ *YHWH will dry up the gulf of the Egyptian sea; with
a scorching wind He will sweep His Hand over the Euphrates
River. He will break it up into seven streams so that men can
cross over in sandals. ¹⁶ There will be a highway for the remnant
of His people that is left from Assyria, as there was for Yisrael
when they came up from Egypt.*" Yeshayahu 11:10-16.

  This prophesy also speaks of an exodus which will
happen in the future and notice that the prophet does not
refer to the church or a group of Christians, but rather the
exiles of Yisrael and the scattered of Yahudah. He clearly
points out the sibling rivalry of the past which led to the
split in the Kingdom of Yisrael and this regathering will
occur in that day when *"the Root of Yeshai will stand as a
banner for the peoples."* He will dry up sea waters and rivers
to make a highway for the remnant to return. This event
has clearly not occurred – it is not something that can or
will be missed.

  This highway will be prepared exclusively
for the Redeemed who will be regathered.
"³ Strengthen the weak hands, and make firm the feeble knees.

⁴ Say to those who are fearful-hearted, 'Be strong, do not fear! Behold, your Elohim will come with vengeance, with the recompense of Elohim; He will come and save you.' ⁵ Then the eyes of the blind shall be opened, and the ears of the deaf shall be unstopped. ⁶ Then the lame shall leap like a deer, and the tongue of the dumb sing. For waters shall burst forth in the wilderness, and streams in the desert. ⁷ The parched ground shall become a pool, and the thirsty land springs of water; In the habitation of jackals, where each lay, there shall be grass with reeds and rushes. ⁸ And a highway will be there and it will be called the Way of Holiness. The unclean will not journey on it; it will be for those who walk in that Way; wicked fools will not go about on it. ⁹ No lion shall be there, nor shall any ravenous beast go up on it; it shall not be found there. But the Redeemed shall walk there, ¹⁰ and the ransomed of YHWH shall return, and come to Zion with singing, with everlasting joy on their heads. They shall obtain joy and gladness, and sorrow and sighing shall flee away."
Yeshayahu 35:3-10.

This highway will be safe passage to Zion for the Redeemed, but those that travel upon it must be clean. In other words, this road is only for those who are obeying the Torah. The remnant will be protected from lions as they return to the Land and walk in truth. This stands in direct contrast to the former Assyrian transplants who attempted to replace the northern tribes but failed to follow the Torah. When this great regathering occurs, we will not only see the scattered tribes returning to the Land but also a restoration of the divided Kingdom.

The prophet Yehezqel gave an illustrative account of how this reunion will occur. *"¹⁵ Again the Word of YHWH came to me, saying, ¹⁶ As for you, son of man, take*

a stick for yourself and write on it: '*For Yahudah and for the children of Yisrael, his companions.*' Then take another stick and write on it, '*For Yoseph, the stick of Ephraim, and for all the House of Yisrael, his companions.*' ¹⁷ Then join them one to another for yourself into one stick, and they will become one in your hand. ¹⁸ And when the children of your people speak to you, saying, 'Will you not show us what you mean by these?' – ¹⁹ say to them, Thus says YHWH Elohim: '*Surely I will take the stick of Yoseph, which is in the hand of Ephraim, and the tribes of Yisrael, his companions; and I will join them with it, with the stick of Yahudah, and make them one stick, and they will be one in My Hand.*' ²⁰ And the sticks on which you write will be in your hand before their eyes. ²¹ Then say to them, Thus says YHWH Elohim: '*Surely I will take the children of Yisrael from among the nations, wherever they have gone, and will gather them from every side and bring them into their own Land;* ²² *and I will make them one nation in the Land, on the mountains of Yisrael; and one king shall be king over them all; they shall no longer be two nations, nor shall they ever be divided into two kingdoms again.* ²³ They shall not defile themselves anymore with their idols, nor with their detestable things, nor with any of their transgressions; but I will deliver them from all their dwelling places in which they have sinned, and will cleanse them. Then *they shall be My people, and I will be their Elohim.* ²⁴ *David My servant shall be king over them, and they shall all have one shepherd;* they shall also walk in My judgments and observe My statutes, and do them.²⁵ Then they shall dwell in the Land that I have given Yaakov My servant, where your fathers dwelt; and they shall dwell there, they, their children, and their children's children, forever; and *My servant David shall be their prince forever.* ²⁶ Moreover I will make a Covenant of peace with them, and it shall be an everlasting Covenant with them; I will

establish them and multiply them, and I will set My sanctuary in their midst forevermore. ²⁷ My tabernacle also shall be with them; indeed I will be their Elohim, and they shall be My people. ²⁸ The nations also will know that I, YHWH, sanctify Yisrael, when My sanctuary is in their midst forevermore." Yehezqel 37:15-28.

This prophecy clearly has not been fulfilled. It is yet another prophecy which links the great regathering and reuniting of the tribes through Messiah – refered to as David, a king, a prince and a servant. The Covenant of YHWH is fulfilled as a Covenant of peace when the Kingdom is restored and under the rulership of Messiah "forever."

Using this same contrast between the House of Yahudah and the House of Yoseph (Yisrael), the prophet Zekaryah confirms this regathering: "⁶ I will strengthen the House of Yahudah, and I will save the House of Yoseph. I will bring them back, because I have mercy on them. They shall be as though I had not cast them aside; for I am YHWH their Elohim, and I will hear them. ⁷ Those of Ephraim shall be like a mighty man, and their heart shall rejoice as if with wine. Yes, their children shall see it and be glad; Their heart shall rejoice in YHWH. ⁸ _I will whistle for them and gather them, for I will redeem them; and they shall increase as they once increased. ⁹ I will sow them among the peoples, and they shall remember Me in far countries; They shall live, together with their children, and they shall return. ¹⁰ I will also bring them back from the land of Egypt, and gather them from Assyria. I will bring them into the land of Gilead and Lebanon, until no more room is found for them. ¹¹ He shall pass through the sea with affliction, and strike the waves of the sea: All the depths of the River shall dry up._ Then the pride of

Assyria shall be brought down, and the scepter of Egypt shall depart. *So I will strengthen them in YHWH, and they shall walk up and down in His Name, says YHWH."* Zekaryah 10:6-12.

The prophecy actually describes how YHWH will regather His people. It sounds alot like the Exodus from Egypt only this time it will be a final regathering of the Redeemed. This regathering will occur in the end when all of the Nations will be punished.

"²¹ I will display my glory among the nations, and all the nations will see the punishment I inflict and the Hand I lay upon them. ²² From that day forward the House of Yisrael will know that I am YHWH their Elohim. ²³ And the nations will know that the people of Yisrael went into exile for their sin, because they were unfaithful to Me. So I hid My face from them and handed them over to their enemies, and they all fell by the sword. ²⁴ I dealt with them according to their uncleanness and their offenses, and I hid my face from them. ²⁵ Therefore this is what the Sovereign YHWH says: 'I will now bring Yaakov back from captivity and will have compassion on all the people of Yisrael, and I will be zealous for My Set Apart Name. ²⁶ They will forget their shame and all the unfaithfulness they showed toward me when they lived in safety in their Land with no one to make them afraid. ²⁷ When I have brought them back from the nations and have gathered them from the countries of their enemies, I will show Myself holy through them in the sight of many nations. ²⁸ Then they will know that I am YHWH their Elohim, <u>for though I sent them into exile among the nations, I will gather them to their own Land, not leaving any behind. ²⁹ I will no longer hide my face from them, for I will pour out My Spirit on the House of Yisrael, declares the Sovereign YHWH.</u>" Yehezqel 39:21-29.

As the children of Yisrael were redeemed from Egypt, so the House of Yisrael (also referred to as Yoseph or Ephraim) will be gathered in grand fashion in order to demonstrate the power of YHWH and reveal His Name to the world. Just as Egypt was punished through the deliverance of Yisrael, so too, the nations of the Earth will be punished when Yisrael is regathered.

As the children of Yisrael sang the song of Mosheh after they were delivered from Egypt, in the future, the Redeemed will sing a song given by Mosheh specifically for the great regathering – the Final Exodus.[128]

17

In the End

In the beginning Adam was created in the Image of YHWH. He was given a Bride named Hawah who was taken from His side. They were allowed to partake of the Tree of Life and dwell in the Garden of YHWH - as long as they obeyed. They disobeyed and were exiled from the Garden.

The Scriptures provide us with an account of man's journey to regain entrance into paradise and dwell with YHWH. In the end, some of mankind will be permitted to return to the Garden and once again, partake of the fruit of the Tree of Life – these are the Redeemed.

After man was exiled from the Garden YHWH looked for a people who would obey His commandments and follow His Torah. He found that person in Avraham who lived in a pagan land, but through his obedience was brought to a new Land. He lived a life exemplified by obedience and was willing to give up everything – even his own promised son.

As a result, he enterd into a Covenant relationship with the Creator of the Universe. YHWH declared that through the offspring of that promised son: "⁴ *. . . all nations on earth will be blessed, ⁵ because Avraham obeyed Me and kept*

My requirements, My commands, My decrees and My Torah."
Beresheet 26:4-5.

YHWH made a covenant with Avraham, which was a promise of engagement that would later result in a marriage at Sinai with all of those who were redeemed from Egypt. The nations were truly blessed as the children of Yisrael, along with the mixed multitude, were delivered from slavery.

The Redeemed were all those who obeyed YHWH. Those who were committed to following and obeying YHWH were brought by YHWH to dwell with Him into the Promised Land - the marital residence. Sadly, Yisrael was an unfaithful bride. She whored after other lovers which resulted in separation and divorce.

The pattern was established and clear from the beginning – obey and live or disobey and die. Since YHWH is the source of life, in order to live forever we must dwell in His presence, otherwise we experience death, which is the inevitable result of being separated from Him.

Whenever man disobeys, he brings judgment which involves separation and death. This is why Adam and Hawah eventually died, because they received judgment for their disobedience. They were no longer permitted to live in the presence of YHWH and partake of the Tree of Life. Just as Adam and Hawah were exiled, so too, Yisrael was exiled.

Despite this separation, YHWH was not finished with His Bride. He divided Yisrael and scattered her to the four corners of the earth. He did this to fulfill His promise that all of the nations would be blessed, because just as He scattered Yisrael into all of the nations, so YHWH told of

a future time when He would miraculously regather His Bride out from all of those nations.

They could not be regathered until the price of their wickedness had been paid and they were cleansed from their filth. As was demonstrated through the pattern of Avraham, YHWH would allow the blood of His Son, the Lamb of Elohim, to be shed to atone for their sin.

It is important to remember that this was a necessary and critical part of the Covenant made between YHWH and Avraham. Only YHWH passed through the pieces of the Covenant so only YHWH was subject to the penalty of death associated with breaking the Covenant by either party.

YHWH, through His Son, paid the price and by that blood He redeemed His Bride. This is, after all, the essence of being redeemed, which is ga'uley (גאולי) in Hebrew. The redemption process involves payment and remember that both people and land can be redeemed. (Vayiqra 25). Yahushua came as a kinsman Redeemer to purchase both the Land and the people of the Kingdom of YHWH.

Yahushua, as the Son of YHWH and the King of Yahudah came to redeem and restore the Kingdom of YHWH. (Galatians 3:13-14). Just as Adam "birthed" a Bride from his side during a death and resurrection experience - so a Bride was birthed from the death and resurrection of Yahushua as the blood and water poured from His side onto the Earth.

This Bride is still Yisrael – the Redeemed – who were once redeemed from Egypt and in the future will be redeemed from the entire planet. Yisrael was originally called to be a set apart nation serving the Set Apart Elohim,

the Creator of the Universe. "*Speak to all the congregation of the children of Yisrael, and say to them: You shall be set apart, for I YHWH your Elohim am set apart.*" Vayiqra 19:2. Another way of saying that is: "Be set apart because I am Set apart." In other words, Yisrael was to be like Him.

This was so that all of the world might see YHWH through Yisrael. Just as Adam was made in the image of YHWH, Yisrael through their obedience of the Torah were supposed to be the image of YHWH on earth. They were a chosen people, not because they were greater than other nations, the Scriptures clearly reveal that they were not.

Chosen does not mean that they were better than the rest of the nations. Chosen means that they were selected to shine the light of YHWH to the world so that all might know and obey the Holy One of Yisrael. Once people came to know YHWH, they would become part of the Kingdom of YHWH, the Commonwealth of Yisrael.

Yisrael literally means "The planting of El." The Tehillim declare: "*You have brought a vine out of Egypt; You have cast out the nations, and planted it.*" Tehillim 80:8. The vine is Yisrael, YHWH is the gardener and the Promised Land is the garden.

Yisrael is also called The Olive tree by YHWH: "*YHWH called your name, Green Olive Tree, Lovely and of Good Fruit. With the noise of a great tumult He has kindled fire on it, and its branches are broken.*" Yirmeyahu 11:16. This tree springs from the Root - which is YHWH - and grows branches which are supposed to bear fruit which then turns into oil that flows to the nations.[129]

Sadly, Yisrael failed to bear fruit, so YHWH chose another way to reach the nations.[130] They were scattered

from the Land and the House of YHWH was destroyed
– all appeared to be hopelessly lost. Thankfully, the
Scriptures tell of a time when there will be a new House
constructed in Jerusalem. We are also given a description
of the borders of the Land of Yisrael. (Yehezqel 47-48).

An important point to understand is that in the
future the Land will, once again, be divided according to
the tribes with Yoseph having a double portion. Also, the
stranger that sojourns with Yisrael will be treated as a
native-born. This is the way that it was always supposed
to be, but it is not the case with the modern State of Yisrael
today. While they allow Arabs to be citizens, they will not
allow someone to move there and become a citizen unless
they meet their particular definition of a "Jew" which we
have already seen is an ambiguous concept.[131]

Yisrael is not an exclusive group based upon
genetics, rather it is an inclusive Assembly based upon
hearts - all those with circumcised hearts are welcome into
the Assembly. You cannot have a heart of stone, you must
have a heart of flesh so that the Seed of YHWH can take
root. (Yehezqel 36:26; Luke 8).

They are those that grow and nurture in the Garden
of YHWH and bear His fruit, the fruit of the Spirit. "[13]
*Those who are planted in the House of YHWH shall flourish in
the courts of our Elohim.* [14] *They shall still bear fruit in old age;
They shall be fresh and flourishing,* [15] *To declare that YHWH is
upright; He is my rock, and there is no unrighteousness in Him."*
Tehillim 92:13-15.

The Scriptures show how YHWH has operated
throughout His creation to tend His garden and nurture
those who will follow Him. He is building a Kingdom and
He is looking for citizens and priests for His Kingdom.

He wants a remnant that love Him and want to be set apart unto Him. When all of Yisrael is regathered there will be a great wedding – with Yisrael as the Bride.

"*⁵ For your Maker is your Husband, YHWH of hosts is His Name; and your Redeemer is the Holy One of Yisrael; He is called the Elohim of the whole earth. ⁶ For YHWH has called you like a woman forsaken and grieved in spirit, like a youthful wife when you were refused, says your Elohim. ⁷ <u>For a mere moment I have forsaken you, but with great mercies I will gather you. ⁸ With a little wrath I hid My face from you for a moment; but with everlasting kindness I will have mercy on you, says YHWH, your Redeemer</u>.*" Yeshayahu 54:5-8.

Therefore, the Redeemer is the Husband and the Redeemed are the Bride. "*³¹ <u>Behold, the days are coming, says YHWH, when I will make a renewed Covenant with the House of Yisrael and with the House of Yahudah</u> - ³² not according to the Covenant that I made with their fathers in the day that I took them by the hand to lead them out of the land of Egypt, <u>My Covenant which they broke, though I was a Husband to them, says YHWH</u>.*" Yirmeyahu 31:31-32.

So the Husband will renew the Covenant with His Bride. This was the context of much of the ministry of Yahushua. He came as a Groom seeking His Bride. Betrothal is and always was a two stage process. In the ancient world a groom would first negotiate a bride price and then enter into an engagement agreement. Once that was completed he would return to his father's home and prepare a place for himself and his bride.

Yahushua told His Talmudim: "*I go to prepare a place for you.*" This is what a Hebrew groom would say to his bride before he left her to prepare the bridal chamber in his father's house. This is the context of the passage found

in the Good News according to Yahanan when Yahushua stated "² *In My Father's House are many mansions; if it were not so, I would have told you.* <u>*I go to prepare a place for you.* ³ *And if I go and prepare a place for you, I will come again and receive you to Myself*</u>; *that where I am, there you may be also.⁴ And where I go you know, and the way you know.*" Yahanan 14:2-4.

Once the bridal chamber is completed, the groom returns for his bride "as a thief in the night." This is a joyous occasion when the groom comes and takes his bride to the bridal chamber and consummates the marriage. It is a time full of suspense and excitement which is followed by a wedding feast.

Prior to the groom's coming, the bride must attend to some necessary preparations. She must ready herself and her trousseau - the possessions, such as clothing and linens, that a bride assembles for her marriage. Thus there are preparations which must be performed by both the bride and the groom. If one of them is not ready, then the wedding cannot take place.

The interesting thing about the ancient Hebrew wedding ritual is that the bride was not completely in the dark as to when her groom would be appearing. A loving groom wants his bride to be ready - he wants to get married. The last thing that he wants is to appear and find his bride unprepared. Therefore, he might send friends or messengers to communicate to the bride the day and the hour of his future coming.

This is the case with our Messiah. He has told us that He will be returning as a thief in the night and warns: "*Therefore if you will not watch, I will come upon you as a thief, and you will not know what hour I will come upon you.*"

Revelation 3:3 NKJV. Later in the book of Revelation He states: *"Behold, I am coming as a thief. Blessed is he who watches, and keeps his garments, lest he walk naked and they see his shame."* Revelation 16:15 NKJV.

The clear conclusion from these passages reveals that we need to watch and be ready as a diligent Bride. Yahushua wants us to be ready and He has given us information to help us be ready for His return.

Read how the Groom warns His Bride: *"⁴² Watch therefore, for you do not know (oida) what hour your Master is coming. ⁴³ But know (ginosko) this, that if the Master of the house had known what hour the thief would come, he would have watched and not allowed his house to be broken into. ⁴⁴ Therefore you also be ready, for the Son of Man is coming at an hour you do not expect."* Mattityahu 24:42-44.

The Greek word "oida" means: "intuitive knowledge" while the greek word "ginosko" means: "objective knowledge" or "acquired knowledge with effort." In other words, you had better watch and figure it out, because you do not know intuitively what hour the Master is coming. Remember, He wants us to know when He is coming and the wise servant will be ready for the Master's return. The evil servant, on the other hand, is the one who will be surprised and caught off guard. *"The Master of that (evil) servant will come on a day when he does not expect Him and at an hour he is not aware of."* Mattityahu 24:50.

Can you imagine how a groom would feel after spending months of preparation and planning, his heart aching with anxious anticipation to retrieve his bride only to show up and find his bride sleeping and unprepared. Her state of preparedness reveals her heart. She obviously does

not love the groom as much as he loves her. The groom wants to find his bride as ready and prepared as himself. So it is with our Messiah, the Groom. (Mattityahu 25:1-13).

Every person must examine their own heart to determine if they are ready or even have the desire to make ready. The Redeemed are those who have been bought for a price and are ready for their Redeemer. They are children of Elohim, members of the House of YHWH, the Bride of Messiah – those who have prepared and are watching for their Groom.

Hear the call to the Bride: "¹⁰ *Go through, Go through the gates! Prepare the way for the people; Build up, Build up the highway! Take out the stones, Lift up a banner for the peoples!* ¹¹ *Indeed YHWH has proclaimed to the end of the world: Say to the daughter of Zion, Surely your salvation is coming; Behold, His reward is with Him, And His work before Him.* ¹² *And they shall call them The Holy People, The Redeemed of YHWH; and you shall be called Sought Out, A City Not Forsaken.*" Yeshayahu 62:10-12.

In a clear Messianic Scripture we see how the Prophet Yeshayahu describes the people of Elohim as the Redeemed – A City not Forsaken. The word translated as "city" is ayer (עיר) which can mean a guarded place – just as Adam was to guard – shamar – the garden. This city, after all, is the restored Eden – the Renewed Jerusalem. A place where renewed man, made in the image of YHWH can dwell in His presence.

Read how the Book of Revelation describes this city – the Bride: "⁹ *Then one of the seven angels who had the seven bowls filled with the seven last plagues came to me and talked with me, saying, 'Come, I will show you the Bride,*

the Lamb's wife.' ¹⁰ And he carried me away in the Spirit to a great and high mountain, and showed me the great city, the holy Jerusalem, descending out of heaven from Elohim, ¹¹ having the glory of Elohim. Her light was like a most precious stone, like a jasper stone, clear as crystal. ¹² Also she had a great and high wall with twelve gates, and twelve angels at the gates, and names written on them, which are the names of the twelve tribes of the children of Yisrael: ¹³ three gates on the east, three gates on the north, three gates on the south, and three gates on the west. ¹⁴ Now the wall of the city had twelve foundations, and on them were the names of the twelve apostles of the Lamb. ¹⁵ And he who talked with me had a gold reed to measure the city, its gates, and its wall. ¹⁶ The city is laid out as a square; its length is as great as its breadth. And he measured the city with the reed: twelve thousand furlongs. Its length, breadth, and height are equal. ¹⁷ Then he measured its wall: one hundred and forty-four cubits, according to the measure of a man, that is, of an angel. ¹⁸ The construction of its wall was of jasper; and the city was pure gold, like clear glass. ¹⁹ The foundations of the wall of the city were adorned with all kinds of precious stones: the first foundation was jasper, the second sapphire, the third chalcedony, the fourth emerald, ²⁰ the fifth sardonyx, the sixth sardius, the seventh chrysolite, the eighth beryl, the ninth topaz, the tenth chrysoprase, the eleventh jacinth, and the twelfth amethyst. ²¹ The twelve gates were twelve pearls: each individual gate was of one pearl. And the street of the city was pure gold, like transparent glass." Revelation 21:9-21.¹³²

  Notice that this great city, the renewed Jerusalem, has a wall just as the Garden of Eden was a protected, enclosed space. While Adam was charged with watching and protecting the Garden, he failed by allowing the serpent to enter and tempt the woman. Yahushua as the

second Adam will watch over the Bride.

The renewed Jerusalem will have twelve gates which are guarded and notice the twelve gates have the names of the twelve tribes of Yisrael. There is no gate of the Gentiles or gate of the Christians. You must be joined with a tribe and be part of Yisrael to enter. In fact, we were already provided a pattern for the layout of the City through the encampment of Yisrael in the wilderness.

This is made clear by the following: "*² I saw the Holy City, the renewed Jerusalem, coming down out of heaven from Elohim, prepared as a bride beautifully dressed for her husband. ³ And I heard a loud voice from the throne saying, 'Now the dwelling of Elohim is with men, and He will live with them. They will be His people, and Elohim Himself will be with them and be their Elohim.*" Revelation 21:2-4. Can you hear the prophecy of Hoshea echoing from the past? This is the very fulfillment of his words – this is the restoration of Yisrael.

As the Garden contained the Tree of Life – so too does the renewed Jerusalem. "*In the middle of its street, and on either side of the river, was the Tree of Life, which bore twelve fruits, each tree yielding its fruit every month. The leaves of the Tree were for the healing of the nations.*" Revelation 22:2. Again, you must pass through a gate to partake of the Tree and notice the number of leaves – twelve. This Tree is for Yisrael and only those who partake of the Tree will have everlasting life.

In the end it comes down to whether one is chosen – only the chosen are The Redeemed who constitute Yisrael – also known as Yahshurun. "*¹ But now listen, O Yaakov, My servant, Yisrael, whom I have chosen. ² This is what YHWH says - He Who made you, Who formed you in*

the womb, and Who will help you: Do not be afraid, O Yaakov, My servant, Yahshurun, whom I have chosen. ³ For I will pour water on the thirsty Land, and streams on the dry ground; I will pour out My Spirit on your offspring, and My blessing on your descendants. ⁴ They will spring up like grass in a meadow, like poplar trees by flowing streams. ⁵ one will say, 'I belong to YHWH;' another will call himself by the name of Yaakov; still another will write on his hand, YHWH's and will take the name Yisrael." Yeshayahu 44:1-5.

Yahshurun is the poetic name of Yisrael. "It comes from the root yashar (ישׁר) which means: 'to be level, straight, (up) right, just, lawful, honest, and righteous.' It literally means: 'To go straight or direct in the way'"[133]

In the fullest sense it refers to walking straight by obeying the statutes, ordinances and commandments of YHWH – those that do so are Yahshurun and YHWH is their King. "*And He was King in Yahshurun, when the leaders of the people were gathered, all the tribes of Yisrael together.*" Devarim 33:5.

Therefore, Yahshurun is describing those from all the tribes of Yisrael that belong to YHWH. They are Yisrael regathered - the ones who walk the straight path through obedience to His commandments. The Scriptures are very clear that obedience is the distinquishig factor: "*¹⁴ Blessed are those who do His commandments, that they may have the right to the Tree of Life, and may enter through the gates into the city. ¹⁵ But outside are dogs and sorcerers and sexually immoral and murderers and idolaters, and whoever loves and practices a lie.*" Revelation 22:14-15.

The Prophet Yeshayahu describes those outside as "uncircumcised" and "defiled" as he proclaims: "*¹ Awake, awake! Put on your strength, O Zion; <u>put on your beautiful</u>*

garments, O Jerusalem, the holy city! For the uncircumcised and the unclean shall no longer come to you. ² Shake yourself from the dust, arise; Sit down, O Jerusalem! Loose yourself from the bonds of your neck, O captive daughter of Zion! ³ For thus says YHWH: 'You have sold yourselves for nothing, and you shall be redeemed without money.' ⁴ For thus says the Master YHWH: 'My people went down at first into Egypt to dwell there; then the Assyrian oppressed them without cause. ⁵ 'Now therefore, what have I here,' says YHWH, 'That My people are taken away for nothing? Those who rule over them make them wail,' says YHWH, 'And My Name is blasphemed continually every day. ⁶ Therefore My people shall know My Name; therefore they shall know in that day that I am He who speaks: 'Behold, it is I.' ⁷ How beautiful upon the mountains are the feet of Him Who brings good news, Who proclaims peace, Who brings glad tidings of good things, Who proclaims salvation, Who says to Zion, 'Your Elohim reigns!' ⁸ Your watchmen shall lift up their voices, with their voices they shall sing together; for they shall see eye to eye when YHWH brings back Zion. ⁹ Break forth into joy, sing together, you waste places of Jerusalem! For YHWH has comforted His people, He has redeemed Jerusalem. ¹⁰ YHWH has made bare His holy Arm in the eyes of all the nations; and all the ends of the earth shall see the salvation of our Elohim. ¹¹ Depart! Depart! Go out from there, touch no unclean thing; go out from the midst of her, be clean, you who bear the vessels of YHWH. ¹² For you shall not go out with haste, nor go by flight; for YHWH will go before you, and the Elohim of Yisrael will be your rear guard." Yeshayahu 52:1-12.

From the beginning in the Garden we were given pictures and patterns which will be repeated and fulfilled in the end. In the beginning man lived in the Garden with the Creator. Man was expelled because of disobedience

but through the restorative work of YHWH, in the future some of mankind will be permitted to return. Those who are pure and undefiled will be allowed to pass through the gates into life – they are known as the Bride, Yisrael, the renewed Jerusalem, Zion, Yahshurun – The Redeemed.

Endnotes

[1] The Hebrew word Elohim (אלהים) is technically plural, but that does not mean more than one Creator. The singular form is El (אל) and could refer to any "mighty one," but because the plural is used to describe the Creator, it means that He is qualitatively stronger or more powerful than any singular El (אל). In Hebrew, the plural form can mean that something or someone is qualitatively greater, not just quantitatively greater. We see in the first sentence of the Scriptures that "In the Beginning Elohim created" the Hebrew for "created" is bara (ברא) which literally is "He created." It is masculine singular showing that while Elohim is plural He is masculine singular. For an excellent discussion of the Hebrew Etymology of the Name of Elohim, I recommend *His Name is One* written by Jeff A. Benner, Virtualbookworm.com Publishing 2002.

[2] The word god actually has pagan origins and was used to refer to Teutonic deities. This subject is discussed in the Walk in the Light series entitled "Names." I have heard it argued that since Gad is actually the name of one of the Twelve Tribes of Yisrael then "God" must be acceptable. We are talking apples and oranges here. No one ever worshipped Gad or the Tribe of Gad as the Creator. On the other hand Baal-Gad or Baal-God which literally means: "Lord God" was historically in direct competition for worship with the Creator. That being the case I think that it would be wise to steer away from anything that even has the appearance of impropriety. There are better, more accurate and more Scriptural titles to use. Granted I will use this terminology when I am trying to get a point across to someone who is not familiar with any other term, but in my worship and fellowship I like to avoid improper terms. It is a good habit to get into if you plan on spending eternity with the Creator.

Beresheet is the transliteration of the Hebrew word בראשית which is often translated as Genesis. It means "in the beginning" and it is the name of the first book found in the Scriptures as well as the first word in that book. Keep in mind that I use the word "book" very loosely because in this modern day we use books in codex form which are bound by a spine and generally have writing on both pages. By using the word "book" we create a mental image regarding manuscripts which may not be accurate. Many ancient manuscripts were written on scrolls, so instead of the word book, it is more accurate to refer to the scroll or the sefer (ספר) when referring to these ancient manuscripts. Therefore the "book" of Beresheet would be more accurately described as Sefer Beresheet ספר בראשית since it originally came as a scroll.

The proper transliteration for the name of the person often called Cain in the Scriptures is Qayin (קין) and the proper transliteration for the name of the person often called Abel in the Scriptures is Hebel (הבל). It is very interesting to view the sacrifices which were rendered by these two because it reveals a pattern which is repeated in Scriptures and shows us behavior which is pleasing and that which is displeasing to YHWH. We read in Beresheet that "in the process of time" they both provided an offering to YHWH. In the Hebrew we read miqetz yamiym (מקץ ימים) which literally means "in the end of days." It seems clear that this was an Appointed Time when both knew that an offering was expected of them. The Scriptures reveal that Qayin brought an offering of the fruit of the ground to YHWH and Hebel ALSO brought the firstborn of his flock and their fat. In other words, Hebel brought an offering of the fruit of the ground to YHWH but he also brought the firstborn of his flock. The Hebrew word used for flock is tsone (צאנו) which implies a goat or a lamb. I believe that this was likely the time of the Passover when all are required to offer a goat or a lamb. (Shemot 12:5). Passover is one of three times in the Torah when males are to appear before YHWH at an appointed time and place, to present offering. The two

other major feasts are Sukkot and Shavuot - during both of these feasts they would have been required to present the firstfruits of their labors which they had sown in the field. (Shemot 23:14). During the Passover and the Feast of Unleavened Bread, we bring a lamb or a goat offered with its' fat and in the midst of Unleavened Bread we also present the Firstfruits (resheet – beginning) of our crops. Now many believe that the Appointed Times were created at Sinai but this is not supported by the Scriptures. I believe that the Torah and the patterns found within the feasts go back to the beginning. YHWH repeatedly tells us that He has declared the end from the beginning. (Yeshayahu 41:26, 46:10, 48). His patterns and His ways go all the way back to the beginning and are demonstrated through cycles – one of those cycles being harvests. Throughout the Scriptures we see the terms "in the beginning" (beresheet) referring to the beginning of a harvest or the firstfruits of a harvest and the term "in the end of days" (miqetz yamiym) referring to the end of that harvest. Many interpret this passage with Qayin and Hebel as if to show that raising animals was better than tilling the ground, but that has nothing to do with it. We see that Hebel offered his firstfruits while there was no mention of this for Qayin. Also note that the offering of Hebel involved blood while the offering of Qayin did not. Thus the offering of Qayin was not acceptable – it did not include blood and he did not receive atonement. As a result he was overtaken by sin and he ultimately did shed blood – the blood of his brother. This provides us with the patterns of Messiah's fulfillment of the Passover.

There are at least 47 other instances in the Tanak where Yah (יה) is located in the Hebrew text but all of the modern English versions reflect the title "The LORD" instead of the Name. When people say HalleluYah (הללויה) they are saying a Hebrew word which means "praise be to Yah." Yah is the short form of the full Name of YHWH. While some pronounce it as Yeh, the real debate revolves around how the end of the Name is pronounced. The third Hebrew letter in the Name is vav (ו). While the vav (ו) now has

a "v" sound in Modern Hebrew, it is believed that it had a "w" sound in Ancient Hebrew. Many of our ancestors in the faith contained the Name of YHWH within their names. For instance, the correct Hebrew name of the Prophet called Isaiah is Yeshayahu. It is spelled יְשַׁעְיָהוּ in Hebrew, and it ends with the first three letters of the Name of YHWH. This is not the only name where this occurs and those three letters are usually always pronounced: "yahu" or "yahuw." The final Hebrew letter hay (ה) has an "h" sound. Therefore, many pronounce the Name as Ya-hu-wah. I believe that a key to the correct pronunciation is found in the name commonly called "Judah." The first time that we see the name Judah in the Scriptures is when Leah conceives her fourth son: *"And she conceived again and bore a son, and said, 'Now I will praise YHWH.' Therefore she called his name Judah."* Beresheet 29:35. The name Judah, properly pronounced Yahudah, stems directly from her statement *"Now I will praise YHWH."* Many people interpret Yahudah to simply mean "praise," but as we can see, this is not correct. The name which is commonly spelled and pronounced Judah in English is spelled 𐤄𐤃𐤅𐤄𐤉 in ancient Hebrew or יהודה in Modern Hebrew. Notice the similarity between יהודה (YHWDH) and יהוה (YHWH). The only difference is the dalet (ד) which has a "D" sound. If we take the dalet (ד) out of Yahudah we are left with YHWH, the Name of the Creator. Therefore, if you believe that the Name of YHWH consists of all consonants then it would likely be pronounced Yahuwah rather than Yahweh. It also seems consistent with the name of the first woman whose name meant "life giver." Remember that the name Hawah (חוה) actually ends with the same two letters as YHWH (יהוה) so Yahuwah would be a consistent pronunciation. There are many different people who believe in many different pronunciations. "John H. Skilton, *The Law and the Prophets*, pp. 223, 224, prefers 'Yahoweh'. The Assyrians transcribed the Name as 'Ya-u-a', so Mowinckle and other scholars prefer 'Yahowah'. Some scholars prefer 'Yehowah', because that is the way the Massoretes vowel-pointed it. (Whether this vowel pointing of the Name was done in truth, or whether it was done to 'disguise' the Name, in accordance with the instruction given in the Mishnaic text of *Tamid* vii.2 (= *Sota* vii.6), we do not know for certain. There is also the Rabbinical interpretation of the Massoretic text saying that the vowels e, o and a were added to the Name as a *Qere perpetuum* which means that the reading of Adonai or Elohim is to be used instead. However, there is no definite proof that the Massoretes originally did it for this reason)." (*The Scriptures*, Institute for Scripture Research, 1998, p. xii.) In this period of restoration which the Assembly is currently experiencing, it is important to remain teachable. I have very good friends who have different opinions and I certainly do not consider the pronunciation to be a point of contention since it is still the subject of debate and speculation. Some pronounce it Yahweh while others pronounce it Yahuwah - still others pronounce it Yahovah and Yahavah. The point is that we are all trying to get it right.

6 Hawah (חוה) means "giver of life" or "mother of all living." It is interesting to note that Adam did not name his wife until after their transgression.

7 The Torah (תורה) is generally found within and consists of the first five books of the Hebrew and Christian Scriptures. Traditionally, it is contained in a Scroll and the first scroll was written by Moses (Mosheh) and placed within the Ark of the Covenant. The Torah is often referred to as "The Law" in many modern English Bibles. Law is not a very accurate word to describe the Torah which often results in the Torah being confused with the laws, customs, and traditions of the religious leaders as well as the laws of particular countries. The Torah is more accurately defined as the "instruction" of YHWH for His set apart people. The Torah contains instruction for those who desire to live righteous, set apart lives in accordance with the will of YHWH. Contrary to popular belief, people can obey the Torah. (Deuteronomy 30:11-14). It is the myriads of regulations, customs and traditions which men attach to the Torah that make it impossible and burdensome for

people to obey. The names of the five different "books" are transliterated from their proper Hebrew names as follows: Genesis - Beresheet, Exodus - Shemot, Leviticus - Vayiqra, Numbers - Bemidbar, Deuteronomy - Devarim.

8   For a more detailed discussion of the effect of tradition on mainstream religion see the Walk in the Light series book entitled "Restoration." In particular the reader is directed to Chapter 15 which gives a number of examples of traditions which do not meet the test of truth.

9   For a more detailed discussion of covenants see the Walk in the Light series book entitled "Covenants."

10   Avram (אברם) was the original name of our Patriarch who is often called Abram. His name was later changed to Avraham (אברהם).

11   Interestingly, many believe that the Torah was given to Israel at Mount Sinai through Moses (Mosheh) but that is obviously contradicted by the fact that Avraham obeyed the Torah. It is very likely that mankind always knew the Torah and at Sinai it became the basis for a marriage covenant with Israel.

12   The Torah provides instructions regarding what is considered to be food. Not all animals were meant to be consumed. The Creator made certain animals that can be eaten and others which are not meant to be eaten because their particular function would make them inappropriate to be eaten. These instructions are meant for our good to keep us healthy, they are not meant to deprive us of any delicacies. Christians have missed considerable health blessings because of their treatment of this subject. They believe that since they are not "under the law" they can now eat anything. Sadly, nothing could be further from the truth. The New Testament Scriptures actually state that "Jesus declared all foods clean" but this particular passage does not provide for the abolition of the dietary instructions as so many believe. Let us take a closer look at the passage in the Good News according to Mark from the NIV Translation. *"¹⁴ Again Jesus called the crowd to Him and said, 'Listen to Me, everyone, and understand this. ¹⁵ Nothing*

outside a man can make him unclean by going into him. Rather, it is what comes out of a man that makes him unclean.' [17] *After He had left the crowd and entered the house, His disciples asked him about this parable.* [18] *'Are you so dull?' He asked. 'Don't you see that nothing that enters a man from the outside can make him unclean?* [19] *For it doesn't go into his heart but into his stomach, and then out of his body. (In saying this, Jesus declared all foods "clean.")"* Mark 7:14-19 NIV. Notice the information in parenthesis at the end of this passage of Scripture. The parenthesis means that this statement is not in the original manuscript but rather it was a translator's notation, a very ignorant one at that! The Messiah was not declaring all foods clean in this Scripture and He never made that statement. It is simply astounding that a translator would put such an erroneous notation at the end of a passage where the Messiah specifically asks "Are you so dull?" It is as if the Messiah is asking that question of the translator. The point of His teaching was that it is the heart that gets defiled, not the body. Eating something unclean does not turn someone into an unclean being. Eating pig does not turn a person into pig, they are still human. They do not turn into the unclean animal – instead their body eventually eliminates the unclean thing. Regardless, eating a pig is still considered an abominable act because swine is not defined as "food" in the Torah. There are various other quotes from Shaul which people use to justify violating the dietary instructions. None of them accomplish that goal when they are translated correctly and read within their proper context. The subject of the Scriptural dietary instructions is discussed in detail in the Walk in the Light series book entitled "Kosher."

[13] The exact boundaries of the Promised Land are hotly disputed because the specific location of the reference points are not all known. What is clear is that the Land Covenant has never been completely fulfilled and we look forward to the future fulfillment of this covenant.

[14] Ancient Hebrew was a visual language wherein every letter has a visual meaning and told a story. When those letters were put together, their meanings combined to form

concepts. I have made it a part of my studies to look beyond the Modern Hebrew to the Ancient Hebrew pictographs to find out the original concepts behind various words. This adds a whole new dimension to the study of the Scriptures which is both exciting and authentic. I highly recommend that you visit www.ancient-hebrew.org which has a lot of valuable information.

15 The Creator's reckoning of time is discussed at length in the Walk in the Light series book entitled "Appointed Times." It is critical that anyone who claims to follow YHWH understand His times and seasons in order to synchronize their lives with His plan.

16 The birth of Yitshaq at Passover is supported by the Targums, which were Aramaic translations of the Torah that often extrapolated facts implied or understood to be part of the Torah, likely through tradition.

17 The Third Day, known as Yom Shliyshiy (יום שלישי) has great significance in the Scriptures and should be the subject of much study for the serious student.

18 Revelation 1:8, 21:6 and 22:13 provide a critical key to this mystery of the Aleph Taw (את). While Greek translations of these texts have the Messiah saying: "I am the Alpha (A) and the Omega (Ω)" it is quite apparent that this Hebrew Messiah was speaking to His Hebrew Disciple in Hebrew or Aramaic. Therefore The Messiah would have declared: "I am the Aleph (א) and the Taw (ה)." The Messiah is the Aleph Taw (את) which is imbedded throughout the Tanak, and particularly the Torah. Therefore, when you read the Hebrew Scriptures you will find the Messiah embedded throughout the pages, often times un-translated but at critical points. The Targums also provide a translation from the Aramaic which describe "The Memra" which is translated into the English as "The Word". The Memra is another vivid example of the Messiah in the Scriptures which is often overlooked in modern English translations. One final intriguing element is the mysterious Urim and Thurrim used by the High Priest. In Hebrew the word Urim starts with aleph (א) and the word Thurrim starts

with taw (ת) so there is clearly a connection.

19 The Hebrew Scriptures are the original texts and the Hebrew language was uniquely chosen by the Creator to transmit His message. There is critical information below the surface of the text which often gets lost, particularly when you start translating this ancient eastern language into a modern western language. As a result, I encourage students of the text to learn and study in the original Hebrew whenever possible.

20 Yisrael (ישראל) is the English transliteration for the Hebrew word often spelled Israel.

21 Succot, also spelled Sukkot, was the first place that the children of Israel camped when they left Egypt. Sukkot is not only a place, it is also a very special Appointed Time. The Seventh month of the Scriptural calendar contains the Appointed Times commonly referred to as "the Fall Feasts." These appointed times include the Day of Trumpets, The Day of Atonement and Sukkot (The Feast of Tabernacles). Sukkot is one of three Appointed Times that adult males were commanded to go to Jerusalem each year. These are shadow pictures or rehearsals of things to come and they will include the return of the Messiah, Judgment, and Him dwelling (tabernacling) with His people. The prophet Zechariah states that Sukkot will be observed from year to year throughout the millennial reign. (Zechariah 14:16). During Sukkot we are commanded to go to Jerusalem and build sukkas – which are temporary dwellings – also called a booth or a manger. This was possibly the structure that Messiah was born in when *the Word became flesh and tabernacled among us.*" Yahanan 1:14. These Appointed Times are discussed in more detail in the Walk in the Light Series book entitled "Appointed Times."

22 Shemot (שמות) is the transliteration for the Hebrew word which is often written Exodus in English Bibles. Shemot actually means: "names."

23 Egypt is the modern word used to describe the land inhabited by the descendents of Mitsrayim, who was the son of Ham (Beresheet 10:6). Thus, throughout this text the

word Mitsrayim may be used in place of the English word Egypt since that is how it is rendered in the Torah.

Mosheh (משׁה) is the proper transliteration for the name of the Patriarch commonly called Moses.

The first born is a very important subject, especially in ancient days. The first born was typically entitled to a "double portion" of the father's estate and was expected to carry on in the father's stead after death. In the Exodus we see YHWH killing the firstborn of all in Egypt that were not under the "covering" of the blood of the slaughtered lambs and kids of the first year. Because of this incident, the Tribe of Levi was later set apart to YHWH. "*11* *YHWH also said to Mosheh,* *12* *'I have taken the Levites from among the Israelites in place of the first male offspring of every Yisraelite woman. The Levites are mine,* *13* *for all the firstborn are mine. When I struck down all the firstborn in Egypt, I set apart for myself every firstborn in Yisrael, whether man or animal. They are to be mine. I am YHWH."* Bemidbar 3:11-13.

The union between a man and a woman is specifically provided by the Creator as an example of the intimate relationship or "knowledge" that He desires to have with His creation. The connection between Creator and creation was lost after Eden and both man and the rest of creation have suffered ever since. Sinai was a step in the direction of restoring that connection between the Creator and His creation. Yisrael was "chosen" as a bride to bring about the restoration of the nations. What happened at Mt. Sinai was a marriage ceremony between YHWH and His Bride – Yisrael. After delivering her from bondage He then gave her the opportunity to become His Bride - if she agreed to obey the Torah. The Torah was, in essence, a marriage contract or a ketubah. The people declared: *"All that YHWH has spoken we will do."* Shemot 19:8. In other words, "I Do" or rather "We Do." They agreed to the marriage and were commanded to prepare for the marriage ceremony by cleansing and consecrating themselves. After hearing the Ten Commandments they could not take it anymore and asked Mosheh to relay the Words of YHWH.

Mosheh ascended the mountain while the people waited and ultimately got impatient. They decided to make up their own celebration to YHWH and create a golden calf, just as they had seen in Egypt. They had already been instructed not to make any images and if they had only waited and listened a bit further, they would have heard the instruction regarding an altar and the prohibition against gold and silver gods which was commanded immediately after the 10th commandment. Regardless, they committed adultery before they even consummated the marriage. In very crude terms, it was like a bride excusing herself during the wedding feast and having sex with an old boyfriend while the groom is waiting for her to go on their honeymoon. It was understandably infuriating to YHWH. As a result, the covenant was broken, and Mosheh literally broke the Tablets which contained the covenant. Mosheh thereafter went up to YHWH to make atonement (Shemot 32:30). The covenant was later renewed and placed upon new tablets, this time cut by Mosheh instead of YHWH which provided a vivid picture of the Messiah and the future renewed Covenant, although the terms were written by YHWH and remained the same – the Torah. The desire of YHWH is for His Bride to know Him. In fact, you must "know YHWH" to be married to Him and this "knowledge" is much more than a handshake or friendly introduction. The Hebrew word for know is yada (ידע) which has a variety of meanings but in this context means intimate relations. The example which is provided through the Scriptures is the intimate "knowledge" shared between a husband and a wife. While YHWH was always a faithful Husband to His Bride, Yisrael was not always a faithful bride. She went whoring and the House of Yisrael was actually divorced from YHWH. As a result, before the restorative work of YHWH can be completed, He must renew the covenant with Yisrael, His Bride - not the Church.

[27] Beresheet 33:17
[28] Succot, also known as the Feast of Booths or the Feast of Tabernacles is specifically mentioned as a celebration which

will occur every year when the Messiah reigns from Zion. All the Nations, not just Jews, will be required to celebrate or they will be punished. This is perfectly consistent with the notion that the Appointed Times belong to YHWH and that it is the time when His Creation will meet with Him. It is commanded in Shemot 23:16; Shemot 34:22; Vayiqra 23:34; Devarim 16:16 and Devarim 31:10. We know from the Prophet Zechariah (Zekaryah) that all of the nations of the Earth will be required to celebrate this feast when Messiah reigns. "[16] *Then the survivors from all the nations that have attacked Jerusalem will go up year after year to worship the King, YHWH Almighty, and to celebrate the Feast of Tabernacles.* [17] *If any of the peoples of the earth do not go up to Jerusalem to worship the King, YHWH Almighty, they will have no rain.* [18] *If the Egyptian people do not go up and take part, they will have no rain. YHWH will bring on them the plague he inflicts on the nations that do not go up to celebrate the Feast of Tabernacles.* [19] *This will be the punishment of Egypt and the punishment of all the nations that do not go up to celebrate the Feast of Tabernacles.*" Zekaryah 14:16-19.

[29] Yisrael was to be a set apart people, a kingdom of priests so that they could be an example to the rest of the nations. YHWH spoke the following to Mosheh at Sinai: "[5] *Now if you obey Me fully and keep My Covenant, then out of all nations you will be my treasured possession. Although the whole earth is Mine,* [6] *you will be for me a kingdom of priests and a holy nation.*" Shemot 19:4-6

[30] Vayiqra (ויקרא) is the transliteration for the Hebrew word which is often written Leviticus in English Bibles. Vayiqra means: "called."

[31] *Ancient Egypt*, Lorna Oakes and Lucia Gahlin, Barnes & Nobles Books, 2003, Page 283.

[32] The word "Bible" has traditionally been the word used to describe the collection of documents considered by Christianity to be inspired by Elohim - I prefer the use of the word Scriptures. The word Bible derives from Byblos which has more pagan connotations than I prefer, especially when referring to the written Word of Elohim. This subject

is discussed in greater detail in the Walk in the Light Series book entitled "Scriptures."

The Scriptures provided Appointed Times which are described by YHWH as "My Appointed Times" (Vayiqra 23:2. In other words, they belong to Him. The Appointed Times described in Vayiqra 23, as well as other portions of the Torah, are often erroneously referred to as the Jewish Holidays. This is a grave mistake because YHWH specifically says that these are "My appointed times." They belong to no ethnic or religious group. This topic is discussed in greater detail in the Walk in the Light series book entitled "Appointed Times." "Shavuot was a shadow of things to come for the body of Mashiach. Consider the "Appointed Times" we should be observing, as we have been enjoined to YHWH as Yisrael through His Covenant (Eph. 2:8-13). These are listed as the Sabbath (weekly), Passover, Unleavened bread, Shabuoth (called "Pentecost"), and the appointments of the seventh moon, Yom Teruah, Yom Kaphar (Kippur), and Sukkoth (Tabernacles), and are carefully explained so all Israel will observe them and see YHWH's redemption plan for them. YHWH uses agricultural metaphors to represent His "redemption plan" for Yisrael, and Yahushua's work is accomplishing that redemption through all of these "shadows." They are literally shadows (metaphoric teachings) for Yisrael. Now, consider the following correction of the translation we are all familiar with: "Let no man therefore judge you in meat, or in drink, or in respect of a festival, or of the new moon, or of the Sabbath days which are a shadow of things to come for the body of Messiah." Colossians 2:16-17. Normally we see the word but in the last phrase. However, these "shadows" are intended to be for the body of Mashiach, not ignored as Christianity has done. The word commonly translated as but instead of for is the Greek word "de", and can mean a variety of things in English. It is a primary particle that can mean: but, and, or, also, yet, however, then, so, or FOR. In the last phrase, the word is does not exist in any of the received Greek texts; it is in italics in the KJV because is was

added, and not in the Greek Received Text). These festivals are shadows of things to come, and certainly are for the body of Messiah. The body of Mashiach is Yisrael. Shavuot is an "annual" Sabbath day, a shadow of our Redemption. Through the Covenant we are wedded to Yahushua, our Redeemer, the Husband of all Yisrael." - Contributed by Lew White.

34 The concept of "The Trinity" is one which derives from pagan father, mother, son worship. Examples of trinitarian worship can be traced back to Babylon. For more detail on this important subject see the Walk in the Light series book entitled "Restoration."

35 This is why Torah observance is critical – it teaches us distinctions between acceptable conduct and unacceptable conduct. It tells us how to live righteous lives. We often hear about a person acknowledging that they are a sinner but the only way to know if you are a sinner is from the Torah.

36 The Tanak is the compilation of Scriptures commonly referred to as The Hebrew Bible or The Old Testament in Christian Bibles. It consists of the Torah (Law), Nebi'im (Prophets) and the Kethubim (Writings), thus the Hebrew acronym TNK which is pronounced tah-nak. I believe that the term "Old Testament" is terribly misleading because it gives the impression that everything contained therein is old or outdated. While growing up in a mainline Christian denomination I was given the distinct impression that it was full of great stories, but it applied to "The Jews" and it was replaced by the "New Testament" which contained the important Scriptures for Christians. While this may or may not have been done intentionally, I believe that it is a notion which is pervasive throughout much of Christianity. Without a doubt, the Tanak is essential to the faith and these are the Scriptures which must be at the core of our belief system. If these truths are not at the foundation and considered completely relevant for today, then people are prone to be misled and follow false and twisted doctrines. This problem is amplified by the fact that most of the

source texts for the "New Testament" derive from copies of Greek or Latin manuscripts which are western languages and have often been translated in such a fashion that the Eastern concepts of the faith are lost or distorted. The issue is discussed at length in The Walk in the Light Series book entitled "Scriptures."

37   The prophets Jeremiah and Ezekiel often referred to the "backsliding" of Yisrael. For example, "*You have rejected me, declares YHWH, you keep on backsliding.*" Jeremiah 15:6. The Hebrew word translating as "backsliding" is achor (אחור) which means "backward" so literally Yisrael went backward instead of forward. (see Jeremiah 2:19; 3:22; 14:7; 15:6, Ezekiel 37:23).

38   For a detailed discussion of the Covenants found within the Scriptures see the Walk in the Light series book entitled "Covenants".

39   Bemidbar (במדבר) is the Hebrew word for the text often referred to as "Numbers." The word Bemidbar actually means: "in the desert."

40   Yahudah (יהודה) is the proper English transliteration for the Hebrew name often pronounced as Judah.

41   There is much debate concerning the exact transliteration and pronunciation of this name – especially since it is the same name as the Messiah. Some spell the name as Yeshua or Y'shua but I believe that these are shortened versions of the Name and fail to adequately represent the Name of YHWH which is clearly part of the Name. This subject is discussed in greater detail in the Walk in the Light book entitled "Names."

42   Since there is no "J" in the Hebrew language the name Joseph is more accurately rendered as Yoseph.

43   The reason that I point this out is because it is very significant and prophetic. The fact that these two sons were born in a pagan context and later adopted by Yisrael speaks to their future redemption.

44   The story of Ruth is truly a story for our day - you should stop and read it now. It is not a difficult story to read and understand so I will simply point out some things to think

about when you read it. Notice that the family of Naomi were from Bethlehem in the Land of Yahudah. They were from the Tribe of Yahudah although they were in the land of Moab because Yisrael was under a famine. Yisrael had no king – they were in the period of the judges yet the name of Naomi's husband Elimelech means: "my Elohim is King" which gives us a hint that this story is about YHWH as King. The only reason Yisrael would be in famine is if they were being cursed which means that they were not obeying the terms of the Covenant made at Sinai and renewed at Moab. So where does Naomi and her family go - back to the Torah - they went to Moab. There Naomi's two sons marry Moabite women - who would then become part of their family. We read that not only did Naomi's husband die while they were in Moab but so did her sons. Typically when one son would die he would take on the responsibilities of his brother's family but in this case all of the men had died and the women and their hope of producing offspring had effectively been "cut off." The women were free to leave their connection with Yisrael and remain in Moab but Ruth "clung" to Naomi and took Naomi's Elohim as her own. They then return to Yisrael together and the story of Ruth coming to the Land of Yisrael starts "in the beginning" (beresheet) of the barley harvest. This is highly significant because we know that it is around the beginning of the first month because the first month coincides with Aviv barley and the harvest. The barley is harvested as the people gather their firstfruits and prepare, among other things, for the Passover, the Feast of Unleavened Bread and Firstfruits. In Vayiqra 23, we are provided a detailed account of what are traditionally known as the Feasts of YHWH which are divided into two groups; the early harvest and the latter harvest. The latter harvest feasts all occur in the seventh month and immediately preceding their description, the Torah provides something specific concerning these times. "*When you reap the harvest of your land, you shall not wholly reap the corners of your field when you reap, nor shall you gather any gleaning from your harvest. You shall leave them for the poor*

and for the stranger: I am YHWH your Elohim." Vayiqra 23:22.
YHWH is specifically showing that He will make provision
for the Gentiles through His Appointed Times and this sets
the stage for the process of being redeemed and grafted in
by Ruth who was previously joined to Yisrael and cut off.
Ruth was gleaning the fields of Boaz and she went about
the business of redemption with Boaz at the threshing floor.
(Ruth 3).

The mikvah is where the Christian doctrine of baptism
derives although it did not begin with Christianity and
was commanded by YHWH long before Messiah came. It
was a natural thing for Yisraelites to do. In fact, there were
numerous mikvaote (plural form of mikvah) at the Temple
and it was required that a person be immersed in a mikvah
prior to presenting their sacrifice. The Hebrew word for
baptize is tevila (טביל) which is a full body immersion
that takes place in a mikvah (מקרה) which comes from the
passage in Beresheet 1:10 when YHWH "gathered together"
the waters. The mikvah is the gathering together of flowing
waters. The "tevila" immersion is symbolic for a person
going from a state of uncleanliness to cleanliness. The
priests in the temple needed to tevila regularly to insure that
they were in a state of cleanliness when they served in the
Temple. Anyone going to the Temple to worship or offer
sacrifices would tevila at the numerous pools outside the
Temple. There are a variety of instances found in the Torah
when a person was required to tevila. It is very important
because it reminds us of the filth of sin and the need to be
washed clean from our sin in order to stand in the presence
of a holy, set apart Elohim. Therefore it makes perfect sense
that we be immersed in a mikvah prior to presenting the
sacrifice of the perfect lamb as atonement for our sins. It
also cleanses our temple which the Spirit of Elohim will
enter in to tabernacle with us. The tevila is symbolic of
becoming born again and is an act of going from one life
to another. Being born again is not something that became
popular in the seventies within the Christian religion. It is a
remarkably Yisraelite concept that was understood to occur

when one arose from the mikvah. In fact, people witnessing an immersion would often cry out "Born Again!" when a person came up from an immersion. It was also an integral part of the Rabbinic conversion process, which, in many ways is not Scriptural, but in this sense is correct. For a Gentile to complete their conversion, they were required to be immersed, or baptized, which meant that they were born again: born into a new life. Many people fail to realize that this concept is not a Christian concept because of the exchange between Messiah and Nicodemus. Let us take a look at that conversation in the Gospel according to Yahanan: *"¹ Now there was a man of the Pharisees named Nicodemus, a ruler of the Yahudim. ² He came to Yahushua at night and said, 'Rabbi, we know you are a teacher who has come from Elohim. For no one could perform the miraculous signs You are doing if Elohim were not with him.' ³ In reply Yahushua declared, 'I tell you the truth, no one can see the kingdom of Elohim unless he is born again.' ⁴ 'How can a man be born when he is old?' Nicodemus asked. 'Surely he cannot enter a second time into his mother's womb to be born!' ⁵ Yahushua answered, 'I tell you the truth, no one can enter the kingdom of Elohim unless he is born of water and the Spirit. ⁶ Flesh gives birth to flesh, but the Spirit gives birth to spirit. ⁷ You should not be surprised at my saying, You must be born again. ⁸ The wind blows wherever it pleases. You hear its sound, but you cannot tell where it comes from or where it is going. So it is with everyone born of the Spirit.' ⁹ 'How can this be?' Nicodemus asked. ¹⁰ 'You are Yisrael's teacher,' said Yahushua, 'and do you not understand these things? ¹¹ I tell you the truth, we speak of what we know, and we testify to what we have seen, but still you people do not accept our testimony. ¹² I have spoken to you of earthly things and you do not believe; how then will you believe if I speak of heavenly things? ¹³ No one has ever gone into heaven except the One who came from heaven - the Son of Man. ¹⁴ Just as Mosheh lifted up the snake in the desert, so the Son of Man must be lifted up, ¹⁵ that everyone who believes in him may have eternal life.'"* Yahanan 3:1-15. Nicodemus was not surprised by the fact that a person needed to be "born again." His first question: *"How can a man be born when he is old?"*

demonstrated he did not see how it applied to him, because he was already a Yahudim. His second question *"How can this be,"* only affirmed that fact. And this is why Yahushua asked: *"You are Yisrael's teacher and do you not understand these things?"* In other words, "you're supposed to be the one teaching Yisrael about these spiritual matters and you're not. You think only the Gentiles need to be immersed and born again, but you all need it because you are all sinners and this needs to be taught to everyone, not just the Gentiles." So you see, being born again through immersion was not new to Yisrael. This is why many readily were immersed by Yahanan the Immerser - they understood their need. It was often the leaders who failed to see their need for cleansing because they were blinded by the notion that their Torah observance justified them. It is important to note that the tevila must occur in "living waters" - in other words, water which is moving and ideally which contains life. These living waters refer to the Messiah. In a Scriptural marriage, a bride would enter the waters of purification prior to her wedding. These are the same waters that we are to enter when we make a confession of faith and become part of the Body of Messiah - His Bride. Also, a bride traditionally enters the waters of separation when her niddah period has ended so that she can be reunited with her husband.

46 Judges, known as shoftim, were those appointed to mete out justice and right rulings among the Yisraelites. They always existed from Mosheh onward but became increasingly important after the death of Joshua (Yahushua) to the time of King David during which time there were individual "judges" who were raised up to lead Yisrael. Since Yisrael was divided into twelve tribes the judges added some cohesiveness to an often divided nation.

47 The "book" of Deuteronomy would be more accurately described as Sefer Devarim, ספר דברים, since it originally came as a scroll. Devarim means "words" in Hebrew.

48 The name of the man often called Samuel in English translations of the Scriptures is more accurately pronounced Shemuel (שמול). In modern Hebrew it is often written and

pronounced as Sh'muel.

The Tabernacle, better known as the Mishkan was constructed by Mosheh and the skilled craftsmen of Yisrael while they travelled through the Wilderness. It was made to be moveable – as a tent and it was the House of YHWH. The physical appearance and layout of the Tabernacle is a pattern of the Garden of Eden. It also provides an image of a person's body and is intended to show us how YHWH desires to dwell or "tabernacle" within us. These two concepts of the Tabernacle combined show us how YHWH desires to dwell <u>with</u> us and <u>in</u> us. The description of the building of the Tabernacle is provided in Shemot 25 – Shemot 28.

We repeatedly see the word shamar (שמר) throughout the Scriptures although we do not always recognize the consistency because it can be translated as "watch," "guard," "keep" etc. The word is meant to stress to us that we are to act as watchmen over the commandments so that we are diligent to obey. Adam did not watch over the Garden as he was commanded and the serpent entered and deceived Hawah and himself – the consequences were devastating. As the Son of Adam we see that Messiah did what Adam failed to do. Where Adam failed in the Garden of Eden Yahushua stepped in and broke the cycle in another Garden. Right before the death of Yahushua we see Him keeping vigil in the Garden of Gethsemane as He is about to complete His mission. While He stays awake and prays - His disciples kept falling asleep. In the Hebrew Mattityahu we get a vivid picture of His instructions as He tells His disciples the same thing that the Creator instructed Adam - He tells them to <u>watch </u>and He gives them something <u>to do</u>. In Mattityahu 26:38 He says: "*Support me and <u>watch</u> with me.*" The word for watch is shamar. In Mattityahu 26:40 He asks: "*So you are unable to <u>watch</u> with Me one hour?*" Again the word is shamar. In Mattityahu 26:41 He states: "*<u>Watch</u> and pray – lest you fall into temptation.*" Again we see the word shamar. In each case this presents the picture of a watchman keeping guard. And notice the connection - <u>Watch and pray lest you</u>

fall into temptation. Adam failed in his duty to watch, just as the disciples did, and as a result both he and the woman fell into temptation. Yahushua the Messiah stayed awake and watched - like a watchman over Yisrael just as was written: "*He who watches (shamar) over Yisrael will neither sleep nor slumber.*" Psalms (Tehillim) 121:4. The purpose of His watching is to preserve and protect and guard our souls - our very lives - we read this in Psalms (Tehillim) 121:7-8. Again to watch over (shamar) our souls is to keep and to protect us. He also instructs <u>us</u> to watch and an important part of our watching involves the Torah. Over and over again we are instructed to <u>keep</u> the commandments and to <u>watch</u> the commandments and to <u>guard</u> the commandments. This is the same word <u>shamar</u> and we are given this instruction so that we stay within the hedge of protection provided by the Torah - <u>so that we don't fall into temptation - so that we are kept from evil.</u> The purpose of a hedge is to make a separation between those things on one side and those things on the other side. The Torah provides us with distinctions and draws a line for us to understand <u>right from wrong, clean from unclean, righteous</u> conduct from <u>abominable</u> conduct. <u>On that foundation the Kingdom is established and it will only be populated with those who will also OBEY.</u>

[51] Tehillim (תהלים) is a proper transliteration for the word Psalms. The Book of Psalms would thus be rendered Sefer Tehillim. King David repeatedly extolled the Torah throughout the Tehillim. In fact, the entire Tehillim 119, the longest of the Tehillim, is about the Torah. I would encourage every reader to read this portion of Scripture, recognizing that the entire text is about the Torah.

[52] We know from the text that Avraham went to the "region" or "land" of Moriah better translated as Moriyah (מריה) which means "shown by YHWH." Tradition holds that this was the same site that the altar was built on before the Temple built by Solomon, although the Scriptures do not specifically state that fact.

[53] There are two similar, but also differing accounts of David's

purchase of the threshing floor of Araunah. According to 2 Shemuel 24:18-25: "[18] *On that day Gad went to David and said to him, 'Go up and build an altar to YHWH on the threshing floor of Araunah the Jebusite.'* [19] *So David went up, as YHWH had commanded through Gad.* [20] *When Araunah looked and saw the king and his men coming toward him, he went out and bowed down before the king with his face to the ground.* [21] *Araunah said, 'Why has my lord the king come to his servant?' 'To buy your threshing floor,' David answered, 'so I can build an altar to YHWH, that the plague on the people may be stopped.'* [22] *Araunah said to David, 'Let my lord the king take whatever pleases him and offer it up. Here are oxen for the burnt offering, and here are threshing sledges and ox yokes for the wood.* [23] *O king, Araunah gives all this to the king.' Araunah also said to him, 'May YHWH your Elohim accept you.'* [24] *But the king replied to Araunah, 'No, I insist on paying you for it. I will not sacrifice to YHWH my Elohim burnt offerings that cost me nothing.' So David bought the threshing floor and the oxen and paid <u>fifty shekels of silver</u> for them.* [25] *David built an altar to YHWH there and sacrificed burnt offerings and fellowship offerings. Then YHWH answered prayer in behalf of the land, and the plague on Yisrael was stopped.*" The weight of the silver was around 1 ¼ pounds or .6 kilograms. According to 1 Chronicles 21:25-26: "[25] *David paid Araunah <u>six hundred shekels of gold</u> for the site.* [26] *David built an altar to YHWH there and sacrificed burnt offerings and fellowship offerings. He called on YHWH, and YHWH answered him with fire from heaven on the altar of burnt offering.*" The amount is a weight equivalent to about 15 pounds or seven kilograms. Notice the difference in prices which appears, on the surface, to be a discrepancy but at second glance is not. The writer in Shemuel simply stating that David purchased the threshing floor and the oxen to sacrifice and paid 50 shekels of silver for them – meaning the oxen. The writer in I Chronicles was concerned about the site and indicated the price for the threshing floor was six hundred shekels of gold. Notice also that fire came down from heaven, as with Eliyahu.

[54] http://en.wikipedia.org/wiki/Threshing_floor

[55] It is important to note that the House of YHWH was

built upon a threshing floor. This is significant because all of the adult males of Yisrael were commanded to appear before YHWH three times a year at the place where He chose to put His Name – In other words - where He lived. That place has been Jerusalem ever since David set up the Tabernacle there. The Appointed Times were centered around the harvests and no one was to come empty handed. In other words, they were supposed to bring the best – their firstfruits – just as Hebel had done long ago. It is there, at the threshing floor of YHWH, that the hearts of men would be sifted as they did business with their Elohim

56 There are significant parallels between the Tabernacle in the Wilderness and the House which David planned to build for YHWH. The House of YHWH took a journey with Yisrael and was portable while Yisrael was moving and even during the period of the shoftim. It was only when David became King and established his throne in Jerusalem that we see the transition of the House of YHWH from a movable tent to a permanent building. This is significant and is a Messianic reference to a future time when Messiah will rebuild the House as foretold to David: "*7 YHWH declares to you that YHWH Himself will establish a house for you: 12 When your days are over and you rest with your fathers, I will raise up your offspring to succeed you, who will come from your own body, and I will establish His kingdom. 13 He is the one who will build a house for My Name, and I will establish the throne of His kingdom forever.*" 2 Shemuel 7:11-14. This House built by Messiah will be the New Jerusalem, only He will be the Chief Cornerstone (Capstone) (Yeshayahu 28:16; Zekaryah 10:4; Ephesians 2:20; 1 Peter 2:6) and He will build this House with Living Stones (1 Peter 2:5).

57 Shlomo (שלמה) is the proper English transliteration for the Hebrew name which is traditionally pronounced as Solomon.

58 This is all that YHWH asks of His people and they continually refuse to do what He says. There are rich blessings for those who obey – like David. There are also curses for those who disobey – like Shlomo.

59   Interestingly, what Jeroboam did is exactly what Christianity has done to the true worship of YHWH. Jereboam established places of worship other than Jerusalem, he got rid of the Levite priests and set up his own priesthood, he worshipped false gods and he established new holidays. The Roman Catholic Church, from which most of modern Christianity derives, has established Rome as their headquarters, rather than Jerusalem. They have established a priesthood separate from the Levitical priesthood. They celebrate Christmas, Easter and numerous holidays with pagan origins, all the while ignoring the Appointed Times of YHWH. They have replaced the Sabbath with Sunday and set up images which are adored and worshipped – all contrary to the Torah. As of June 29, 2008, the Congregation for Divine Worship and the Sacraments by explicit directive of Pope Benedict XVI has prohibited the use of YHWH in Catholic worship. Instead, it has been directed that the Name should be replaced by the Latin "Dominus," Greek "Kyrios," Hebrew "Adonai" or a word of "equivalent meaning" in the local language. See www.catholicnewsagency.com. I could go on, but trust that the point is abundantly clear, the Christian faith, including the Catholic Church and its' progeny in the Protestant factions have fallen into the same error as Jereboam and the House of Yisrael.

60   This is where it gets confusing for some due to the fact that the Northern Tribes carried the name Yisrael, rather than say – Joseph. While the united Kingdom is called Yisrael, the northern tribes are also referred to as Yisrael, the House of Yisrael, Joseph and Ephraim.

61   www.uhcg.org

62   Yehezqel (יהזקאל) is the proper Hebrew transliteration for the Prophet commonly called Ezekiel.

63   The dates concerning the exile of Yahudah are subject to debate in academia. The dates provided in this book have been determined through extensive research by a friend in Jerusalem who is using historical information, mathematics, eclipse data, computer simulations and other scientific methods to lock in time and refine these dates. As a result,

these dates will likely not agree with many accepted sources, but they are believed to be more accurate. The same will also hold true with many of the dates found in this book and other Walk in the Light resources. For more information see www.torahcalendar.com.

64 It was already discussed that the patriarch commonly referred to as Joshua was originally named Hosea, which means "salvation." As with other name changes in the Scriptures, it is important to take note when it occurs. In the case of Hoshea, his name simply meant "salvation." When his name was changed, the Name of YHWH was added as a proclamation that "YHWH saves His people!" So then, the Name of the Messiah is the same name as Joshua, who left Egypt, spied out the Land and gave a good report then wandered in the wilderness with Yisrael for 40 years. He was the one, along with Mosheh, who renewed the covenant with Yisrael at Moab. He then led the children of Yisrael across the Jordan River as a community mikvah and directed their circumcision. He led them in their first Passover in the Land and he was the one who led them into battle as they conquered their enemies, took the Land and again renewed the covenant at Shechem. The patterns are profound and more than mere coincidence. How appropriate that the Messiah of Yisrael would bear the same Name as this great patriarch.

65 Fausset's Bible Dictionary, Electronic Database Copyright (c)1998 by Biblesoft.

66 There is an amazing tendency for people to suppress the Name of YHWH or even replace it with the names of false gods. The Jewish religion has continued and propagated a false tradition concerning the ineffability of the Name. They will often use the title "Adonai" or "Ha Shem" when referring to the Name. Some ancient scribes would leave a blank or vowel point the Name as Adonai. In English translations of the Bible, translators have chosen to replace Elohim with "God" and YHWH with "The LORD." Amazingly, the use of the terms "God" and "Lord" can be linked to pagan worship. I have been shown copies of

English Bibles which have been translated into foreign languages where they actually insert Allah in place of God. This is simply unbelievable because they have, in effect, altered the Scriptures by referring to a different god. Allah is not YHWH – Allah is the name of a muslim deity. It is completely inappropriate to replace the Name of YHWH with a title or the name of another god. This appears to be a conspiracy to suppress the Name of YHWH and should give anyone pause over this very important issue. For a more detailed discussion of this subject see the Walk in the Light series book entitled "Names."

67 Yeshayahu (ישעיהו) is the proper transliteration for the Prophet commonly called Isaiah. His name in Hebrew means "YHWH saves."

68 See also Yeshayahu 35 and 65

69 Yirmeyahu (ירמיהו) is the proper transliteration for the Hebrew name of the prophet commonly called Jeremiah.

70 Just as the generation at Sinai was unable to enter into the Land due to their idolatry, so it would be with the House of Yisrael. The adulterous generation would have to die off and allow a new generation – a generation of virgins, so to speak, which would be the Bride Yisrael and enter into a renewed Covenant with YHWH her Husband.

71 A Ketubah (כתובה) is simply a marriage contract. It was quite common in ancient cultures and continues to be common primarily in eastern cultures. It established the rights and responsibilities of the parties and often included the damages for a parties' breach of the contract. In western culture similar contracts are used and called pre-nuptial agreements.

72 Those that continue to attempt to argue that the regathering has already occurred are typically motivated by a particular prejudice, doctrine or position. Some are from the Yahudim who are attempting to position themselves as "first class" citizens and relegate the rest of the Redeemed to "economy class" as Gentile Believers – which is a contradiction in terms. Some are Christians that do not want to have anything to do with the "Old Testament" and would

rather consider themselves "Spiritual Israel" or "The Church" thus elevating themselves above Yisrael or at least putting themselves into a different category. Whatever their motivation, their teachings are divisive and clearly in contradiction to the prophecies which indicate that this regathering will occur at the end of times and Messiah will rule over the united kingdom from that point on. See Chapter 16 for numerous examples of these prophecies.

⁷³ The Christian religion practices Replacement Theology which comes fashioned in a variety of doctrinal teachings. Replacement Theology basically teaches that the church replaced Yisrael. The Yisrael that we read about in the "Old" Testament was "physical" Yisrael while the "church" is "spiritual" Israel. The word "church" is a man-made word generally associated with the Catholic and Christian religions. In that context, it is typically meant to describe the corporate body of faith. It is used in most modern English Bibles as a translation for the Greek word ekklesia (εκκλεσια) which generally refers to the "called out assembly of YHWH." The word "church" derives from pagan origins and its misuse is part of the problem associated with Replacement Theology which teaches that the "Church" has replaced Yisrael, which in Hebrew is called the qahal (קהל): "the called out assembly of YHWH." The Hebrew "qahal" and Greek "ekklesia" are the same thing: The Commonwealth of Yisrael. Therefore, the continued use of the word "church" is divisive and confusing. It gives the appearance that "the Church" is something new or different from Yisrael.

⁷⁴ The collection of writings commonly called "The New Testament" is better called The Messianic Scriptures because they describe the past and future work of the Messiah. The New Covenant, more accurately called the Renewed Covenant is found in the Tanak, which is just as relevant today as the Messianic Scriptures. They fit together as a complete package and the "New" does not replace or supersede the "Old". In fact, early Believers only had the Tanak as the complete Messianic Scriptures were not

written for decades after the resurrection of the Messiah. I believe that the Torah is the foundation for faith in YHWH and therefore I avoid using the "Old" and "New" distinctions which tend to diminish the Tanak. This subject is described in greater detail in the Walk in the Light Series books entitled "The Scriptures" and "Covenants."

75 Jesus is the English version of the Hellenized Greek name Iesous, spelled Iesus in Latin. Some say that this name has no specific meaning, while others indicate that it refers to different pagan deities. One thing is for certain, Jesus was not a Hebrew name and the Messiah was not called Jesus when He walked the Earth. Nor is it a translation of the Hebrew Name Yahushua. Notice that the English name Jesus is not even a transliteration of the Greek or Latin spellings because it starts with a "J" sound. Whether in English, Greek or Latin, it bears little resemblance to the correct Hebrew Name although it is strikingly similarity to the name Iaso, also spelled Ieso, the Greek goddess of healing, who is directly related to sun god worship. In fact, according to Greek mythology, the father of Ieso was Asclepius, the deity of healing. His father was Apollo, the sun god. "Iaso is Ieso in the Ionic dialect of the Greeks, Iesous being the contracted genitive form. In David Kravitz's, *Dictionary of Greek and Roman Mythology*, we find a similar form, namely Iasus. There are four different Greek deities with the name Iasus, one of them being the Son of Rhea." *The Scriptures*, Institute for Scripture Research, (1998) p. 1216.

76 Hellenization was something advanced by Alexander the Great in the fourth century B.C.E. and later into the first century B.C.E. which involved conquering nations and imposing Greek civilization and customs upon them. Often times the conquered nation would maintain its individual characteristics while absorbing aspects of Greek culture including the worship of many gods. This continued for hundreds of years and many of the early Believers of Yahushua lived within these Hellenized cultures. In time, many pagan concepts crept into the faith which has been perpetuated and compounded throughout the last two

thousand years.

77   Eliyahu is the correct transliteration of the Hebrew name for the prophet of Yisrael commonly called Elijah. The name means: "YHWH is Elohim." If you examine the Greek manuscripts from which we derive our English New Testament you will find Helias in the Greek when referring to Eliyahu. This was also done in the Septuagint. How interesting that a Greek rendering of this prophet that was swept up in a fiery chariot would be the same as the pagan sun god that was often depicted as riding a chariot into the sun.

78   For a more detailed examination of the Name of the Messiah see the Walk in the Light series book entitled "Names."

79   For more information on the birth of Yahushua see the Walk in the Light Series books entitled "The Messiah" and "Appointed Times."

80   December 25 is not the birth date of Yahushua, rather it used to be the date that the winter solstice fell upon. As such most pagan religions treated that as the birth date of their sun god. It is a pagan holiday which Christianity adopted as their own. For a more detailed discussion on Christmas and other such pagan days see the Walk in the Light series book entitled "Pagan Holidays."

81   The name of the Prophet commonly called Micah (מיכה) is the contracted form of Michayahu (מיכיהו) and means: "who is like Yah."

82   Mattityahu (מתתיהו) is the proper transliteration of the Hebrew name which is often spelled Matthew in English. The name contains the Name of YHWH and means "gift of Yah."

83   Adoption is a very important concept to understand. I have been blessed with having adopted two children as Yisrael adopted two children – Ephraim and Manasseh. Through this process I have learned just how powerful it is to adopt a child because it is a choice that we make – we choose to love and the love that I have for my children could not be any stronger. We choose to take the child as our own and we even elevate that child to a first born status. This is the

love that YHWH shows for us and He demonstrates very vividly how He is willing to take us – who were not His people and make us His sons – "Sons of Elohim." Ephraim and Manassah were born in Egypt and adopted by Yisrael, Mosheh was born in Egypt and adopted into the family of Pharoah – even Messiah was adopted by Yoseph. Following this example, we all need to be ready to be adopted. This is why Shaul wrote: "*22 We know that the whole creation has been groaning as in the pains of childbirth right up to the present time. 23 Not only so, but we ourselves, who have the firstfruits of the Spirit, groan inwardly as we wait eagerly for our adoption as sons, the redemption of our bodies.*" Romans 8:22-24. He also wrote about Yisrael: "*4 Theirs is the adoption as sons; theirs the divine glory, the Covenants, the receiving of the law, the temple worship and the promises. 5 Theirs are the patriarchs, and from them is traced the human ancestry of Messiah, who is Elohim over all, forever praised! Amen.*" Romans 9:4-5.

84 *The "Lost" Ten Tribes of Israel . . . Found!* Steven M. Collins, CPA Book Publisher 1995 4th Printing p.268.

85 *Antiquities of the Jews*, 11.5.2, from The Works of Josephus, translated by Whiston, W., Hendrickson Publishers 1987 13th Printing. p 294.

86 It is believed by many that this was the great sign in the sky as described in Revelation 12:1-2: "*Now a great sign appeared in heaven: a woman clothed with the sun, with the moon under her feet, and on her head a garland of twelve stars.*" NKJV. The Hebrew word which describes the stars and constellations is mazzaroth. There is much that we can learn from the celestial bodies which were given for "signs" among other things. (Beresheet 1:14). For more information concerning these matters a good starting point would be: *Mazzaroth* by Frances Rolleston Weiser Books 2001; *The Witness of the Stars* by E.W. Bullinger Kregel Publications; *The Gospel in the Stars*, Joseph A. Seiss, Kregel Publications 1972.

87 It is worthy to note that David, known as a man after Elohim's heart, could not build the House of YHWH. The reason is provided in the Scriptures by David himself: "*7 My son, I had it in my heart to build a house for the Name of YHWH*

my Elohim. [8] *But this word of YHWH came to me: 'You have shed much blood and have fought many wars. You are not to build a house for My Name, because you have shed much blood on the earth in My sight."* 1 Chronicles 22:7-9. That being the case we must question the status of the "Second Temple" of Herod. Now this Temple was actually built by Zerubbabel and the remnant of Yahudah who returned but is often attributed to Herod because he spent many years and much money rebuilding it, most likely as a monument to himself than a tribute to YHWH. There is nothing in the Scriptures indicating that YHWH commissioned Herod with this task as He had done with Shlomo. Also, Herod was a tyrant with even the blood of his own family on his hands. So I doubt that Herod was qualified to rebuild the Temple and since it did not even contain the Ark, the entire Temple service was defective – thus appropriately representing the status of things in Jerusalem at that time.

[88] en.wikipedia.org/wiki/Sadducees.

[89] en.wikipedia.org/wiki/Pharisees. For an excellent treatment of the rise of Rabbinic Judaism I recommend the book *Rabbi Akiba's Messiah: The Origins of Rabbinic Authority* by Daniel Grubner, Elijah Publishing (1999).

[90] According to Josephus: "The Pharisees have delivered to the people a great many observances by succession from their fathers, which are not written in the laws of Moses; and for that reason it is that the Sadducees reject them, and say that we are to esteem those observances to be obligatory which are in the written word, but are not to observe what are derived from the tradition of our forefathers." *Antiquities of the Jews* 12.10.6 (13.297), Josephus Flavius, [Whiston Translation p. 281].

[91] I grew up thinking that John the Baptist was the first Baptist. He is actually better referred to as John the Immerser although the concept of "immersion" or "mikvah" in no way originated with him. He was the son of a priest which meant that he was also a priest although he was not serving in the Temple. He was in the wilderness immersing people which was a common practice for those who desired to

repent and prepare themselves to worship YHWH. Many in those days rejected the Temple in Jerusalem as corrupted, so those who were looking for True Spiritual cleansing went to him. As a priest and a Yisraelite he was a Hebrew and therefore he had a Hebrew name, not the English name John. Yahuhanan (יהוחנן) is a name which means "YHWH has given." Many pronounce his Hebrew name as Yochanan (יוחנן) but that pronunciation loses the Name of YHWH. According to McClintock and Strong it is "a contracted form of the name Jehohanan." Therefore, in an effort to keep the original flavor of the name I use Yahonatan, Yahuhanan or Yahanan when referring to Yahanan the Immerser or the disciple of Yahushua called John.

The doctrine of baptism is often thought to be something new to the religious scene and uniquely Christian but according to the Scriptures Yahushua never baptized anyone with water and John the Baptist (Yahanan the Immerser) was not a Christian. In actuality, baptism is nothing new and was commanded by YHWH long before Messiah came. "Baptisms in the sense of purifications were common in the Old Testament The "divers washings" (Greek "baptisms") are mentioned in Hebrews 9:10, and "the doctrine of baptisms," Hebrews 6:2. The plural" baptisms" is used in the wider sense, all purifications by water; as of the priest's hands and feet in the laver outside before entering the tabernacle, in the daily service (Shemot 30:17-21); of the high priest's flesh in the holy place on the day of atonement (Vayiqra 16:23); of persons ceremonially unclean (Vayiqra 14; 15; 16:26-28; 17:15; 22:4-6), a leper, one with an issue, one who ate that which died of itself, one who touched a dead body, the one who let go the scapegoat or [gathers] the ashes of the red heifer, of the people before a religious festival (Bemidbar 19:10; Yahanan 11:55). The high priest's consecration was threefold: by baptism, unction, and sacrifice (Shemot 29:4; 40:12-15; Vayiqra 8:1). "Baptism" in the singular is used specially of the Christian rite." (from Fausset's Bible Dictionary, Electronic Database Copyright (c)1998 by Biblesoft – Names of Scriptures corrected for consistency). It was a natural and significant thing for Yisraelites to purify themselves through immersion. The Hebrew word for baptize is tevila (טביל) which is a full body immersion that takes place in a mikvah (מקוה) which comes from the passage in Beresheet 1:10 when YHWH "gathered together" the waters. The mikvah is the gathering together of flowing waters. To qualify as a mikvah, the waters must be living waters, they must be moving and they must contain life. It is interesting that Yahanan immersed people in the Yarden (Jordan) River which is a living water that flows into the Dead Sea which is literally dead. There is no life in the Dead Sea so it is not a mikvah, as if the sins of the people literally washed into the Sea of Death. There were numerous mikvahs at the temple and it was required that a person be immersed in a mikvah prior to presenting their sacrifice. Therefore, the tevila or baptism was common and full of meaning for a Yisraelite.

93 The Renewed Covenant is an extremely misunderstood concept because many have misnamed it the "New Covenant." Make no mistake about it, Yahushua did not make a <u>new</u> or <u>different</u> Covenant, instead He reconfirmed or renewed the Covenant at what is commonly referred to as "The Last Supper." "*In the same way, after the supper He took the cup, saying, 'This cup is the renewed Covenant in My blood, which is poured out for you.'*" Luke 22:20. Many modern translations of that statement state: "*this cup is the new covenant*" which is an incorrect translation. The word translated as "new" is kainee (καινη) which means: "refreshed or renewed." If the intent was to invoke a brand new covenant the word neo (νεο) would have likely been used in the Greek text. This interpretation is completely consistant with the language used by Yirmeyahu, Yeshayahu and Yehezeqel. In Hebrew the word for renew is hadashah (חדשה) and the word for Covenant is brit (ברית). Thus the renewed Covenant is referred to as the Brit Hadashah. YHWH gives us a wonderful example of renewal through His creation. Despite the fact that much of the world reckons time according to a solar calendar,

the Scriptural calendar revolves around the moon. Months begin at the sighting of the "new moon" which is referred to as hodesh (חדש). We know when we see the "new moon" that it is really not a brand new moon which appears approximately every 28 days (the number of days in a cycle depends upon whether you are measuring according to the synodic cycle (29.5 days) or the sidereal cycle (27.1 days) thus the average is 28 days). Rather it is a renewed moon or a refreshed moon. Notice the similarity between the words hadashah (חדשה) and hodesh (חדש). They share the same root meaning of renewal and the only difference is the hey (ה). Therefore just as the moon is refreshed in its time so the Covenant is refreshed in YHWH's time. Yahushua was the mediator of the Renewed Covenant just as Mosheh was the mediator of the Sinai Covenant. Notice that there were no Gentiles at the table during the Last Supper, there were only Yisraelites. Not all twelve tribes were present at the table, but they were clearly represented, just as was done during the rededication of the Temple by Nehemiah and Ezra. (Ezra 6:17). Therefore, the Renewed Covenant was prophesied to Yisrael and it was made with Yisrael. The notion that YHWH is somehow done with Yisrael is absurd, because if He is done with Yisrael then the Covenants are finished and there are no promises for us to rely upon for redemption. History shows us that the Christian religion has attempted to hijack the Renewed Covenant and somehow replace Yisrael, but the Christian Church was never a party to any Covenant. You cannot separate Yisrael from the Renewed Covenant because without Yisrael there is no Renewed Covenant. Paul (Shaul) clearly stated: "⁴ the people of Yisrael. *Theirs is the adoption as sons; theirs the divine glory, the Covenants, the receiving of the Torah, the temple worship and the promises.* ⁵ *Theirs are the patriarchs, and from them is traced the human ancestry of Messiah, who is Elohim over all, forever praised! Amen."* Romans 9:3-5. The promises and the Covenants belong to Yisrael. This is why we see many Christians with such an identity crisis. There are literally hundreds of denominations, sects and cults - all with differing rules, regulations, hierarchies and beliefs from the others - each one believing that they have the "full gospel." They don't know how to deal with each other – let alone Yisrael. Most all of them removed the Torah from their tents and sprinkled what little was left with "grace" to the point where what Christians perceive as the Renewed Covenant is something very different from Mosheh and the Prophets. Gentiles only enter into the Renewed Covenant through Yisrael and simply put - if you have been taught anything different - you have been taught a lie. If you recognize this truth then you may actually see the fulfillment of prophecy occur in your life. The Prophet Yirmeyahu immediately after prophesying concerning the fishers and the hunters stated: "*19 . . . the Gentiles shall come to you from the ends of the earth and say, Surely our fathers have inherited lies, worthlessness and unprofitable things. 20 Will a man make gods for himself, which are not gods? 21 Therefore behold, I will this once cause them to know, I will cause them to know My hand and My might; and they shall know that My Name is YHWH.*" Yirmeyahu 16:19-21.

[94] We are instructed in the Torah to wear tzit tzit on the four corners of our garments. (Bemidbar 15:38-39; Devarim 22:12). The Yahudim have traditionally fulfilled this instruction by wearing tallits which are also known as prayer shawls. Tefellim are also known as phylacteries and are worn in obedience to the Torah which instructs us to bind or tie the commandments on our hands and our foreheads. (Devarim 6:8; 11:18). Yahushua referred to both of these acts of obedience in Mattityahu 23:5 and criticized the manner in which the teachers of the Torah and the Pharisees obeyed because they did so to impress men – their hearts were not right. He did not say that we are not to obey the Torah and all children of Yisrael should be following these instructions. A prophecy in the Tanak speaks of the Messiah as follows: "*The Sun of Righteousness shall arise with healing in His wings.*" Malachi 4:2 NKJV. These "wings" are kanaph (כָּנָף) in Hebrew and refer to the edge of a garment, which is the tzitzit. We read in the Good News according

to Luke: "*43 Now a woman, having a flow of blood for twelve years, who had spent all her livelihood on physicians and could not be healed by any, 44 came from behind and touched the border of His garment. And immediately her flow of blood stopped.*" Luke 8:43-44 NKJV. The Greek word used to describe a border is kraspedon (κρασπεδον) which means a fringe or tassel. In other words, she grabbed His tzitzit which He was wearing in obedience to the Torah and He came with healing in His tzitzit just as was foretold by the Prophet Malachi. Also, in Mattithyahu 14:35-36 we read: "*35 And when the men of that place (Gennesar) recognized Him, they sent out into all that surrounding country, and brought to Him all who were sick, 36 and begged Him to let them only touch the tzitzit of His garment. And as many as touched it were completely healed.*" We see in these passages not only a beautiful fulfillment of prophecy, but also an example of the Torah observance of Yahushua which has been obscured due to translation inconsistencies and ignorance on the part of translators. By grabbing hold of the tztizit – which represent the commandments, the terms of the Covenant – people were shown that healing and blessings come through the Torah which is what Messiah came to teach and fulfill.

Most of us that grew up in the age of television are largely influenced by the images that we see on television and at the movies. Most movies that we see about the life of Yahushua show a Messiah with relatively older Talmudim. We know that Yahushua began his ministry when He was 30 years of age which was fairly customary for rabbis. In fact, according to Mishnah Aboth 5, 21 there were three levels of education 1) Mikra, 2) Mishnah and 3) Talmud. A child would begin their study of the Torah at an early age. By the age of 15 they typically made the decision to pursue in depth study or take on a vocation. Marriage would generally occur by 18. It appears that Kepha was the only one who was married thus implying that the others were under 18. While most of the Talmudim of Yahushua were in a vocation they also were young enough and eager enough to follow a Rabbi. Their actions and comments were often immature reflecting a younger age and Yahushua often called them "children" (Yahanan 21:5), "babes" (Mattityahu 11:25) and "little children" (Yahanan 13:33). In Matthew 17:24-27 we read of an incident where Yahushua paid the "Temple tax" for Himself and Kepha. According to Shemot 30:14: *"Everyone passing over to be registered, from twenty years old and above, gives a contribution to YHWH."* The contribution was a half sheqel per person. Since Kepha found a sheqel he had enough to pay for himself and Yahushua. Again, the implication is that the others were under the age of 20 so they did not need to pay the contribution. Having this information certainly might change the way that we look at the Scriptures and better help us understand the way that Yahushua taught and dealt with His Talmudim.

96 For the purposes of this discussion, it is important to point out that the Feast of Pentecost takes place 50 days after the Feast of Firstfruits which occurs during the Feast of Unleavened Bread. Pentecost, also known as Shavuot (weeks), is one of three Feasts which all males are commanded to go up to Jerusalem. While at the Feast, you would go to the Temple, or rather House of YHWH, for prayer and offerings, particularly during the morning (9:00 am) and evening (3:00 pm also known as the 9th hour). Contrary to popular belief, on the day of Pentecost, the Talmudim were not huddled in the upper room, which was no doubt quite small. Rather they were in the House of YHWH at 9:00 am for the Feast. This is how such a crowd from around the world could gather to witness the outpouring and the speaking in many languages. These were all of the Torah observant Yisraelites who were present for the Feast. The Scriptures record that 3,000 were added to the faith and baptized, or rather immersed. There were many mikvahs at the Temple where people would cleanse themselves before entering the House of YHWH, this is how they were able to immerse so many people.

97 In my opinion, there is no other passage of Scripture that more succinctly demonstrates the focus of Yahushua's teaching than on the issue of washing of the hands. First read

the account and then I will elaborate. *"¹ Then the Scribes and Pharisees who were from Jerusalem came to Yahushua, saying, ² 'Why do Your disciples transgress the tradition of the elders? For they do not wash their hands when they eat bread.' ³ He answered and said to them, 'Why do you also transgress the commandment of Elohim because of your tradition?' ⁴ For Elohim commanded, saying, 'Honor your father and your mother' and, 'He who curses father or mother, let him be put to death.' ⁵ But you say, 'Whoever says to his father or mother, 'Whatever profit you might have received from me is a gift to Elohim' - ⁶ then he need not honor his father or mother.' Thus you have made the commandment of Elohim of no effect by your tradition. ⁷ Hypocrites! Well did Yeshayahu prophesy about you, saying: ⁸ 'These people draw near to Me with their mouth, and honor Me with their lips, but their heart is far from Me. ⁹ And in vain they worship Me, teaching as doctrines the commandments of men.'"* Mattityahu 15:1-9. To fully understand what is going on in this text it is helpful to understand the historical background as well as to go beyond the English text. The Pharisees had developed their own religious traditions apart from the Torah. The laws and traditions which constitute the oral Torah are specifically known as the takanot (תקנות) and ma'asim (מעשים). The word takanot means "enactments" and refers to the laws enacted by the Pharisees. Ma'asim literally means "works or deeds" and refers to the precedents of the Rabbis that provide the source for Pharasaic rulings along with subsequent rulings based on those precedents. Over the centuries, these enactments and precedents developed into a powerful set of rules and regulations that have operated to define and control the religion now known as Judaism, which is quite different than the faith of ancient Yisrael. These enactments and precedents established by the Rabbis and the Pharisees were given the same, if not greater weight, than the Torah. One of these was the man-made commandment concerning the washing of the hands. While many who read this passage believe that there is actually a commandment concerning the washing of hands in the Torah - they are wrong. This is really nothing more than a

man-made tradition – you will not find this commandment anywhere in the Torah. Regardless, the tradition exists to this day known as Netilat Yadaim. After the washing ceremony a prayer is said as follows: "Blessed are You Hashem (the Master) our G-d (Source of our strength) Ruler of the universe, Who has made us holy (special to Him) through His commandments, and commanded us concerning washing (our) hands." Notice that in their prayer they state that YHWH commanded us concerning washing our hands – which He did not. While it is certainly not a bad idea to wash your hands before you eat, it is not a commandment. If you examine the Hebrew text of Mattityahu the essence of the conflict is crystal clear. The Pharisees first confront Yahushua by asking Him: "*Why do your talmudim transgress the takanot of antiquity by not washing their hands before eating?*" Amazingly, they considered it a transgression to disobey a takanot. Yahushua responded to them by asking: "*Why do you transgress the Words of Elohim because of your takanot?*" Notice He calls it <u>their</u> takanot which is absolutely correct. It is not in the Torah and the takanot is not from YHWH - it is from men. Yahushua was giving the religious elite a lesson in the Torah. He was also rebuking them for placing their own traditions above the Torah and, in fact, replacing the Torah and making it of no effect. A remarkable aspect of this passage is that Yahushua quotes the Prophet Yeshayahu during part of the rebuke which goes to show that the conduct of the Pharisees was nothing new - it had been prophesied hundreds of years in advance.

98   Kepha is the proper transliteration for the Hebrew name of the disciple commonly called Peter.

99   Shaul (sha ool) is the proper transliteration for the Hebrew name of the apostle commonly called Paul.

100   The road to Damascus experience was not a conversion as many like to describe it. Shaul did not convert to Christianity as Christianity did not even exist until centuries later. Contrary to popular belief, the Christian religion is not the same faith as that which was practiced by the first disciples

of the Messiah and Yisrael. All of the original disciples were
Yisraelites and all of the original Believers were Yisraelites.
Early Gentile converts were "grafted in" to the Olive
Tree which represents The Commonwealth of Yisrael
(Romans 11). Over the decades and centuries that followed
the death and resurrection of Messiah, pagan doctrines
and anti-Semitism infiltrated and divided the Assembly
of Believers. The historical persecution of the Yisraelites
by the Roman Empire led to the demise of the Yisraelite
Believers (commonly called Nazoreans or Natzrim) and
the surge of Christianity, which perpetrated the concept
that "The Church" had replaced the Elect of Elohim,
which is Yisrael. The Christian Religion was officially
established by the Roman Empire in the Third Century
by Emperor Constantine – a pagan who worshipped the
sun god Mithra. By that time there had been a significant
departure from the original faith presented in the Scriptures
by Avraham, Yitshaq, Yaakov, Mosheh, the Prophets and
the Messiah. The new religion called Christianity was a
mixture of the truth, anti-Semitism and sun god worship
which has twisted and distorted Scriptures for centuries to
become a religion of lawlessness that, in many ways, stands
diametrically opposed to the will and commandments of
Elohim. Therefore, Shaul never converted to anything. He
remained a Yisraelite who stopped persecuting followers of
Yahushua because he realized that Yahushua was indeed
the Messiah. Once he got straightened out he then traveled
to teach this truth to others.

When Shaul met the Messiah he was humbled so that he
could learn the error of his ways. Through his zeal he had
become blinded by hate: "*But he who hates his brother is in
darkness and walks in darkness, and does not know where he is
going, because the darkness has blinded his eyes.*" 1 Yahanan
2:11. It was through this experience that Shaul was able to
understand and then teach what was happening to Yisrael
as follows: "*⁷ Yisrael has not obtained what it seeks; but the elect
have obtained it, and the rest were blinded. ⁸ Just as it is written:
'Elohim has given them a spirit of stupor, eyes that they should not
see and ears that they should not hear, to this very day.'*" Romans

11:7-8. Therefore, Shaul was not converted to a new religion, there was no new religion to convert to. Rather, he was able to understand the Scriptures and their true meaning.

102 Few people realize the continuing significance of Sinai throughout the Scriptures. This is the place where the Torah was given through Mosheh to the nation of Yisrael. It is also the place where Eliyahu fled, a forty day journey, in one day and met with the Word of YHWH. (1 Kings 19:8-9). While the traditional location of Mount Sinai has been in the Sinai Peninsula there is overwhelming archeological evidence pointing to Saudi Arabia. Beyond the physical evidence it certainly concurs with Shaul going to Sinai as he comments in Galatians 1:17 of going to Arabia after his encounter with Yahushua on the road to Damascus. Mattityahu 4:1-11 recounts the wilderness experience of Yahushua and refers to an exceedingly high mountain which I believe could have been Horeb (Sinai).

103 *Our Father Abraham, Jewish Roots of the Christian Faith*, Marvin R. Wilson William B. Eerdmans Publishing Company, Grand Rapids Michigan 1989 p. 65.

104 Rabbinic Judaism is not the same religion as that of the Yisrael that we read in the Scriptures. Rabbinic Judaism is a religion which was developed largely because of the Great Revolt. After the siege on Jerusalem and the destruction of the Second Temple by Titus in 70 A.D., the Pharisees and possibly only surviving Sanhedrin Yochanan ben Zakkai founded an Academy at Yavneh which became the center of Rabbinic Authority. His predecessor Gamaliel II continued to solidify the power base of the Pharisaic Sect of the Hebrews who, through their cooperation with the Roman Empire, were able to survive the near annihilation which was suffered by the other Yisraelite sects such as the Sadducees, the Zealots, the Sicarii and the Nazoreans. There were still other sects of Yisraelites which history provides scant detail such as the Therapeutae and those who composed the "Odes of Solomon." In any event, the Pharisees, through the enhancement of Rabbinic authority and the leadership of Rabbi Akiba developed into the leading Yisraelite sect

which is now known as Rabbinic Judaism. While Rabbinic Judaism claims to stem directly from Yisrael it is not much different from the Roman Catholic church claiming a direct line of "Popes" to Shimon Kepha. These claims of authority are quite meaningless as neither religious system represents the pure faith found in the Scriptures. Rabbinic Judaism, while it may consist of mostly genetic descendents of Avraham, Yitshaq and Yaakov, is not Yisrael. In other words, you do not have to convert to Judaism to become part of the Commonwealth of Yisrael (i.e. the Kingdom of Elohim) nor do you have to accept Talmudic teaching to follow Elohim. Rabbinic Judaism does not have a Temple nor a priesthood and their Rabbinic power structure is not supported or condoned by the Scriptures. This is why the Talmud, which is not Scripture, is so important in Rabbinic Judaism, because it lends credence to their newly devised system. When the Messiah returns He will set things straight. He will find and lead His sheep and he will not need any Catholic Priests, Christian Pastors, or Jewish Rabbis to help Him.

[105] en.wikipedia.org/wiki/Bar_Kokhba's_revolt. There are many problems with both Bar Kokhba and Rabbi Akiba and to properly understand the development of Judaism and Christianity it is critical to understand the essence of the Revolt. Rabbi Akiba, the father of Rabbinic Judaism supported a man who was clearly a false Messiah. He even manipulated facts to support the Messiahship of Bar Kokhba whose real name, ironically, was Bar Kosiba which can mean: "son of a liar." For a very good discussion on this subject see *Rabbi Akiba's Messiah: The Origins of Rabbinic Authority* by Daniel Gruber, Elijah Publishing (1999) ISBN: 0-9669253-1-9.

[106] The use of the term "Gentile Converts" is used simply to describe a person who was once a Gentile that repented and joined with Yisrael. It is not meant to imply that they converted to the religions of Christianity or Judaism, which did not actually exist at that time.

[107] Erubin 21b. Whosoever disobeys the rabbis deserves death

and will be punished by being boiled in hot excrement in hell. Hagigah 27a. States that no rabbi can ever go to hell. Baba Mezia 59b. A rabbi debates God and defeats Him. God admits the rabbi won the debate. All quotes and sources taken from *Quotes 'With Attitude' from the Jewish Talmud Commentary* By Don Talbot.

108 Read what the 12th Century Babylonian Sage Maimonides, also known as Rambam, wrote concerning this issue: "If there are 1000 prophets, all of them of the stature of Elijah and Elisha, giving a certain interpretation, and 1001 rabbis giving the opposite interpretation, you shall 'incline after the majority' (Shemot 23:2) and the law is according to the 1001 rabbis, not according to the 1000 venerable prophets. And thus our Sages said, 'By God, if we heard the matter directly from the mouth of Joshua the son of Nun, we would not obey him nor would we listen to him!' . . . And so if a prophet testifies that the Holy-One, Blessed be He, told him that the law of a certain commandment is such and such, or [even] that the reasoning of a certain sage is correct, that prophet must be executed . . . as it is written, 'it is not in heaven' (Devarim 30:12). Thus God did not permit us to learn from the prophets, only from the Rabbis who are men of logic and reason." Gordon, Nehemia, *The Hebrew Yeshua vs. The Greek Jesus*, Appendix 3, Page 83. In my opinion, Rambam "destroyed the Torah" through this interpretation. In Torah study, it was common to refer to a bad interpretation as "destroying the Torah" while a good interpretation would "fulfill the Torah." Rambam misquoted Scripture in an effort to derive from it what he wanted – an excuse to solidify the power of the Rabbis. Rambam used this reasoning to justify the execution of any prophet who prophesied that the Rabbis are wrong on any point of interpretation.

109 *Come Out of Her My People*, C.J. Koster, Institute for Scripture Research (1998) p. 65.

110 http://www.mechon-mamre.org/jewfaq/gentiles.htm.

111 In Israel if you visit the remains of Korazim in the Galilee region you will find the head of Medusa engraved in the

wall of the synagogue. You can also find pentagrams and hexagrams engraved on synagogues in the region – both of these symbols have long been associated with the occult. For further discussion on the hexagram read: *Six-Pointed Star: Its Origin and Usage* by O. J. Graham, The Free Press 777, 2001.

Many Christians cringe when you imply that there might be a problem with their translation of the Scriptures. I know many who describe themselves as "King James Only" types. In other words, they believe that the English King James translation is the perfect and infallible translation. While it is certainly a great text that has helped countless individuals read the Scriptures in the English language, it is not perfect. There are clearly issues which the translators did not understand that effected the translation and there are even outright errors. This is the task of textual critics, to find and correct those errors in order to have the most accurate translation possible. Textual criticism is a necessary aspect of restoration when the motivation of the "critic" is to discern the original meaning of a document. This is particularly important concerning the "New Testament" manuscripts because there are no original "autographs" of any "New Testament" manuscripts. Today, there are somewhere around 25,000 to 30,000 texts, some of which are merely fragments, all of them being copies of copies of copies. There are numerous variations in these texts which require diligent efforts to discern which variation best represents the original text. Most of the time these variations are inconsequential syntax matters but there are some very important variations that can effect doctrinal issues. Sadly, some textual critics endeavor upon their quest with the exclusive purpose of disproving the validity of the Scriptures. I find it to be an exciting endeavor and it in no way diminishes my faith to admit that the New Testament copies are not perfect. I understand the realities of the fact that we are dealing with writings almost 2,000 years old. It is incredible that we have so many texts of documents that involve our faith. This issue and others related to the origin,

accuracy and reliability of the Scriptures is discussed in the Walk in the Light series book entitled "Scriptures."

113 The causes of division and the subject of restoration is discussed in detail in the Walk in the Light series book entitled "Restoration."

114 Many believe that the Greek language is the "original" language of all of the New Testament but this is not necessarily the case, particularly when referring to the Good News according to Mattityahu. The existence of the Hebrew version of Mattityahu has caused quite a stir in the scholarly community as well as those who believe in the "original Greek." Many people treat Greek as if it were a holy language in the same sense that Hebrew is the holy tongue. Not so - the Greek language was a pagan language and was generally considered to be an "unclean" language among Yisraelites. Therefore, we should not be surprised to find Messianic texts written in Hebrew since the early Assembly likely consisted of mostly all native Yisraelites. That is not to say that these Yisraelites did not speak Greek because some of them probably did, but I would expect that there were many texts written in Hebrew that have since been lost or destroyed. Strangely, it was with the great influx of Greek speaking Gentile converts that likely caused the high volume of Greek copies which resulted in our ability to preserve so many of these writings and determine the original meaning – even though we do not have the original documents. The Good News according to Mattityahu is special because we have numerous witnesses to the fact that it was originally written in Hebrew. "Papias (ca. 60-130 CE), bishop of Hierapolis wrote that 'Matthew collected the oracles in the Hebrew language, and each interpreted them as best he could.' Irenaeus wrote in Adv. Haer. 3.1.1: 'Matthew also issued a written Gospel among the Hebrews in their dialect while [Kepha] and [Shaul] were preaching at Rome and laying the foundations of the [Assembly]' Origen quoted by Eusebius, H.E. 6.25.4 wrote: 'As having learnt by tradition concerning the four gospels, which alone are unquestionable in the [Assembly of Elohim] under heaven,

that first was written that according to [Mattityahu], who was once a tax collector but afterwards an apostle of [Yahushua Mashiach], who published it for those who from Judaism came to believe, composed as it was in the Hebrew language.' Eusebius, H.E. 3.24.6 wrote: '[Mattityahu] had first preached to Hebrews, and when he was on the point of going to others he transmitted in writing in his native language the [Good News] according to himself, and thus supplied by writing the lack of his own presence to those from whom he was sent.'" Quoting from *Hebrew Gospel of Matthew* by George Howard, Mercer University Press 1995 pp. 157-158. The source text for The Hebrew Gospel of Matthew translated by George Howard derives from a treatise entitled Evan Bohan (אבן בוחן) which means: "The Touchstone." It was written by Shem-Tob ben-Isaac ben-Shaprut in the 14th Century. It was not intended to be favorable toward Christianity, in fact, it was meant to assist Jews to argue the Scriptures with Christians. This is why some Believers have a problem with the text because it uses the slur (יש"ו) Yesu whenever referring to Yahushua.

¹¹⁵ The Septuagint is the common name for the Greek translation of the Hebrew Scriptures - The Tanak. Septuagint often rendered as LXX means "70" because tradition has it that 72 scholars translated the text. The Septuagint can be extremely useful when we study the "New Testament" because it acts as a bridge between the New Testament Greek and the Hebrew in the Tanak.

¹¹⁶ Fausset's Bible Dictionary, Electronic Database Copyright (c)1998 by Biblesoft.

¹¹⁷ In modern society we are operating on a system of reckoning time which is not the same as the Creator established from the beginning – although He is still operating on His calendar. As a result, we often see people giving credence and importance to dates on the Gregorian Calendar which likely have no significance on the Creator's Calendar. The Creator's Calendar is discussed in more detail in the Walk in the Light series book entitled "The Appointed Times." To find out more on dates you can also view the Creator's

Calendar at www.torahcalendar.com.

¹¹⁸ Some anti-Israel Orthodox Jewish groups are known as Neturei Karta web address: <u>www.nkusa.org</u>. Also True Torah Jews Against Zionism web address: <u>www.jewsagainstzionism.com</u>. The author is not endorsing either of these groups but merely provides this information due to their unique and often unknown perspective.

¹¹⁹ Many of the issues concerning the Palestinian question are propaganda, fabrications and distortions of the truth which are an attempt to inhibit the progression and legitimization of the State of Israel. Palestine was simply a term given to the land which now encompasses portions of various newly formed ethnically Arab nations and includes the modern state of Israel. Palestinian was a word used to describe both Arabs, Jewish and other persons who lived in the area called Palestine. The word Palestinian is currently used in such a way that the general public will think that the Palestinians are a separate nation of people, like the Jews, when in fact, they are Arabs who lived in Palestine, just as much of Jordan are Arabs who lived in Palestine. They are only Jordanians because they lived in Transjordan when it was formed in 1922. The current "Palestinian" problem has been perpetrated by Arab nations who have refused to assimilate their fellow Arab brothers and sisters and instead have let them remain in refugee camps until the day when they "drive the Jews into the sea" and everybody can return to "their land" and live happily ever after. The "Palestinian" problem was created by Arabs who told these people to leave their homes while they destroyed Israel. The Arabs left and Israel won the war. As a result, the Arabs that left had no homes to return to and the Arabs who made the grand promises failed to make good and made them stay in refugee camps. The Palestinian problem exists because the Arab nations want it to exist. The Arab nations have been able to use the Palestinians to spew their hate at the Jews indirectly without getting their hands dirty.

¹²⁰ It is important to remember that some of the House of Yisrael went to Jerusalem to sacrifice after Jereboam

initiated his system of false worship. Did they stay in Judea or return home – we do not know. We do know that all of the House of Yisrael was eventually removed from their Land. According to the Scriptures, the Land vomited them out because of their abominations. Prior to that time we read during the beginning of the reign of Hezekiah how he reestablished the Temple worship and invited some of the other tribes to come to Jerusalem and worship – which they did – at least Asher, Manasseh and Zebulun. The reign of Hezekiah straddled the period when the Northern Tribes were being exiled. This may have been a final opportunity for some to repent before they were taken by the Assyrians. *The Settlers' Crisis, and Israel's,* Hillel Halkin, Commentary Volume 119, Number 3, March 2005, Page 41.

The blessings that will be bestowed upon Yisrael when the finally return are clearly delineated in the Torah as follows: "*1 When all these blessings and curses I have set before you come upon you and you take them to heart wherever YHWH your Elohim disperses you among the nations, 2 and <u>when you and your children return to YHWH your Elohim and obey him with all your heart and with all your soul according to everything I command you today, 3 then YHWH your Elohim will restore your fortunes and have compassion on you and gather you again from all the nations where he scattered you. 4 Even if you have been banished to the most distant land under the heavens, from there YHWH your Elohim will gather you and bring you back. 5 He will bring you to the land that belonged to your fathers, and you will take possession of it. He will make you more prosperous and numerous than your fathers. 6 YHWH your Elohim will circumcise your hearts and the hearts of your descendants, so that you may love him with all your heart and with all your soul, and live. 7 YHWH your Elohim will put all these curses on your enemies who hate and persecute you. 8 You will again obey YHWH and follow all his commands I am giving you today. 9 Then YHWH your Elohim will make you most prosperous in all the work of your hands and in the fruit of your womb, the young of your livestock and the crops of your land. YHWH will again delight in you and make you prosperous, just as He delighted in your fathers, 10 if you obey YHWH your</u>*

Elohim and keep His commands and decrees that are written in this Scroll of the Torah and turn to YHWH your Elohim with all your heart and with all your soul." Devarim 30:1-10.

123 Yom Teruah is a very interesting Appointed Time which is often called Rosh Hashanah – "Head of the Year." It is found, among other places at Vayiqra 23:24-25. *"²⁴ Say to the Yisraelites: On the first day of the seventh month you are to have a day of rest, a sacred assembly commemorated with trumpet blasts. ²⁵ Do no regular work, but present an offering made to YHWH by fire."* You have to know when the first month begins before you can determine the seventh month. Also, you must know when a month begins. On the Creator's Calendar a month begins at the new moon, better known as the renewed moon or Rosh Chodesh in Hebrew. Yom Teruah is the only Appointed Time that occurs concurrently with the sighting of the new moon. Historically, it was virtually impossible to determine the exact day the crescent moon would first be visible, so it could not be precisely calculated to occur on a specific date as with others. It calls for the blasting of trumpets and shofars and precedes the great Appointed Times of Yom Kippur and Sukkot. It will be a day of great significance in the future, as it is a day and an hour which no man "intuitively" knows (oida) and we are to keep watch for it. When we see the sign we are to sound the trumpet. This should make us think of the words of Messiah as He repeatedly warns: *"Therefore keep watch, because you do not know (oida) the day or the hour."* Mattityahu 25:13 (see also Mark 13:32-37).

124 Christianity and Judaism are currently littered with pagan influences. Christianity has rejected the Scriptural Appointed Times and has adopted pagan holidays such as Christmas and Easter. Christianity has rejected the seventh day Sabbath and replaced it with SunDay worship – the traditional day for sun worship. These issues and many others are discussed throughout the Walk in the Light series including "Restoration," "The Sabbath," "Appointed Times" and "Pagan Holidays."

125 Sukkot (Succot), also known as the Feast of Booths or

the Feast of Tabernacles is specifically mentioned as a celebration which will occur every year when the Messiah reigns from Zion. All the Nations, not just Jews, will be required to celebrate or they will be punished. This is perfectly consistent with the notion that the Appointed Times belong to YHWH and that it is the time when His Creation will meet with Him. (see Zecharyah 14).

[126] This subject is discussed in greater detail in the Walk in the Light series book entitled "The Appointed Times."

[127] According to Vayiqra 25:1-7: "¹ YHWH said to Mosheh on Mount Sinai, ² 'Speak to the Yisraelites and say to them: When you enter the Land I am going to give you, the Land itself must observe a sabbath to YHWH. ³ For six years sow your fields, and for six years prune your vineyards and gather their crops. ⁴ But in the seventh year the land is to have a sabbath of rest, a sabbath to YHWH. Do not sow your fields or prune your vineyards. ⁵ Do not reap what grows of itself or harvest the grapes of your untended vines. The land is to have a year of rest. ⁶ Whatever the land yields during the sabbath year will be food for you - for yourself, your manservant and maidservant, and the hired worker and temporary resident who live among you, ⁷ as well as for your livestock and the wild animals in your land. Whatever the land produces may be eaten." The seventh year is commonly referred to as the Shemitah year. While there are currently some in the modern State of Israel that are attempting to obey this command, they are unable to obey it because the knowledge of the Scriptural 50 year Jubilee Cycle has been lost in history. Rabbinic Judaism follows a man-made 49 year cycle that, by their own admission, is not Scriptural. (see *Smittah 5768 A Practical Guide*, Council of Young Israel Rabbis in Israel, Written by Rabbi David Marcus). There are some in Israel who are attempting to subvert this command by growing their crops and then exchanging their products with those from other countries so that their produce, which is grown in Israel, is not actually sold in Israel. Sadly, this is a commandment which was intended to visibly reveal the blessings of YHWH to the world, but those in the Land apparently do not have the desire, the faith

or the knowledge to see it come to fruition. The Land in the modern State of Israel is currently producing incredible bounty for the people and one way or another, it will receive its' rest. (2 Chronicles 36:21). The restoration of the 50 year Jubilee Cycle and the 7 year Shemittah cycle will likely be restored by Eliyahu the Prophet, before Yahushua the Messiah returns according to the prophecy in Mattityahu 17:11.

[128] Revelation 15 indicates that the song of Mosheh will be sung by The Redeemed prior to the seven bowls of wrath. It might be a good idea to learn this song which can be found at Devarim 32.

[129] See Zekaryah 4

[130] Just as YHWH foretold Yisrael, either way they would reach the Nations, either through blessing or through a curse. If they had obeyed the Torah they would have been blessed which would have drawn men to them. As a curse they would be scattered throughout those very Nations and then draw them back to YHWH when they are regathered.

[131] See Yehezqel 47-48

[132] The size of the New (Renewed) Jerusalem is enormous. I believe that this may be the actual dimensions and ultimate fulfillment of the Land Covenant made with Avraham.

[133] Theological Wordbook of the Old Testament. Copyright (c) 1980 by The Moody Bible Institute of Chicago.

Appendix A

Tanak Hebrew Names

Torah - Teaching

English Name	Hebrew	English Transliteration
Genesis	בראשית	Beresheet
Exodus	שמות	Shemot
Leviticus	ויקרא	Vayiqra
Numbers	במדבר	Bemidbar
Deuteronomy	דברים	Devarim

Nebi'im - Prophets

English Name	Hebrew	English Transliteration
Joshua	יהושע	Yahushua
Judges	שופטים	Shoftim
Samuel	שמואל	Shemu'el
Kings	מלכים	Melakhim
Isaiah	ישעיהו	Yeshayahu
Jeremiah	ירמיהו	Yirmeyahu
Ezekiel	יחזקאל	Yehezqel
Daniel	דניאל	Daniel
Hosea	השוע	Hoshea
Joel	יואל	Yoel

Amos	עמוס	Amos
Obadiah	עבדיה	Ovadyah
Jonah	יונה	Yonah
Micah	מיכה	Mikhah
Nahum	נחום	Nachum
Habakkuk	חבקוק	Habaquq
Zephaniah	צפניה	Zepheniyah
Haggai	חגי	Chaggai
Zechariah	זכריה	Zekaryah
Malachi	מלאכי	Malachi

Kethubim – Writings

Psalms	תהלים	Tehillim
Proverbs	משלי	Mishle
Job	איוב	Iyov
Song of Songs	שיר השירים	Shir ha-Shirim
Ruth	רות	Ruth
Lamentations	איכה	Eikhah
Ecclesiastes	קהלה	Qohelet
Esther	אסתר	Ester
Ezra	עזרא	Ezra
Nehemiah	נחמיה	Nehemyah
Chronicles	דברי הימים	Divri ha-Yamim

Appendix B

The Walk in the Light Series

Book 1   Restoration – A discussion of the pagan influences that have mixed with the true faith through the ages which has resulted in the need for restoration. This book also examines true Scriptural restoration.

Book 2   Names – Discusses the True Name of the Creator and the Messiah as well as the significance of names in the Scriptures.

Book 3   Scriptures – Discusses the origin of the written Scriptures as well as many translation errors which have led to false doctrines in some mainline religions.

Book 4   Covenants – Discusses the progressive covenants between the Creator and His Creation as described in the Scriptures which reveals His plan for mankind.

Book 5   The Messiah – Discusses the prophetic promises and fulfillments of the Messiah and the True identity of the Redeemer of Yisrael.

Book 6   The Redeemed – Discusses the relationship between Christianity and Judaism and details how the Scriptures identify True Believers. It reveals how the Christian doctrine of Replacement Theology has caused confusion as to how the Creator views the Children of Yisrael.

Book 7   The Law and Grace – Discusses in depth the false doctrine that Grace has done away with the Law and demonstrates the vital importance of obeying the commandments.

Book 8   The Sabbath – Discusses the importance of the Seventh Day Sabbath as well as the origins of the tradition concerning Sunday worship.

Book 9   Kosher – Discusses the importance of eating food prescribed by the Scriptures as an aspect of righteous living.

Book 10   Appointed Times – Discusses the appointed times established by the Creator, often erroneously considered to be "Jewish" holidays, and critical to the understanding of prophetic fulfillment of the Scriptural promises.

Book 11   Pagan Holidays – Discusses the pagan origins of some popular Christian holidays which have replaced the Appointed Times.

Book 12   The Final Shofar – Discusses the walk required by the Scriptures and prepares the Believer for the deceptions coming in the End of Days.

The series began as a simple Powerpoint presentation which was intended to develop into a book with twelve different chapters but ended up being twelve different books. Each book is intended to stand alone although the series was originally intended to build from one section to another. Due to the urgency of certain topics, the books have not been published in sequential order.

For anticipated release dates, announcements and additional teachings go to:
www.shemayisrael.net

Appendix C

The Shema

Deuteronomy (Devarim) 6:4-5

Hear, O Israel: The LORD our God, the LORD is one!
You shall love the LORD your God with all your heart,
with all your soul, and with all your strength.

Traditional English Translation

שמע ישראל יהוה אלהינו יהוה אחד
ואהבת את יהוה אלהיך בכל לבבך ובכל נפשך ובכל מאדך

Hebrew Text

Shema, Yisra'el: YHWH Elohenu, YHWH echad!
V-ahavta et YHWH Elohecha b-chol l'vavcha u-v-chol
naf'sh'cha u-v-chol m'odecha.

Hebrew Text Transliterated

The Shema is arguably the most important prayer in
Judaism and the Messiah stated that it was the First of all
commandments.
(Mark 12:29-30).

Appendix D

Shema Yisrael was originally established with two primary goals: 1) The production and distribution of sound, Scripturally based educational materials which would assist individuals to see the light of Truth and "Walk in the Light" of that Truth. This first objective was, and is, accomplished through Shema Yisrael Publications; and 2) The free distribution of those materials to the spiritually hungry throughout the world, along with Scriptures, food, clothing and money to the poor, the needy, the sick, the dying and those in prison. This second objective was accomplished through the Shema Yisrael Foundation and through the Foundation people were able to receive a tax deduction for their contributions.

Sadly, through the passage of the Pension Reform Act of 2006, Congress severely restricted the operation of donor advised funds which, in essence, crippled the Shema Yisrael Foundation by requiring that funds either be channeled through another Foundation or to a 501(c)(3) organization approved by the Internal Revenue Service. Since the Shema Yisrael Foundation was relatively small and operated very "hands on" by placing the funds and materials directly into the hands of the needy in Third World Countries, it was unable to continue operating as a Foundation with the tax advantages associated therewith.

As a result, Shema Yisrael Publications has effectively functioned in a dual capacity to insure that both objectives continue to be promoted, although contributions are no longer tax deductible. To review some of the work being accomplished you can visit www.shemayisrael.net and go to the "Missions" section.

We gladly accept donations, although they will not be tax deductible. To donate, please make checks payable to: Shema Yisrael Publications and mail to:

Shema Yisrael
123 Court Street • Herkimer, New York 13350
1-866-866-2211

Printed in Great Britain
by Amazon